Robin Hood
FAQ

Robin Hood FAQ

All That's Left to Know About England's Greatest Outlaw and His Band of Merry Men

Dave Thompson

APPLAUSE
THEATRE & CINEMA BOOKS
An Imprint of Hal Leonard LLC

Published in 2017 by Applause Theatre & Cinema Books
An Imprint of Hal Leonard LLC
7777 West Bluemound Road
Milwaukee, WI 53213

Trade Book Division Editorial Offices
33 Plymouth St., Montclair, NJ 07042

All images are from the author's collection unless otherwise noted.
The FAQ series was conceived by Robert Rodriguez and developed with Stuart Shea.
Printed in the United States of America

Book design by Snow Creative

Library of Congress Cataloging-in-Publication Data

Names: Thompson, Dave, 1960 January 3– author.
Title: Robin Hood FAQ : all that's left to know about England's greatest outlaw
    and his band of merry men / Dave Thompson.
Description: Milwaukee : Applause Theatre & Cinema books, 2017. | Includes
    bibliographical references and index.
Identifiers: LCCN 2016052091 | ISBN 9781495048227 (paperbck)
Subjects: LCSH: Robin Hood (Legendary character) | Robin Hood (Legendary
    character)—In literature. | Robin Hood (Legendary character)—In motion
    pictures. | Outlaws—Great Britain—History—To 1500.
Classification: LCC PR2129 .T56 2017 | DDC 820.9/351—dc23
LC record available at https://lccn.loc.gov/2016052091

www.applausebooks.com

To Captain Tobias Wilcox—gone to Barbados

Contents

Acknowledgments   ix
Introduction: In Merrye Englande in Ye Days of Olde   xi

1   Riding Through the Glen: A Veritable Flock of Robins   1
2   The Rise of Robin Hood: From Tiny Yeomen, Great Earls   12
    Are Grown
3   Earls and Elsewhere: Further Fables, Theories, and Thoughts   23
4   The Death of Robin Hood: (Reports of Which Would Appear   30
    to Be Greatly Exaggerated)
5   A Swift Historical Diversion: An Earlier Robin Awakens   38
6   What Did Robin Have Against the French?
7   Robin Hood and the Holiest War: A Brief History of the Crusades   53
8   Robin Hood and the Band of Brothers (Part One): Introducing   65
    The Merry Men—the Big Three
9   Robin Hood and the Band of Brothers (Part Two): Merrier   76
    and Merrier Still
10 A Maid Called Marian: The Fairest Flower of the Forest   89
11 Shooting at the Sheriff: Nottingham, Gisborne, and   98
    a Few Other Fiends
12 Robin Hood and Religion: A Real Love/Hate Relationship   112
13 Into the Woods We Go: Robin Hood and the Mystery   122
    of the Forest
14 Another Historical Interlude: Later Robins from Ludd   151
    to Courtenay
15 The Ballads of Bold Robin Hood: With a Hey Nonny-no,   166
    to the Greenwood We Shall Go
16 A Robin Hood Broadside: Later Laments and Sensational   183
    Sonnets
17 From Ballads to Books: The Legend Continues . . .   192
18 Robin Hood, the Opera: Did Somebody Mention Songs?   199
19 From Sherwood to Shenandoah: Robin Hood in America   212
20 The Swash is Buckled: Fairbanks and Flynn—the Merriest   223
    of Men

21 Hammer and Sword: The Endless Cinema Show   235
22 Robin Gets Raunchy: The Original Men In Tights   249
23 Robin in Your Living Room: From Lincoln Green   263
    to Richard Greene

Epilogue   281
Appendix One: Robin in Song   285
Appendix Two: Robin on Screen   305
Index   331

Acknowledgments

Firstly, before the swords start clashing and the arrows begin flying, thanks to all the family and friends for whom a chorus of "Robin Hood, Robin Hood, riding through the glen" will *never* get old.

Neither will "Robinnnnnnnnnnnn . . . thehoodedman."

But especial thanks to Amy Hanson, for watching the movies and hearing the songs more often than anyone ought to; Jo-Ann Greene, who once drove through Sherwood Forest and thought it ought to be bigger (it was, once); Jen Swan for filling in some gaps; and Grey Malkin and Hester NicEilidh for their thoughts on Francis James Child and his ballads.

To all at FAQ Central Headquarters, but most especially John Cerullo, Marybeth Keating, Wes Seeley, Lon Davis and Debra Davis; to Alan Merrill, Karen and Todd; Linda and Larry; Betsy, Steve and family; Jen; all at Captain Blue Hen in Newark; Chrissie Bentley; Dave and Sue; Tim Smith, Gaye Black, Oliver, Trevor and the King of the Deep; Barb East; Bateerz and family; the Gremlins who live in the heat pump; and to John the Superstar, the demon of the dry well.

Author's note

Across the unfolding centuries, many of the names familiar in this story have undergone subtle (and sometimes, not-so-subtle) change. We can all see how Robyne (and occasionally Robert) Hode has become Robin Hood, but we may never agree on the correct way to spell Allen a Dale . . . is it Allan or Alan? Or even Allin? O'Dale or -a-Dale? Maid Marian or Marion or Maud?

Is it Gisborne or Gisbourne? Scarlet or Scarlett (or Scathlock or Stukley or a myriad more variations)? Loxley or Locksley?

For the most part, this book adheres to the spellings utilized by Francis James Child in his monumental *The English and Scottish Ballads* collection of antique verse.

Those (and several more) alternate/earlier spellings live on, however, in direct quotations from, and reference to earlier manuscripts and ballads, a reminder that until the invention of the printing press began to standardize spelling and punctuation, peeple were once free too spel wurds any wey they liked. Rather like modern text messaging.

Introduction

In Merrye Englande in Ye Days of Olde

> So it is: yet let us sing,
> Honour to the old bow-string!
> Honour to the bugle-horn!
> Honour to the woods unshorn!
> Honour to the Lincoln green!
> Honour to the archer keen!
> Honour to tight little John,
> And the horse he rode upon!
> Honour to bold Robin Hood,
> Sleeping in the underwood! .
> Honour to maid Marian,
> And to all the Sherwood-clan!
> Though their days have hurried by
> Let us two a burden try.
>
> —*John Keats, "Robin Hood"*

The story is simple, and it should be familiar to all.

In 1192, Robin of Loxley, the Earl of Huntingdon, returned to his English homeland from the Holy Land, where he fought gallantly alongside his king, Richard I, the Lionheart, against the Saracen hordes.

Largely centered upon modern Israel, the Holy Land at that time was regarded as a realm of almost Graustarkian intrigue, romance, and violence, newly invaded by a cunning, perfidious foe who would kill a Christian as soon as look at him, but whose savagery and fighting prowess was beyond measure.

It was, most westerners believed, a just war; one nobly targeted at expelling Moslems and Jews alike from the Holy Land, and preserving its

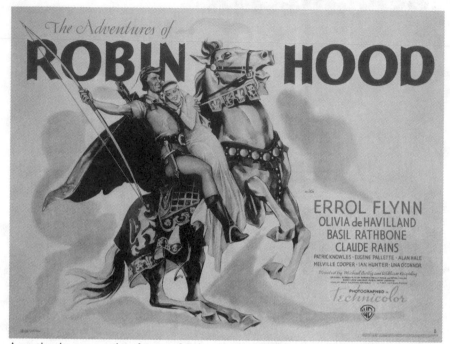

A captivating promotional poster for the classic 1938 Warner Bros. Technicolor production, *The Adventures of Robin Hood*.   *Photofest*

most sacred sites—centered upon, but by no means limited to, the city of Jerusalem—for the followers of one religion, and one religion alone.

But it was also an expensive war, a conflict which levied greater and ever more punitive taxes upon the people back home; while crueler, and ever more wicked men took advantage of the king's absence to seize power and money for themselves.

For all his gallantry and religious fervor, King Richard had been no saint. He had rebelled against his father, King Henry II (1154–1189) and had himself imposed some monstrous taxes in order to finance his journey to the East.

However, he was a positive paragon of virtue when compared to the man who affected to rule in his stead—Prince John, the king's avaricious, ambitious younger brother.

No matter that Richard had appointed a trusted regency to rule the country throughout his absence. He had also gifted certain areas to John, and these became the prince's *de facto* kingdom.

Noblemen loyal to the rightful monarch had their lands confiscated under the flimsiest of pretexts, and handed instead to men who supported the prince.

Officials who refused to swear allegiance to John were likewise cast out of their positions, and replaced by more of the prince's henchmen.

Taxation was increased, ostensibly to continue financing the king's wars, but in reality, to benefit the men who collected them.

Existing laws were strengthened, new laws were introduced. Crimes that might once have merited no harsher punishment than a few hours in the stocks suddenly became capital offenses. Anything resembling "due process" was suspended, to be replaced by summary justice, meted out on the spot by the military.

England was a land under siege—and the besiegers were its own government.

That was the world to which Robin returned. A world which was all but unrecognizable.

Loxley had certainly changed. Robin arrived in his home town to discover that his lands were now controlled by the evil Sir Guy of Gisborne; that the entire neighborhood was in thrall to a newly installed, and utterly brutal, Sheriff of Nottingham.

In vain, Robin tried to reason with the usurpers, but that was an argument that he was never going to win. Instead, he was thrown into jail and, although he escaped easily enough, his situation only worsened. For now he was an outlaw . . . literally, a man who lived outside of the law, outside of the *protection* of the law.

He could be shot on sight by anybody who wanted to claim the reward that the sheriff had placed on his head; and, if he survived capture, then he could be executed without trial.

Robin fled into the depths of Sherwood Forest, the vast and sometimes impenetrable woodland that surrounded the city of Nottingham. There, he gathered together a band of similarly fated felons—a disgraced friar named Tuck; a giant of a man called Little John; Much, the son of the miller who raised Robin as a child; Allen a Dale; Will Scarlet; and Maid Marian, a ward of the Sheriff who had known Robin since childhood, and who seemed fated to be betrothed to every tyrannical nobleman in the land, but whose heart belonged to Robin alone.

It was Marian's aid that permitted Robin to survive and prosper. There could scarcely be a footfall in the castle of which she did apprise him. Information on the sheriff's movements, the actions of his troops and, most

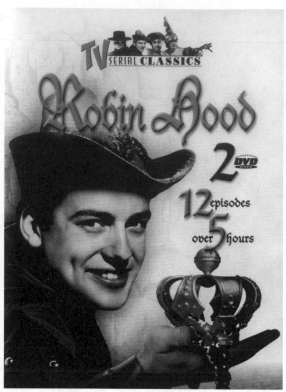

Richard Greene fronts this DVD selection of Robin's 1950s television adventures.

importantly, the comings and goings through the city gates. Shipments of gold, the delivery of taxes, wealthy visitors—anything that might aid Robin in his chosen quest of robbing from the rich and giving to the poor.

It's a wonderful story, packed with action, brimming with excitement, a thrill-a-minute saga of derring do. Across the cycle of stories that relay the adventures of Robin Hood, the man in green is warrior and spy, protector of the weak, slayer of the wicked, fearless, agile, intrepid, dynamic. Scrupulously fair and unimpeachably honest. A lover and a fighter.

He's probably the best-known outlaw in history, and one of the most heroic, too. Nobody who learns his story, whether from printed word or moving picture, can fail to be thrilled, even inspired, by his deeds, and though one might occasionally deplore his methods, it cannot be denied that his heart is in the right place. Unless, of course, you are among the rich from whom he steals.

But who was he, this robbing hood named Robin Hood?

Well, he wasn't the man we know from the stories.

Not the story as we all know it, anyway.

He might, indeed, have been a nobleman coming home from foreign wars, to discover his birthright had been stolen by some scheming ne'er-do-well.

But he may also have been a poacher or a peasant, coerced by circumstance into a life of crime.

He might have been a member of the royal court, disgraced for a crime he never committed. Or one for which he was wholly responsible.

battling the onslaught of the Industrial Revolution. William Courtenay, leading Kentish farmers against the newly instituted Poor Laws. George Orwell's Winston Smith, striking against Big Brother.

They all effectively tell the same story, of one man against the machine, fighting for the betterment of all.

A man named Robin Hood.

He still lives.

Just a couple of years ago, in 2015, an English housing benefit officer, distributing welfare to the local needy, was revealed to have handed out some £55,000 in bogus payments to claimants who didn't actually qualify for the benefits. He was, said the *Daily Express* newspaper, "a modern Robin Hood."

So was Jamaican drug lord Christopher "Dudus" Coke. "He lives in a poor area, and because of his sale of cocaine, he basically plays the Robin Hood role," University of Miami adjunct professor David Rowe told CNN.

So was another Englishman, jailed in 2009 for undertaking a six-month spree of armed robberies on banks and bookmakers. At least some of the proceeds, he claimed, would be distributed to the needy, and he even wrote a letter to the local newspaper, following one of his raids. It read: "I will continue to take from the rich and give to the poor," and it was signed, "R. H."

Needless to say, the authorities treated these modern Robins with scarcely more forbearance than their medieval counterpart regarded the original one. Or, for that matter, anybody who appeared to be following in his footsteps.

In 1439, after the outlaw Piers Venables masterminded an audacious jailbreak in Derbyshire, a petition to Parliament in London accused:

> havynge no liflode ne sufficeante of goodes, gadered and assembled unto him many misdoers . . . and, in manere of insurrection, wente into the wodes in that contré, like as it hadde be Robyn-hode and his meyné.
>
> [Having no livelihood or goods, he assembled a band of many misdoers . . . and took to the woods, there to live as Robin Hood and his men.]

In 1441, an army of peasants took to blocking roads in the county of Norfolk, and chanting "We are Robynhodesmen—war, war, war."

In 1469, separate uprisings against the crown were led by men who called themselves Robin of Holderness and Robin of Redesdale.

In 1498, one Roger Marshall was arrested after leading an uprising in the town of Willenhall, in Staffordshire. He called himself Robin Hood.

And so on. In America, Bonnie and Clyde; in Australia, Ned Kelly, and in the modern world, the forces of Anonymous have all been compared to history's favorite brigand.

But Robin Hood (and his Merry Men)'s criminal tendencies are not the only quality for which they are admired.

He may not be a style icon, for example, but when actress and singer Dana Gillespie first introduced her boyfriend, a young David Bowie, to her parents in 1964, "he was in Sherwood Forest Robin Hood–type suede things."

He may not be one of the world's great romantics, but the tale of Robin and his consort, Maid Marian, is one of the world's most beloved love stories—and on stage and screen, the role has attracted some of the profession's most beautiful actresses, just as the part of Robin Hood has lured some of its most handsome actors.

He was certainly an Englishman, but he belongs to the world. Robin Hood's story is as well known in Japan and Russia as it is in the UK and the USA. In Jamaica, long before Dudus the drug lord arrived on the scene, Robin Hood was already a popular hero among the island's disaffected, and there is a teetering pile of old reggae records to be built from the songs that invoke his memory.

And, again, he may not ever have existed. But when the original edition of the British *Dictionary of National Biography* was published in sixty-three volumes between 1885–1900, Robin Hood was featured alongside both the greats and the ghastlies of the island story—the only figure among thousands of inclusions whose existence could not be unequivocally vouchsafed; or, as the editors of the index put it, whose "historical authenticity is ill-supported." (Hood appears in volume twenty-seven, by the way.)

Ultimately, though, none of that matters. His memory lives, his spirit lives, his legend lives. This book is the story of those lives.

Robin Hood
FAQ

Riding Through the Glen

A Veritable Flock of Robins

It is one of the most diverting pastimes in modern scholastic endeavor. Who, from a multitude of possibilities, was the original Robin Hood? Nobody knows. But there are a lot of possibilities.

The earliest surviving historical reference to an outlaw (or, at least, a criminal) named Robin Hood . . . not necessarily *our* Robin Hood, just *a* Robin Hood . . . dates to somewhere between the years 1213 and 1216.

That was when one of the Abbot of Cirencester's servants, a certain Rob*ert* Hood, was found guilty of murdering a man named Ralph during a quarrel in the abbot's garden.

We will accept here that the names Robin and Robert were often interchangeable in the writings of those times (as were the names Maud, Matilda, and Marian).

It's a pleasant coincidence of names, but it is a long jump between what appears to have been a common killer and an heroic freedom fighter . . . even longer than the distance between Cirencester, deep in the heart of the Cotswolds, and Yorkshire and Nottingham, Hood's traditional stomping grounds.

Safely we can say this was not our man, just as he is unlikely to have been any of the other Robin Hoods whose thirteenth century existence has been vouchsafed by sundry other historical documents. The fact is, Robinhood (all one word) appears to have been a reasonably common surname.

No matter. We find another just a decade later in Yorkshire, deep within the records of the periodic courts, or assizes, that were held around the country, at which traveling magistrates would distribute justice upon the felons of the realm. There we learn that one "Robert Hod, fugitive," who also went by the name of Hobbehod, had been forced to forfeit "chattels" (property) to the not-inconsiderable value of one pound, twelve shillings, and sixpence, in partial payment of a debt to the Liberty of St. Peter's York.

There is also a strong body of opinion that then links the unfortunate "Robert Hod, fugitive" to another local criminal, Robert of Wetherby "outlaw and evildoer of our land"—a man whose capture and execution ultimately cost the local judiciary some six pounds, ten shillings, or four times the value of the confiscated chattels.

We know not precisely from what, aside from debt, Robert Hod may have been a fugitive. Nor of what evil doings the evildoer Robert of Wetherby might have been guilty. But one fact is assured. Leading the hunt for this miscreant was Eustace of Lowdham, now the Sheriff of Yorkshire but, hitherto, the deputy sheriff of the neighboring county of Nottinghamshire.

Robert Hod? The sheriff of Nottinghamshire? It's almost too good to be true.

And so it is. Robert Hod is revealed as the historical record's first possible Robin Hood. But he is not its last.

The View from North of the Border

In court documents dating from half a century later, in 1262, one William le Fevre, an outlaw in the county of Berkshire, was named as William Robehod; while another candidate (or, as the law might put it, suspect) for the role of the real-life Robin is found lurking within that vast historical tract known today as Wyntoun's *Chronicle of Scotland*, written around 1420.

Andrew of Wyntoun was both a poet and a holy man, a canon of St. Andrews, near Dundee in Scotland. Written largely, and most impressively, in eight-syllable couplets, his *Orygynale Cronykil of Scotland* is the oldest history of that land known to survive today, its span reaching from the earliest days of myth and fable to what Andrew knew as "the present day," the death of the Duke of Albany, Robert Stewart, in 1420.

Scrupulously dated, it covers, also, noteworthy events taking place south of the border in northern England and, for 1283, Andrew writes

> Lytill Ihon and Robyne Hude
> Waythmen ware commendyd gude;
> In Yngilwode and Barnysdale
> Thai oysyd all this tyme thare trawale

—meaning that the two men, Little John and Robin Hood, were widely regarded as "wight yeomen" or good hunters, and were familiar sights around Inglewood and Barnsdale, in the bordering county of Cumberland.

Certainly, the coincidence of those two names is one to conjure with. But are these really our men? Merely hunting well is scarcely a qualification for becoming history's greatest outlaw.

Nevertheless, Scottish historians remained fascinated by Robin Hood. A couple of decades later, another Scots chronicler, Walter of Bower, placed Robin in the forefront of one of the periodic rebellions that shook his nation's southern neighbor during the reign of King Henry III (1216–1272), the successor to evil King John.

In 1263, a disaffected baron, Simon de Montfort, made a serious play for the throne, rallying a vast army—the so-called "disinherited"—to his standard, and marching against the king.

At first, all went well—Henry himself was captured, alongside his son Edward, at the Battle of Lewes, in 1264. But Edward escaped and, regrouping the army, routed the rebels in turn at the Battle of Evesham. Simon de Montfort was killed, Henry was restored to the throne, and the rebel army scattered to the winds.

Simon de Montfort led one of the rebellions that *may* have produced the true Robin Hood.

According to Walter of Bower's *Scotchronicon*, Robin Hood was one of those soldiers, a "famosus siccarius" (a well-known cutthroat), and one whose fame, it seems, lived on. For, almost two centuries later, Bower complained, "[F]oolish people are inordinately fond of celebrating [him] in tragedy and comedy," a reference we cannot help but immediately relate to the multitude of Robin-related ballads and plays that we know were circulating at that time.

Bower then repeats some of Robin Hood's most notable achievements.

> Once on a time, when, having incurred the anger of the king and the prince, he could hear mass nowhere but in Barnsdale, while he was devoutly occupied with the service, (for this was his wont, nor would he ever suffer it to be interrupted for the most pressing occasion,) he was surprised by a certain sheriff and officers of the king, who had often troubled him before, in the secret place in the woods where he was engaged in worship as aforesaid. Some of his men, who had taken the alarm, came to him and begged him to fly with all speed. This, out of reverence for the host, which he was then most devoutly adoring, he positively refused to do. But while the

rest of his followers were trembling for their lives, Robert, confiding in Him whom he worshipped, fell on his enemies with a few who chanced to be with him, and easily got the better of them; and having enriched himself with their plunder and ransom, he was led

With Jonas Armstrong as Robin, the BBC's 2006 TV series both updated the saga and stayed true to its roots.

from that time forth to hold ministers of the church and masses in greater veneration than ever, mindful of the common saying, that "God hears the man who often hears the mass."

Nowhere in these ballads or plays (or, at least, those that have survived), however, do we hear of Robin battling at, or even talking about, Lewes and Evesham, or any of the other engagements that punctuated that short-lived war; and nowhere in the English chronicles of the day is he mentioned as having taken part.

Perhaps we should assume that he didn't. But before we cross to that conclusion, there is one further detail to take into account.

Also numbered among de Montfort's "disinherited" was a soldier named Adam Gordon. He, too, lost his lands; he, too, adopted the life of an outlaw; he, too, made his home in a forest close to an imposing castle (at Farnham in Surrey, some 150 miles south of Nottingham); and he, too, devoted his life to plaguing the authorities, bedeviling the garrison and robbing the rich.

Sound familiar?

Adam's reputation rapidly spread, and admiration was not slow to follow. First a local hero, then a regional one, word spread further and further until finally he came to the attention of the king's son, Prince Edward.

Intrigued by the legend, Edward gathered together a small army of men and made his way southwards, to flush the outlaw from his lair. And what a lair it was, at least according to the old ballad "Prince Edward and Adam Gordon."

> . . . he doth dwell in a dreary haunt
> Remote from humankind
> Among the wolds and deep morass
> His lodging he hath ta'en
> And never that wandering wight went in
> That e'er came out again
> So dark, so narrow and so drear
> The windings all about
> That scarce the birds that skim the air
> Can find their way throughout.

Nevertheless, the prince located his prey. But, instead of unleashing his soldiers on the lone outlaw, he instead challenged Adam to a duel. He even commanded his own men not to intervene, no matter how grim things might become.

Full many a warrior stood around
That marvelous fight to see
While from their wounds, the gushing blood
Ran like the fountain free

In the event, the prince won, but only just, and was so impressed by his adversary's strength and courage that he granted Gordon an unconditional pardon, and restored to him his title and property alike.

Yet, while the chronicles of the period overflow with tales of Adam Gordon, and this incident in particular, just that one ballad has been passed down to us to commemorate his fame.

Or has it?

The Tale of the Unpunished Porter

Next up for consideration is one Robert Hood, an outlaw hailing from the town of Wakefield, in Yorkshire, who was exiled to live in Barnsdale Forest following the Battle of Boroughbridge in 1322.

Like Walter of Bower's Robin Hood, Robert chose the wrong side in the latest spot of baronial unrest, this time in support of Thomas, earl of Lancaster, against the reigning King Edward II (Henry III's grandson, who reigned 1307–1327).

This particular king was a prodigious traveler, constantly riding around his kingdom, and among the many names recorded as members of the regal retinue was a porter named Robin Hood, who served the king from March 24, 1323 to November 22, 1324—when he was paid off because he was, apparently, no longer able to work.

So what? Robin, like Robert, was scarcely an uncommon name in fourteenth-century England, and Hood continued ubiquitous, too, particularly in the north of the country, in the county of Yorkshire.

But the plot thickens. The earliest surviving ballad to name our hero *as* a hero, "A Lyttel Geste of Robyn Hode," is set during one of that same king's perambulations, undertaken between April and November of 1323, and during which he encounters, pardons and ultimately employs an outlaw whose name you have probably already guessed.

According to the ballad, Hode remains in the king's employ for around fifteen months, before tiring of the court life and returning to his former occupation. Assuming that the initial meeting took place early into the king's travels (and assuming a certain fluidity around those "fifteen months"), his employment could easily have come to an end in November 1324, the same month in which the aforementioned porter quit his job.

But wait! There is more!

The legwork for this investigation is not a recent construct. Rather, it dates from a pamphlet published in 1852 by the antiquarian Joseph Hunter (1783–1861), a Unitarian minister fascinated by the history, legends, and genealogy of his native South Yorkshire.

The Great Hero of the Ancient Minstrelsy of England, Robin Hood; his Period, real Character, etc., investigated and perhaps ascertained combined all three of these fascinations into what for many people remains the most cohesive of all attempts to place the legend of Robin Hood into some form of historical context.

Outlawing's a youngster's game. Still both in their forties, Sean Connery and Audrey Hepburn played Robin and Marian in retirement in 1976. This marked Hepburn's return to films after an eight-year absence. *Photofest*

First he links Robyn Hode to one Robert Hood, a native of Wakefield, Yorkshire, mentioned in local records dated to 1316–1317. Then he reveals that Hood was married to a woman called Matilda, which several early playwrights claim was Maid Marian's real name; and finally, he points out that Wakefield is just ten miles from the village of Barnsdale, which other medieval sources state was the outlaw's birthplace.

Marian's story, too, appears to lend credence to this theory. According, again, to sundry medieval writings, her cousin was Elizabeth de Staynton, the Prioress of Kirklees Priory. So, Hunter revealed, was the real-life Matilda's.

Of course, if it was all that straightforward, we wouldn't be having this conversation. But it isn't.

For a start, subsequent trawls through the court records revealed that Robyn the Porter was working for the king a full year earlier than Hunter's researches suggested, meaning he was already there when any pardons were offered.

Furthermore, much the same story is told in other ballads of this same period, among them "King Edward and the Shepherd" and "King Edward and the Hermit," which suggests that there was no single, definitive text, just a ballad that took for its protagonist whoever the singer fancied.

The inclusion of Maid Marian has to raise further eyebrows; she is generally regarded as a later addition to the story, bused in to provide Robin with some much-needed romantic interest. And finally, although an Elizabeth Staynton was certainly buried at Kirklees during the thirteenth century (her tombstone was discovered in 1706), we have no confirmed evidence that she was ever the prioress.

So close, but yet so far.

Another candidate rides into view just a couple of decades later, a Robin Hood who was thrown into a cell at Rockingham Jail in 1354, on the vague charge of "forest offenses"—which could mean anything from trespass to poaching to being armed with a bow, and sundry other possibilities.

But a lot of people fell foul of the laws that governed the forests, and are recorded in the annals under that very same charge. Like Andrew of Wyntoun's "wight yeomen," one cannot help but believe that a real Robin Hood would have deserved a somewhat more specific accusation than mere "forest offenses."

Robin of Loxley

In November 1992, the American tabloid *Sun* celebrated the success of Kevin Costner's recent *Robin Hood* movie by unearthing the corpse of the man himself . . . Hood's, that is, not Costner's.

According to the published story, a mummified body had been discovered in a grave in Sherwood Forest, still clad in hood and green leggings, and accompanied by a medallion that confirmed his identity for all time: "Robert of Locksley."

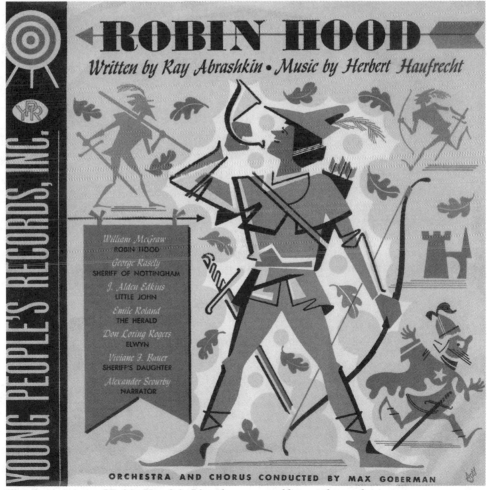

The classic image of Robin Hood, in Lincoln green and bow at the ready.

The story wasn't true, of course—people have allegedly been stumbling across Robin Hood's remains for centuries. But the fictional inscription on that fictional medallion at least confirmed one thing. It confirmed that the most stubborn of all surviving Robin Hood legends is that which opened this book, the tale that places Robin in the village of Loxley, South Yorkshire.

Probably.

There is another Loxley, in Warwickshire—close to Stratford-upon-Avon, the birthplace of another English hero, William Shakespeare, and that has its supporters, too. Pleasant though this contender might be, however, it has little to recommend it to the committed Robin researcher, or many others either. Even Margaret Halsey, doyen of acid-tongued Americans-in-England back in the late 1930s, found nothing more to remark upon there than "a wide sweep of fields and copses," and "a dazzlingly ugly" tea shop.

No, given the wealth of legends concerning Robin Hood that can be found in Yorkshire (and the paucity of them in Warwickshire), the smart money is on the first-named village.

The problem is, we do not have much in the way of authentication.

Loxley was first mentioned as a part of the legend around 1600, in an anonymous text known today as part of the Sloane Manuscripts—so titled because they were once the property of the physician Sir Hans Sloane (1660–1753), and purchased following his death under the same Act of Parliament that established the British Museum in London.

Over four thousand manuscript volumes include early writings on alchemy, chemistry, medicine, botany, magic, mathematics, and religion, many of them stemming from the pens of the greatest minds of the age: John Dee, Sir Isaac Newton, and Sir Thomas Browne among them.

Contemporary records of the great explorers rub pages with horticultural treatises, and deep within this treasure trove of arcane knowledge lies a five-and-a-half page biography of Robin Hood, written in a tiny, cramped hand which, in distilling almost every key element of the existing tales and ballads, in turn becomes the bedrock of almost all subsequent histories of the man.

From *The Sloane Life*, as it is known to researchers, we learn that "Robin Hood was borne at Lockesley, in Yorkshire, or after others, in Nottinghamshire, in the days of Henry the second, about the yeare 1160; but [lived until] the latter end of Richard the Fyrst."

This places him neatly within the time frame of the most common stories and legends.

He appears to have been of good parentage, "but was so riotous, that he lost or [sold] his patrimony, and for debt became an outlawe; then [joining] to him many stout fellows of like [disposition]."

This outlaw band took up residence in Barnsdale Forest and Clomptoun Park, also in Yorkshire, "and other such places," where they practiced with their bow and arrows until "they all excelled all the men of the land."

Soon, Robin's companions numbered "an hundred and a halfe . . . and they were counted invincible." Often, these allies were recruited after a battle—apparently, "wheresoever he h[e]ard of any that were of unusual strength and hardynes[s]," Robin would make their acquaintance, often while disguised as a beggar; somehow induce them to fight him and then, having measured their strength and prowess against his own, he would invite them to join his gang.

Many of these names are now as familiar as Robin's own.

> After such manner he procured the pynder of Wakefeyld to become one of his company, and a freyer, called Muchel, though some say he was an other kind of religious man, for that the order of fryers was not yet sprung up; Scarlock, he induced, upon this occacion: one day meting him, as he walked solitary, and lyke to a man forlorne, because a mayd to whom he was affianced was taken from by the violence of her friends, and giuen to another that was auld and welthy.
>
> Whervpon Robin, vnderstanding when the maryage-day should be, came to the church, as a beggar, and having his company not far of, which came in so sone as they hard the sound of his horne, he toking, the bride perforce from him that was in hand to have maryed her, and caused the preist to wed her and Scarlocke together.

Other writers were quick to "confirm" the evidence of the Sloan Manuscript. In 1637, for instance, John Harrison wrote (in his *Exact and Perfect Survey and View of the Mannor of Sheffield*) of a pasture known as "Little Haggas Croft, wherein is ye [foundation] of a house or cottage where Robin Hood was borne."

And that, aided by a healthy dose of speculation from sundry other interested authors and chroniclers, is how any legend grows. A kernel of truth, or something approaching it, is either embellished in the retelling, or emboldened by scholarship.

Like that old-time parlor game in which a sentence is whispered from one person to the next, undergoing a subtle change with every fresh hearing, the legend of Robin Hood is ever-changing, ever-evolving. His birthplace is no more constant than any other aspect of the story.

2

The Rise of Robin Hood

From Tiny Yeomen, Great Earls Are Grown

owhere is this process better illustrated than by Robin's gradual ascent up the social ladder.

In the earliest retellings of his story, he is just an average guy, usually a yeoman, a social rank that the *Concise Oxford Dictionary* summarizes as "a person qualified by possessing free land of forty (shillings) annual [feudal] value, and who can serve on juries and vote for a Knight of the Shire. He is sometimes described as a small landowner, a farmer of the middle classes."

Other chroniclers portrayed him as the son of a forester, one of the men who worked so diligently to keep the Royal Forests clear of poachers and trespassers.

Hood Senior was also something of an expert bowman, although he also appears to have kept some rather dubious company.

Adam Bell, Clim of the Clough, and William of Cloudesley

One of the most insistent of all early attempts to establish Robin Hood's lineage was made by the anonymous author of the ballad "Robin Hood's Birth, Breeding, Valor and Marriage"—described in the book *A Collection of Old Ballads* (1723) as "the most beautiful and one of the oldest [Robin Hood ballads] extant."

In fact there are several versions of the ballad in existence today (as is the case with many medieval writings—different scribes wrote different words), but one of these also incorporates elements of another ballad, "Adam Bell,

Clim of the Clough and William of Cloudesley," probably written during the first decades of the sixteenth century—and therein hangs a tale.

Like Robin Hood, the titular threesome were outlaws, said to roam Inglewood Forest, near Carlisle, way up in the top left-hand corner of England. Cast adrift from society as a punishment for breaching the laws surrounding hunting (those ubiquitous forestry offenses!), the trio swore allegiance to one another, and embarked upon a life of crime.

It is unclear if their story is based upon actual events, or whether they were simply invented as a local alternative to Robin Hood.

Either way, Bell, Clim, and Cloudesley (it sounds like a law firm) appear to have enjoyed at least a handful of adventures, and in the process grown so popular, at least regionally, that they were soon being allied with the tales of Robin Hood.

Indeed, admirers of fifteenth century satire should consult a Parliament Roll for the county of Wiltshire, dated 1432, in which a list of local dignitaries not only includes Robin Hood, Little John, Much the Miller and Will Scathelock, but is topped by "Adam Belle, Clim O'Cluw, Willyam Cloudesle"; and also includes what might well be a fragment of a then-popular ballad, scrawled in the margin:

Robyn Hode Inne Greenwood Stode Godeman Was He

Anyone who ever wrote random pop song lyrics in their schoolbooks will understand why.

(Wiltshire, incidentally, is at quite the opposite end of the country to Carlisle, suggesting that tales of this trio did spread far and wide.)

Adam Bell and company's connections with Robin Hood himself are weak, but nevertheless both ancient and tenacious. The American author Howard Pyle, in his spellbinding *The Merry Adventures of Robin Hood* (published in 1883) has Little John compare Robin's archery skills to those of Adam Bell, but according to "Robin Hood's Birth, Breeding, Valor and Marriage," written perhaps four centuries earlier, the trio were companions not of Robin, but of his father.

> The father of Robin a forrester was,
> And he shot in a lusty long bow,
> Two north country miles and an inch at a shot,
> As the Pinder of Wakefield does know.
> For he brought Adam Bell, and Clim of the Clugh,
> And William a Clowdeslé

> To shoot with our forrester for forty mark,
> And the forrester beat them all three.

Again we learn that Robin was born "in merry sweet Locksly Town," this time in Nottinghamshire, but now we discover something about his mother—that she was a niece of Sir Guy of Warwick, another legendary hero of the age:

> For he slew the blue bore that hangs up at the gate,
> Or mine host of The Bull tells a lye.

and also the sister of Gamwell of Great Gamwell Hall—the father of the man who would later become Will Scarlet!

> And a noble house-keeper was he,
> Ay, as ever broke bread in sweet Nottinghamshire,
> And a squire of famous degree.

It isn't much to go on. But it confirms Robin's original station in life, in the years before the balladeers, troubadours, storytellers, and filmmakers took his renown so much further afield; before the tales of his heroism became more and more pronounced, and before the legend of his legacy swelled to its modern, massive proportions.

Not all of these elaborations were necessarily wise. In 1737, messrs A. Bettesworth and C. Hitch published a volume whose title, in full, is as follows: *The Whole Life, and Merry Exploits of Bold Robin Hood, Earl of Huntington: Shewing how He Became an Out-law, and Fled to the Forest of Sherwood ; where He and His Gang Shelter'd Themselves for Many Years, Committing Many Notorious Villanies and Robberies, Insomuch that All Passengers Were Forc'd to Pay Them Tribute : and at Last Betook Himself to a Monastery in Yorkshire, where He was Bled to Death by a Monk : to which is Added, Several Songs Not in the Former Impressions: with The Whole History of Johnny Armstrong, of Westmoreland.* (Armstrong being a lesser-known outlaw.)

An early attempt to place the ballads into some kind of overarching chronology, linked with sundry other adventures and observations, *The Whole Life* compensates for tradition's lack of insight into Robin's early years by informing us not only that "his Father and Mother were so fond of him that they let him suck till he was two years old," but that he was also proclaimed "head scholar at school."

A pampered over-achiever, a spoiled brat, a complete and utter mammothrept, as the medieval scribes would have put it. Odd qualities indeed for the boy destined to become King of the Outlaws.

However, he soon conforms to type, inheriting the estate of his uncle, Squire Gamwell, and proceeding to fritter away the ensuing fortune by indulging healthily in what we can only assume was a most hedonistic lifestyle.

Soon, he was all but penniless, and so

> he began to study what Course to take to maintain his Company, for you must think his Expences was very great; at last, he resolv'd upon this. To take from the Rich and be [*charitable*] to the Poor; and it was not long before he put his Thoughts in Practice, and rob all that

Another classic depiction of Robin Hood, seen through the eyes of Walt Disney.

came by that Way; but the Poor he rather reliev'd, than took from them: He grew so famous for Robberies, that every body dreaded to ride that Way, for fear of meeting with Bold Robin Hood; for if the Rich were ever so strongly arm'd it avail'd them nothing.

That's more like it, although purveyors of the sensational might prefer the story told by another old ballad, the seventeenth century survivor "Robin Hood's Progress to Nottingham."

Although this is not an especially heroic tale, either.

Again, the young Robin was of relatively humble stock. But he was something of a braggart, nonetheless.

Falling into conversation with no less than fifteen drunken foresters, Robin makes what they consider to be a very boastful wager, that he could kill a deer from a distance of one hundred rod—that is, about a mile and a half.

Of course they take him up on it, but when he wins, they refuse to pay up, telling him to leave before they beat him up.

So Robin kills them all; then, when a crowd of people converge on him, intending to arrest him, he shows little mercy there, either. As English folk musician Grey Malkin puts it, "This bloodthirsty and positively sociopathic turn of events . . . is clearly not the Robin that the BBC or Disney imagined when constructing their interpretations, nor the one that springs to mind for most people. Robin here is a cold blooded teenage killer, ruthless and proud of it."

> 'You said I was no archer', said Robin Hood,
> 'But say so now again'
> With that he sent another arrow
> That split his head in twain.
> The people that lived in fair Nottingham
> Came runing out amain,
> Supposing to have taken bold Robin Hood,
> With the forresters that were slain.
> Some lost legs, and some lost arms,
> And some did lose their blood,
> But Robin Hood hee took up his noble bow,
> And is gone to the merry green wood.
> They carryed these forresters into fair Nottingham,
> As many there did know;
> They digd them graves in their church-yard,
> And they buried them all a row.

The Earl of Huntingdon

As early as 1569, the printer and scholar Richard Grafton, writing his *Chronicle at Large*, took issue with the traditional portrayal of Robin merely as yeoman, citing as evidence:

> In an olde and auncient Pamphlet I finde this written of the sayd Robert Hood. This man (sayth he) discended of a nobel parentage: or rather beyng of a base stocke and linage, was for his manhoode and chivalry advaunced to the noble dignité of an Erle.
>
> Excellyng principally in Archery, or shootyng, his manly courage agreeyng therunto: But afterwardes he so prodigally exceeded in charges and expences, that he fell into great debt, by reason wherof, so many actions and sutes were commenced against him, wherunto he aunswered not, that by order of lawe he was outlawed, and then for a lewde shift, as his last refuge, gathered together a companye of Roysters and Cutters, and practised robberyes and spoylyng of the kynges subjects, and occupied and frequentede the Forestes or wilde Countries.
>
> The which beyng certefyed to the King, and he beyng greatly offended therewith, caused his proclamation to be made that whosoever would bryng him quicke or dead, the king would geve him a great summe of money, as by the recordes in the Exchequer is to be seene.

The notion that Robin was an earl, although it appears to be vouchsafed only by an "olde auncient Pamphlet" (that Grafton does not name, and which the centuries have not preserved), quickly became adhered to the legend. Fifteen years later, the author of the poem "Albion's England," William Warner, made a similar claim, at the same time as glancing towards another of the Robin legends, that he was a fighter in the army of Thomas, Earl of Lancaster (see the "Tale of the Unpunished Porter," in the preceding chapter).

The story is relayed in the words of an old hermit. Earl Thomas, on the run following his rebellion's defeat, is hiding out in some woods when he encounters the anchorite, and they fall to discussing the fates of past outlaws. First the hermit sets the scene:

> I have no tales of Robin Hood, though mal-content was he
> In better daies, first Richards daies, and liu'd in Woods as we
> A Tymon [misanthrope] of the world: but not devoutly was he soe,
> And therefore praise I not the man. But for from him did grow
> Words worth the note, a word or twaine of him ere home I go.

He then outlines what we might consider the very heart of the legend: a fallen nobleman who led an army of yeomen in a never-ending quest to rob from the rich and give to the poor:

> Those daies begot some mal-contents: the Principall of whome
> A Countie [earl] was, that with a troope of Yomandrie did rome
> Brave Archers, and deliver men, since nor before so good
> Those tooke from rich to give the poore, and manned Robin Hood.
> Who fed them well, and lodg'd them safe in pleasant Caves and
> Bowers,
> Oft saying to his merrie men, what [lustier] life than ours?

Throughout the 1500s, then, Robin was an earl, a middling rank within the nobility, and at the very end of the century, the Elizabethan playwright Anthony Munday wrote a pair of plays in which his earldom was identified: *The Downfall of Robert, Earl of Huntington* and *The Death of Robert, Earl of Huntington*.

There is no firm historical proof to link Robin Hood with any particular Earl of Huntington; in fact, there is no such person as the Earl of Hunting*ton*. But Hunting*don* is another matter entirely, and with that minor correction in spelling out of the way, a sliver of circumstantial evidence rapidly makes itself felt.

Several slivers, in fact.

Brief mention has already been made of Barnsdale, the Yorkshire village which some say was Robin's original home. But there is another Barnsdale in the county of Rutland, which, in the late twelfth century, fell into the lands held by Waltheof, Earl of Huntingdon. And he fascinates because he led not one but two brief rebellions against King William I, the Norman duke who conquered England in 1066.

A rare example of a Saxon nobleman who was permitted to retain his lands even after the Norman Conquest, Waltheof's first uprising was swiftly quashed. He did not, however, give up and, in 1076, he rose up in violent defiance once more.

Again his rebellion was crushed, only this time, William was taking no chances. He had Waltheof executed and the earldom was greatly reduced in power. It remained in the family, however, passing first to Waltheof's daughter Maud, and then to her husband, Simon de Senlis.

Renowned as the man who built Northampton Castle (he was also the first Earl of Northampton), de Senlis died in France around 1113, and Maud remarried, this time to the future King of Scotland, David I. It is their grandson, also named David, with whom Anthony Munday appears to have been concerned.

For his life can be viewed through a *very* Robin Hood–shaped prism.

As we have already mentioned, one of the most common "historical" elements in the modern tale of Robin Hood (courtesy of Sir Walter Scott's epic novel *Ivanhoe*) places him firmly within that tumultuous period when

The merry menagerie: Robin and company in Disney's best-remembered retelling.

the throne was effectively vacant, while the king, Richard the Lionheart, was away fighting the Third Crusade in the Holy Land.

An interim regency had been set in place by the king, headed up by the Bishop of Durham, Hugh de Puiset, and William de Mandeville, 3rd Earl of Essex (later replaced by Richard's chancellor William Longchamp). But great swathes of the country had also been handed to his brother Prince John, who immediately started scheming a more substantial role. And, of course, more substantial riches.

Robin Hood was one of the men who stood against the prince; he remained a firm supporter of the rightful king; and so, it seems, did the Earl of Huntington; he was involved in Richard's coronation, and also traveled to the Holy Land to fight. As did Robin Hood.

So far, so coincidental. Where things become interesting is in the fact that we do not know how long the earl was away, or even if he did actually go to the Holy Land. Sir Walter Scott's novel *The Talisman* is the main source for that story, and that was written some six centuries later. Earl David simply vanishes from the historical record for close to four years, beginning just two weeks after his marriage, in 1190, to the Earl of Chester's daughter Maud, or Matilda.

This isn't so unusual. The minutia of war overflows with tales of gallant young warriors wedding their sweethearts on the eve of battle. But four years was a long time to be away, even by the standards of medieval warfare.

King Richard himself intended returning home after just a year in the Holy Land, making his departure in September 1192, having arranged a three-year truce with the Saracen leader Saladin. He would have made it home, too, had he not been captured by Leopold V, the Duke of Austria, and imprisoned until February 1194.

But David, Earl of Huntington, might easily have made a safe return at the time of the truce. Could he then have spent the next eighteen months in hiding, in the forest, battling against Prince John and his horrible henchmen as they consolidated their control over the kingdom?

We don't know.

But David bounded firmly back into the spotlight in February 1194, just days before Richard's return, when he joined his father-in-law, the Earl of Chester, in the siege of . . . where else? . . . Nottingham Castle.

Anthony Munday muddies these waters by naming his earl Robert. But the confusion is only slight. David's son was named Robert and, while the boy died in infancy, which means he was highly unlikely to have been an outlaw as well, nevertheless the connection is made.

There are other links between David and the legend.

The earliest known literary reference to Robin Hood appears in the poet William Langland's "Piers Plowman" (1377), where he makes reference to the "rhymes of Robyn Hood and Randolf Earl of Chester"—the real-life Earl of Huntington's father-in-law. And if we hurl chronology to one side, and accept the legend as simply a jumble of facts rearranged into an easy-to-follow narrative (a haphazard approach which sustains way too many television so-called-documentaries today), the earl's career following King Richard's death in 1199 is most instructive.

In 1209, he was fined heavily for "encroachment as a result of the forest eyre of 1207–1209, contrary to the liberties of the Huntingdon honour"—in other words, claiming (or at least using) land that he did not have any legal right to.

Two years later, David was forced to sell off great swathes of property in order to honor a debt to the exchequer, and the year after that, in 1212, he was implicated in a plot to assassinate King John.

His role was not proven, and he was allowed to remain free. But when the barons rose up against King John in 1215, setting the stage for the signing of the *Magna Carta Libertatum* ("the Great Charter of the Liberties"—sometimes described to as the first civil rights document in history), Earl David was firmly on the side of the barons.

Retribution followed. By March of the following year, all of Earl David's lands had been handed to Gerard de Sottenghem, a mercenary soldier in the employ of the king.

Thus do at least a handful of the pieces fall into place. A nobleman deprived of his lands by a rapacious ruler. A loyalist fighting against a usurper. A man with family connections in all the right places . . . Earl David even had blood ties to Gisborne, home of the legend's fiendish blackguardly Guy. And finally, another Scottish historian, John Mair (or Major), writing in 1521, firmly sets the legend of Robin Hood during the reign of King Richard I.

> About this time, as I conjecture, the notorious robbers Robert Hood of England and Little John lurked in the woods, spoiling the goods only of rich men. They slew nobody but those who attacked them, or offered resistance in defense of their property. Robert maintained by his plunder a hundred archers, so skillful in fight that four hundred brave men feared to attack them. He suffered no woman to be maltreated, and never robbed the poor, but assisted them abundantly with the wealth which he took from the abbots.

But too much of David's tale is supposition, clouded by the passage of time and supported only by links drawn almost half a millennium after the fact. In chronological terms, Anthony Munday is barely a century further removed from our time than he was from the era of which he wrote.

And a lot can happen in four hundred years.

3

Earls and Elsewhere

Further Fables, Theories, and Thoughts

In 1742, writer and historian William Stukeley finally solved the mystery of Robin Hood's identity.

Or so he said.

As one of his age's most dexterous researchers, Stukeley was already well accustomed to combing through obscure family records, and delving into the dustiest archives and manuscripts, in search of the most enigmatic historical facts.

Neither was he afraid of getting his hands dirty, sometimes literally.

It is to Stukeley that we owe much of what was once believed to be true about those great prehistoric monuments that lie in southern England, Stonehenge, and Avebury, when he established himself among the first men ever to conduct what we might term a serious archaeological investigation into their original purpose.

He was also the first man to popularize a revival in Druidism, which he claimed to be the religion of the people who built those monuments in the first place.

The son of a lawyer, a Friend of the Royal Society, a Fellow of the Royal College of Physicians, secretary to the Society of Antiquaries and a Freemason too, he wrote an acclaimed biography of the scientist Sir Isaac Newton, and may well have been the first author ever to tell the tale of a falling apple inspiring Newton to formulate his theories of gravity.

It was Stukeley who first described the fossilized remains of a pleisosaur (a marine dinosaur capable of growing to some fifty feet in length) as anything more than a big fish . . . or the bones of a sinner, drowned in Noah's flood, as his local church kept insisting they were.

But it was Stukeley, too, who breathed vivid life into one of the greatest forgeries ever perpetrated upon the learned halls of British academia, when he lent his support, and the weight of his reputation, to a newly discovered fifteenth century manuscript titled *De Situ Britanniae*, which was claimed to be a copy of an otherwise lost history of Britain penned a millennium earlier by a Roman general.

In Stukeley's favor, he was not the only academic who trusted in the discovery; for the next two centuries, *De Situ Britanniae* was regarded as *the* primary source for all subsequent writings on the period, permeating everything from the most learned history to the most basic school lesson. Gibbons's *Decline and Fall of the Roman Empire* is merely the best known of the subsequent works to take *De Situ Britanniae* at face value; the first Ordinance Survey maps simply the most widespread.

It would be deep into the nineteenth century before archaeology (and cartography) could seriously challenge the book's assertions, at which point it became clear that the entire work was a forgery, probably prepared by a historian named Charles Bertram, the man who introduced the work to Stukeley.

Yet Stukeley himself was not above a little academic mischief, either, if he believed his conclusions on a subject to be correct. Many historians have been known to bend facts to fit their theories. Stukeley simply went a few steps further, and invented them.

Robert Fitz Ooth, for instance.

Stukeley's *Palaeographia Britannica or discourses on Antiquities in Britain No. I* was a collection of learned essays on a wide variety of historical mysteries, with the legend of Robin Hood just one of its subjects.

It was one that Stukeley seemed especially fond of, however, as he recalled first encountering the legends as a child, "enraptured [by] an old man who remembered the traditional ballads."

He was intrigued, too, by Anthony Munday's identification of the earl of Huntingdon as a likely candidate for the role of a historical Hood, but perplexed, perhaps, by the playwright's naming of Robert as the earl. Was there, he wondered, another gap in the historical record, one that Munday had plugged, but without explaining how?

No, there wasn't.

So Stukeley invented one, Robert fitz Ooth, a fictional Norman Lord of the genuine Kime, near Lincoln.

Indeed, he did not merely invent Robert. He invented an entire family tree, one that included the aforementioned Waltheof, and many more besides.

He made, however, one major miscalculation. Rightly or wrongly, few of the historians of the day were at all comfortable with the notion that

England's greatest medieval hero and freedom fighter, should not actually have been English.

Robert fitz Ooth is a Norman name, and the Normans were French. Even before the true extent of Stukeley's genealogical deception was uncovered, fitz Ooth did not have a hope of acceptance.

A Knight Templar

A myriad theories nurture a plethora of possibilities, then, all of them vying to firmly and finally pin down Robin Hood.

They might as well be trying to bottle lightning.

But one relatively recent theory is arresting enough to be added to the role call, put forward by writer John Paul David, and expounded in his book *Robin Hood: The Unknown Templar* (2009).

The Knights Templar—or the Poor Fellow-Soldiers of Christ and of the Temple of Solomon, to give them their correct name—are one of those historical realities that, like Robin Hood, have lent themselves to any manner of grand theories, wild legends and, occasionally, unexpected truths.

The order was founded under the auspices of the Church around 1120, a charitable organization that nevertheless produced some of the most ferocious warriors of the age. Fiercely dedicated to the cause of the Crusades, and unmistakably clad in white mantles adorned with a bright red cross, the Knight Templars were present at many of the greatest battles of the era, and were responsible, too, for building some of the most impressive castles and fortifications in the Holy Land.

Headquartered in the Temple of the Holy Mount in Jerusalem (hence the reference to the earlier Temple of Solomon in the organization's name), a once impoverished religious order quickly rose up the medieval pecking order, winning favor with the high and mighty until, in 1129, the Council of Troyes confirmed them as a favored Catholic charity.

Now there was no holding back the Templars. Donations flooded in, both willingly given and passed on under duress, but the order did not accumulate wealth purely for the sake of it.

They made their riches work for them in the most modern sense of the phrase. Behind the scenes and away from the battlefields, the Knights Templar have been credited with all but inventing the concept of modern banking, at the same time as establishing a major power base throughout Europe by the simple means of extending generous loans (and usurious interest repayments) to any worthy who requested one—the Iron Bank in

George R. R. Martin's *Game of Thrones* cycle is itself indebted to the memory of the Templars.

Unfortunately, holding the purse strings of the crowned heads of Europe was not a practice that was guaranteed to win the Templars many genuine friends, particularly once the Crusades were over and the Holy Land was irretrievably lost.

In 1307, one of the Knights Templars' most indebted clients, King Philip IV of France, made his move.

A couple of years earlier, a disaffected former Knight Templar had begun whispering that the order was not as saintly as it liked to appear; that all manner of foul calumnies were enacted in its name, not least of all during the top-secret initiation ceremony which every aspiring Knight needed to undertake.

Errol Flynn, swash, buckled, and suave, in *The Adventures of Robin Hood*.   *Photofest*

Nobody actually believed these allegations—the complainant had himself been dismissed from the order for sundry misdeeds. But Pope Clement V felt duty bound to at least be seen to investigate them, so he asked King Philip for his assistance.

The king, seeing a very satisfactory way of ensuring that his debts were utterly wiped out, agreed.

The first wave of arrests took place at dawn on Friday, October 13, 1307 (the superstitions attendant on that date are sometimes said to be a reminder of these events), and one can only marvel at the imagination displayed by the interrogators who were entrusted with exacting the truth from the prisoners.

There were the religious charges, that themselves were regarded as utterly unforgivable. The Templars, it was said, habitually spat on the cross and denied Christ. They had abandoned God, and worshipped instead a series of false idols, one of which was Baphomet, a supposed goat-headed man not at all dissimilar to contemporary depictions of the devil; another was the mummified head of John the Baptist, which the Knights were said to have discovered during their years in residence at the Temple.

Homosexuality, fraud, extortion—there was no end to the charges leveled at the unfortunate Knights, and no end, either, to the grisly tortures devised to drag the truth from the prisoners. By November, the pope was so convinced of the Knights' guilt that he ordered all Christian monarchs in Europe to seize the order's assets and arrest its followers.

More torture, more confessions, and more deaths ensued, but now the pope was growing suspicious. He had heard of Henry's indebtedness, and was certainly worldly enough to wonder if the French king was not, perhaps, following his own agenda.

The pope established his own court of justice, to hear again the testimony of the arrested men, and was astonished at how many recanted their confessions the moment the torture stopped. He became even more convinced that there was more to this affair than met the eye.

Philip was not to be held back, however. Without going so far as to accuse the pope of being in league with the Knights Templar, he nevertheless demanded that the original confessions be acted upon, and threatened military action if the pope refused.

Clement, while still dubious of the charges, could not see a way out of the ensuing dilemma. He agreed to disband the order, not because he believed a word of the confessions, but on the grounds that regardless of whether

Robin in action, from a 1795 engraving by Thomas Bewick.

the accusations were true, the scandal that had erupted around them had damaged the Knights Templar beyond any hope of redemption.

In 1312, he turned their possessions over to another order, the Hospitallers, and allowed Henry's cruel justice to take its course.

And that should have been the end of it.

But it wasn't.

Legends sprang up almost immediately, not merely of great Templar treasure troves that awaited discovery, but also the nature of those treasures.

The Templars, it was said, had discovered and secreted the Holy Grail and the Ark of the Covenant. The order itself was said to have lived on in the deepest secrecy, its power and influence still a force to be reckoned with (Freemasonry, whose own rituals borrowed much from the Templars, is one of the organizations that are believed to have emerged from their ashes).

Vast conspiracy theories have been woven around the Templars' story, and some of the most esoteric best sellers of recent years, too—*The Holy Blood and the Holy Grail*, *Focault's Pendulum,* and *The Da Vinci Code* are deeply entrenched in Templar lore.

So where does Robin Hood fall into this?

The evidence is circumstantial, but no less compelling for all that. The ballads tell us of Robin's religious faith, and mention, too, his skill as a banker—in that earliest of tales, for example, "A Lyttel Geste of Robin Hood," Robin is more than happy to extend a loan to an impecunious knight. Both of these are qualities that bound together the Knights Templars.

If we accept those theories that place a living Robin early in the fourteenth century, during the reign of King Edward II, then he would have lived, too, through the turmoil that led up to the death of the Knights Templars, and been affected, too, by the king's response to the pope's commands. Across England, county sheriffs were instructed to arrange the arrest and imprisonment of every Templar in the country.

However, the histories record no more than 153 men being taken into custody in England, suggesting either that the sheriffs did not do a particularly good job of things, or that a lot of men evaded capture.

These men would have become outlaws as a matter of course; evading the soldiers, hiding out in forests, living off the land and the money they could steal. But some of them, perhaps, might have retained sufficient of the old order's charitable instincts to also make gifts of food to the poor.

We do not have a name for the particular knight who might have become Robin Hood; nor any concrete details to raise this theory above the mere fanciful. But sometimes, the search for hard fact blinds us to the realities that are bound up in circumstance and supposition. Because truth is only as true as the existing evidence allows it to be, we may never learn the *true* truth about Robin Hood.

The Death of Robin Hood

(Reports of Which Would Appear to Be Greatly Exaggerated)

So much for the life of Robin Hood, what about his death?

The legends are, for once, more or less in agreement over that.

Suffering from an unnamed sickness, Robin believes the only remedy lies in being bled, once a common cure for a great many ailments. Based on the belief that the body functioned according to the balance of its "humors" . . . that is, blood and all the other bodily fluids . . . it therefore followed that sickness was caused when the humors fell out of balance. Too much of one could cause any number of problems, and blood was the most common culprit.

Any number of respected physicians supported this claim—among the ancients, Erasistratus (304–250 BC), Caecilius (in the early first century AD) and Galen (129–216 AD) were all dedicated proponents of the practice, and one assumes it met with considerable success, because physicians were still relieving the humors as late as the nineteenth century, and the practice lives on in the modern language as well. When somebody is described as being "good-" or "ill-humored," the expression originated not from how much they laugh when they see an elephant in a tutu, but from their state of physical well-being, too.

There were few hospitals, as such, in the medieval world. However, several religious orders practiced healing, and Robin decided to visit one of these.

In the most famous, and widespread, of the legends, he selected Kirklees Priory, where (it is said) Maid Marian's cousin Elizabeth de Staynton was the prioress. However, it was not his only choice, at least according to the eighteenth century ballad "Robin Hood and the Valiant Knight."

The ballad begins in what we might call typical fashion, with an unnamed king deciding that he has heard enough complaints about "Robin Hood and his merry men all," particularly from the clergy.

Time and again the outlaws had been "too bold," so the king convened a council of nobles to decide what should be done. Inevitably they agreed upon the ultimate solution, calling up "a trusty and worthy knight . . . Sir William by name," and bidding him:

> "Go you from hence to bold Robin Hood,
> And bid him, without more a-do,
> Surrender himself, or else the proud elf
> Shall suffer with all his crew.
>
> "Take here a hundred bowmen brave,
> All chosen men of might,
> Of excellent art for to take thy part,
> In glittering armor bright."

Sir William accepted the mission and, that midsummer day, he rode out at the head of his army, positioned his archers, and battle commenced.

> . . . their fight did last
> From morning till almost noon;
> Both parties were stout, and loath to give out;
> This was on the last [day] of June.

Stalemate ensued, and the two sides separated. But Robin, it seems, was injured.

> At length they went off; one part they went
> To London with right good will;
> And Robin Hood he to the green-wood tree,
> And there he was taken ill.

A monk was called for, and his diagnosis was swift—Robin needed to be bled. But whether by malice or sheer incompetence, the procedure went tragically awry.

> Thus he that never feared bow nor spear
> Was murdered by letting of blood;
> And so, loving friends, the story doth end
> Of valiant bold Robin Hood.
> There's nothing remains but his epitaph now,
> Which, reader, here you have;
> To this very day, and read it you may,
> As it was upon his grave.

In truth, it's not the greatest ballad that was ever written, and the ending is certainly a grotesque anti-climax—barely three verses in all cover Robin Hood's death, and there is no mention whatsoever of any last words or actions the dying man might have enacted.

So we turn back to back to Elizabeth de Staynton, the Prioress of Kirklees Abbey—for in her story, there is no room whatsoever for equivocation or uncertainty. Robin considered her a friend, a trusted ally. Unfortunately, Elizabeth's sympathies did not necessarily rest in the same direction.

> Robert Hood, beyng . . . troubled with sicknesse, came to a certein Nonry in Yorkshire called Bircklies, where desirying to be let blood, he was betrayed and bled to deth. After whose death the Prioresse of the same place caused him to be buried by the high way side, where he had used to rob and spoyle those that passed that way.
>
> And upon his grave the sayde Prioresse did lay a very fayre stone, wherin the names of Robert Hood, William of Goldesborough and others were graven. And the cause why she buryed him there was for that the common passengers and travailers knowyng and seeyng him there buryed, might more safely and without feare take their jorneys that way, which they durst not do in the life of the sayd outlawes. And at eyther end of the sayde Tombe was erected a crosse of stone, which is to be seene there at this present.
>
> *Richard Grafton, Chronicle at Large (1569)*

A Cistercian nunnery that once stood proud among the most beautiful buildings in West Yorkshire (almost all trace of it has now vanished), Kirklees Priory was founded in 1155 by the Norman nobleman Reiner de Fleming. Fittingly, it was dedicated to the Virgin Mary—as was Robin himself, according to various medieval texts.

The priory is first mentioned in connection with Robin Hood in that earliest of surviving ballads, "A Lyttel Geste of Robyn Hode," and would go on to figure frequently in subsequent legends, both ancient and modern—a possible consequence of the notoriety that attached itself to the establishment during the early 1300s.

Apparently, three of the nuns who lived there, Alice Raggid, Elizabeth Hopton, and Joan Heton, were in the habit of regularly entertaining menfolk despite their vows of chastity. Of course this created a monstrous scandal at the time; indeed, it is quite possibly the reason the priory came to occupy such a prominent, but disreputable, part of the Robin Hood legend.

Ballad writers were nothing if not up on the news of the day; in fact, many were their listeners' sole contact with events in the wider world. How

Another year, another Robin. In 2010, Russell Crowe donned the mantle.

much more topical could a performer be than to include the latest headlines in his latest song, and to give them such a prominent role as well?

One ballad, the unequivocally titled "The Death of Robin Hood," depicts the prioress as being in league, and possibly also having an affair, with a local nobleman, Red Roger of Doncaster.

Red Roger is not necessarily a name pulled from thin air. The Elizabethan Anthony Munday's play *The Death of Roberte, Earl of Huntingdon* names a *Sir* Doncaster as one of Robin Hood's most ferocious foes, and while Munday may simply have lifted the name from the earlier ballad, it also suggests that there was some form of historical enmity that bound these two characters together.

Munday's Sir Doncaster is certainly vituperative. He tells the prioress,

> I hate thy cousin, Earle of Huntington,
> Because so many love him as there doe,
> And I myselfe am loved of so fewe.
> Nay, I have other reasons for my hate;
> He is a foole, and will be reconcilde
> To anie foe he hath; he is too milde

Too honest for this world, fitter for heaven.
He will not kill these greedie cormorants,
Nor strippe base pesants of the wealth they have;
He does abuse a thieves name and an outlawes,
And is indeede no outlawe, nor no theefe—

Douglas Fairbanks was not Hollywood's first Robin, but his remains one of the definitive
visions.
Wikimedia Commons

He is unworthy of such reverent names.
Besides, he keeps a paltry whinling girle,
And will not bed, forsooth, before he bride.
Ile stand too't, he abuses maidenhead,
That will not take it, being offered,
Hinders the common wealth of able men.
Another thing I hate him for againe:
He saies his prayers, fastes eves, gives alms, does good.
For these and such like crimes, sweares Doncaster
To work the speedie death of Robin Hoode.

Doncaster's hatred towards him was not unknown to Robin and his men. Neither was the man's relationship with the prioress; according to the ballad, Will Scarlet even insisted that if Robin truly intended visiting her, he should take fifty bowmen with him for protection.

Robin, however, disagreed. He would be accompanied by Little John alone.

The pair had only just set out, amusing themselves with some target practice, when they came across a stretch of black water, over which a plank of wood has been laid. And here we run into one of those little linguistic twists that nobody has satisfactorily explained. According to the ballad,

Kneeling on the plank an old woman
Was banning Robin Hoode;
"Why dost thou bann Robin Hoode?" said Robin

And answer there comes none, because the next two lines of the ballad are missing.

"Banning" has two meanings. Either the old woman was cursing him, and was thus, in a way, responsible for all that would transpire later; or she was warning him, and it was his own stubbornness that led to his demise. Different scholars offer different interpretations. Either way, we rejoin the ballad in time for the beldame to complete her lamentation, and the outcome will be the same:

"Wee weepen for his deare body,
That this day must be lett bloode."

Robin, however, brushes her concerns (or her curse) to one side.

"The dame prior is my aunt's daughter,
And nie vnto my kinne;
I know shee wold me noe harme this day,
For all the world to winne."

Taking their leave of the old woman, Robin and Little John journey on, and soon reach Kirklees. There, Robin offers the prioress a donation of twenty pounds, and promises there will be more when he is cured. She sets to work.

> And downe then came dame prioresse,
> Downe she came in that ilke,
> With a pair off blood-irons in her hands,
> Were wrapped all in silke.
> 'Sett a chaffing-dish to the fyer,' said dame prioresse,
> 'And stripp thou vp thy sleeue:'
> I hold him but an vnwise man
> That will noe warning leeve.
>
> Shee laid the blood-irons to Robin Hoods vaine,
> Alacke, the more pitye!
> And pearct the vaine, and let out the bloode,
> That full red was to see.
>
> And first it bled, the thicke, thicke bloode,
> And afterwards the thinne,
> And well then wist good Robin Hoode
> Treason there was within.

Another missing section confounds us, but we rejoin Robin in time for him to be fighting for his life against Red Roger of Doncaster, who succeeds in running his sword through Robin's side. Robin, however, slices off his assailant's head, before attempting to make his escape.

His wound, however, is mortal. Ignoring Little John's entreaties to burn the priory to the ground, Robin staggers to the gatehouse and, with his dying breath, shoots an arrow through the window. Wherever it lands, he declares, that is where he should be buried.

And about 650 yards away, in the gardens of a nearby private house, an old grave seems unequivocal about its contents.

> Here underneath this little stone
> Lies Robert, Earl of Hungtingdon
> No archer as he was so good
> And people called him Robin Hood
> Such outlaws as he and his men
> England will never see again
> Died 24 December 1247

Which, one might innocently assume, is fairly incontrovertible evidence. Sadly, no.

In common with every other abbey and priory in England, Kirklees was dissolved, or closed, by King Henry VIII, following his break from the Catholic Church over its refusal to allow him to marry Anne Boleyn. In 1539, the incumbent prioress, Joan Kyppes, surrendered the priory and its lands to the throne and, over the next century, the land changed hands several times, before winding up the property of one John de Savile in the early 1600s.

An ambitious man, de Savile was vying for the office of Sheriff of Yorkshire at the time, and like so many politicians before and since, believed that a display of personal glory might enhance his prospects.

So he took himself off to what he thought was an appropriate piece of land, and there placed a newly constructed grave marker, inscribed, "In memory of Robin Hood."

He did not, so far as we know, look to see if Robin (or anybody else, for that matter) was actually buried there, and nobody seems to have checked since then. But he said it was Robin Hood's grave, and so Robin Hood's grave it became.

There is, after all, naught so gullible as a passing tourist.

A Swift Historical Diversion

An Earlier Robin Awakens

The story of William the Conqueror's victory over the English King Harold is one of European history's best known. At a time when the English distrust of their continental neighbors was all but a national pastime (today, by comparison, it is a barely significant minority quirk), Harold's predecessor, Edward the Confessor, was a renowned Francophile, marrying into Norman (from the duchy of Normandy) nobility and elevating a Norman to the prestigious Archbishopric of Canterbury.

When it became clear that Edward would die childless, his decision to name another Norman, Duke William, as his successor to the English throne was, in a way, inevitable.

It was not popular, however, either among the people or the government of the day, the Witan. Indeed, when Edward finally passed away, Harold Godwin, the son of the popular Saxon of Godwin, was the unanimous people's choice for the throne, and the only men who opposed his elevation were the Normans themselves.

The Witan opted for the popular vote, and Harold was duly crowned king. From the other side of the English Channel, Duke William simply seethed, and schemed. Not only had Edward guaranteed the throne to William, after all, but Harold had sworn on sundry holy relics that he would not oppose the duke's accession.

Vengeance, both earthly and divine, was inevitable.

In the fall of 1066, while Harold's army was in northern England fighting off a passing Norwegian invasion, William's Norman army crossed the channel and landed at the coastal village of Pevensey. (Visitors to this picturesque spot can still see parts of the church which the invaders built while they waited for Harold to march his army back down the country to confront them.)

The two armies, the well-rested Norman and the exhausted English, finally met at what is now the village of Battle, a few miles outside the seaside town of Hastings, on October 14, 1066, and despite their exertions, the foot-sore English soldiery was more than a match for the Normans. Taking up position on a small hill, they withstood charge after charge before William finally adopted the subterfuge which would eventually carry the day.

Aware of the long march the English had just completed (indeed, William had himself arranged for the Norwegian assault in the first place); knowing that they wanted nothing more than to get this battle over with and go home, William had his army feign a disorderly retreat, certain that the over-confident English would break ranks in pursuit.

And so they did; only for the Normans to then wheel around and carve their way back to the hill, under the covering fire of their archers. According to tradition, it was one of these archers who killed King Harold, who allegedly perished with an arrow through his eye.

Hereward meets Torfrida, an engraving by C. G. Lewis from the Charles Kingsley novel.

The battle was over.

From Hastings, William's forces marched unopposed towards London, cutting a murderous swath through the peasantry of southeastern England, and winning their submission through force of arms alone. William was crowned King of England on Christmas Day, 1066, and now he turned his attention to bringing the rest of the country under his control.

The invaders brooked no dissent.

We should all, thanks to film and fable, be familiar with the ruthless brutality of the fictional Sheriff of Nottingham. Under the Conqueror, as he worked to consolidate his hold on the country, every local ruler—almost all of whom were appointed by the new king; most of whom shared his Norman heritage—was cut from a similar cloth.

Regardless of the titles they bore, property owners who failed to give fealty to the new ruler were outlawed, imprisoned, or even slaughtered, and their lands given to William's supporters.

Towns, even entire regions, that resisted the onslaught were burned, and all across the land, great castles rose up not as defenses against further invaders, but to keep a close watch on the people who lived around them. Nottingham Castle, which features so heavily in the tales of Robin Hood, was just one of these, originally built within a year of the conquest, and rapidly growing to become a near-impregnable stronghold—as impregnable, in fact, as William's grip on the crown.

Although his reign remained turbulent and troubled, the Conqueror reigned for twenty-one years more, until his death in 1087. His direct dynasty, the House of Normandy, would then survive until the death of his grandson, Stephen, in 1154; his legacy, however, flourishes to this day, in the remains of the castles that he built, and which still draw admiring glances from tourists

So, however, do the legends of the men against whose assaults those castles were built as a defense.

Awake! Awake!

According to "Mother Hodge," a story related in Donald Suddaby's *New Tales of Robin Hood* (1950), the boy who would become Robin Hood grew up entranced by the legends of Hereward the Ever Wakeful. And if we were to place any credence whatsoever in the belief that our childhood fascinations are frequently a signal influence upon the choices we make later in life, then he could have picked no more appropriate role model. For, in terms of heroic English legend, Hereward was not simply one of its first outlaws. He still ranks among its greatest.

Unlike certain other heroes we could name, there is no doubt whatsoever that Hereward existed. Indeed, the very fact that Hereward *did* exist is reason enough for some scholars to deny that Robin Hood ever lived.

For, they ask, how is it that the most authoritative chronicles and histories of Hereward's day abound with contemporary (or near enough) references to his actions, whereas similar sources remain unflinchingly mute on the subject of Robin? Like Adam Gordon, whom we met in chapter one, if he really had been all that the balladeers claimed he was, surely *somebody* would have recorded his deeds?

Hereward, contrarily, is everywhere. Period chronicles document his life, among them the *Domesday Book*, that most fanatically detailed survey of the land, completed in 1086—that is, less than fifteen years after Hereward's death.

The *Anglo Saxon Chronicle* and the *Book of Ely*, too, attest to his life and crimes, while the first biography of the man, the *Gesta Herewardi*, was written as early as 1109, again within living memory of his exploits. Modern researchers might insist that you take some of its tales with a grain of salt, but still the gist of the *Gesta Herewardi* is vouchsated by history.

Hereward was born around 1045 in the eastern English county of Lincolnshire. It is very doubtful indeed that his parents, as some have claimed, were Leofric, the Earl of Mercia, and his wife, Lady Godiva (yes, *that* Lady Godiva). More likely, he was of relatively noble Anglo-Viking birth, and it is generally agreed that his uncle was Abbot Brand of Peterborough. Such connections would prove invaluable later in Hereward's life.

Hereward was twenty-one when the Normans invaded and the land fell beneath the iron fist of William the Conquerer. Hereward, however, was not there to witness it.

The various chronicles disagree on the precise cause, but around the age of eighteen, Hereward was sent into exile by his own father, his sins including disobedience, misbehavior, and upsetting the neighbors.

Neither was that the end of his trials. Again indicating that the boy's family was fairly powerful, the matter came to the attention of King Edward the Confessor, who declared young Hereward an outlaw.

Different accounts relate different adventures. Hereward is said to have spent time in the far southwest of England, in Cornwall, and across the sea in Ireland. By 1066, however, he was serving as a mercenary in the army of

Where Hereward the Wake made his last stand

ELY CATHEDRAL

rises in majesty

A modern rendering of the ever-Wakeful Hereward.

Baldwin V, the Count of Flanders, at which time he married a beautiful, and wealthy, Gallo-Germanic woman named Torfrida.

She, in turn, was destined to be little more than a footnote in most of the period histories, only to be raised to almost Maid Marianic heights in the nineteenth century, when Hereward's life was retold by novelist Charles Kingsley.

And rightfully so. Many of Hereward's heroics and adventures were subpoenaed over the centuries for fresh tales of Robin Hood; it was only fitting that Hereward's tale should be permitted to snatch something back. And if that should happen to be a comely maiden who was as devoted to Hereward's cause as he was, then so be it.

Hereward returned to England around 1069 to discover not only that his family lands had been taken by the Normans, but also that his brother had been brutally slaughtered, with his head then impaled on a spike alongside the front gate.

Instantly, Hereward swore revenge, and he exacted it, too. As the murdering Normans feasted drunkenly one night, Hereward crept in to the hall and killed fifteen of them. He then returned to Flanders for a short time, while he waited for the heat to die down.

An outlaw once again, he was back in England before the year's end, and now his own reign began, a campaign of retaliation and revenge fired by a sense of justice that was no weaker, nor less justified, than Robin Hood's. When the Norman Earl of Surrey's brother-in-law, Frederick, declared that he would personally see to it that Hereward was put an end to, he had barely set out on his quest before Hereward had killed him.

From his secret base on the isle of Ely, at that time a dark, treacherous swamp that was impossible to cross without local knowledge, Hereward and a growing band of supporters sallied forth to attack Norman interests across the region.

On one occasion, it is said, no less a personage than the king himself, William the Conqueror, rode out in search of this human devil. Hereward's arrow at least unseated him from his horse.

Soon, one of several rival claimants for the English throne, the Danish Sweyn Estrithson, had added his own men to Hereward's army, and though small in numbers, they showed no fear. When William dismissed Abbot Brand from Peterborough Abbey and replaced him with a more compliant Norman priest, Hereward immediately led an assault on the abbey, sacking it and making off with its treasures.

It is uncertain what he did with them—some say that the Danes carried them home with them. No matter. Hereward's goal had been to deprive the Normans of the abbey's wealth, and he did so.

Another army joined with Hereward, this time belonging to the former Earl of Northumbria, another man displaced by the invaders, and now the Normans took decisive action. A huge army was dispatched to Lincolnshire to crush the rebellion once and for all, its military might reinforced by some of the finest engineers in the land.

Everybody by now was aware that the Isle of Ely was impregnable by normal standards. But the Normans believed they knew how to defeat it. They would build a mighty wooden causeway across the swamp, and then simply march into Hereward's stronghold.

The plan might have worked, as well. Unfortunately, the weight of the army, in full armor and weaponry, was too great for the causeway. The timbers cracked, the causeway sank. Many men drowned.

It was time for Plan B. In the belief that these simple Englishmen could be cowed by superstition, the Normans procured themselves a witch, built a great wooden tower, and then wheeled it to the edge of the swamp. From the top of this edifice, the witch set about casting spells and blasting curses upon the rebels—who responded by setting fire to the tower. That was the end of the witch.

It is around this point that we see how so many heroic legends of the medieval age may (and only may; it could be mere coincidence) spring from a common source or inspiration.

Anxious to discover the Norman plot, Hereward disguised himself as a potter and insinuated himself into the enemy camp, learning their plans and then escaping back to his base with a wealth of information.

The Scottish hero William Wallace affected a similar disguise when he needed to know what the English were planning. And so too does Robin in the ballad "Robin Hood and the Potter," dated to around 1500.

Of course Robin's intention is primarily to make mischief and further gall the sheriff (in which aim he succeeds admirably); Hereward's had more serious connotations. But he was successful, and so the siege continued.

In the end, Hereward was betrayed by some of the very men he had pledged to aid, a band of monks whom he had brought into his camp to protect them from further Norman assaults on the Church.

Unfortunately, the monks, so accustomed to a life of comfort and greed, swiftly wearied of the hardships that accompany a state of siege; and grew heartily sick of the plain food that was their daily diet.

They sent a message to the Normans, offering to negotiate. A few bribes later, the monks revealed the one safe, secret route into the outlaws' camp.

That was the night that the rebellion was crushed, the defenders massacred. Hereward was more than fortunate to escape with his life.

Undeterred by the defeat, however, he continued to live as an outlaw, fighting the Normans at every opportunity. Or, as Charles Kingsley wrote in 1866,

> And now is Hereward to the greenwood gone, to be a bold outlaw; and not only an outlaw himself, but the father of all outlaws, who held those forests for two hundred years, from the fens to the Scottish border.

Author Charles Kingsley. *Hereward the Wake* was but one of his many classic novels.   *Wellcome Library, London*

Utlages, forestiers, latrunculi, sicarii, sauvages, who prided themselves upon sleeping on the bare ground—they were accursed by the conquerors, and beloved by the conquered. The Norman viscount or sheriff commanded to hunt them from hundred to hundred, with hue and cry, horse and bloodhound. The English yeoman left for them a keg of ale, or a basket of loaves, beneath the hollins green, as sauce for their meal of "nombles of the dere."

With the same friendly yeoman that was "a good felawe," they would lodge by twos and threes during the sharp frosts of midwinter, in the lonely farm-house which stood in the field or forest-clearing: but for the greater part of the year their lodging was on the cold ground in the holly thickets, or under the hanging rock, or in a lodge of boughs.

And they found fair lasses, too, in time, . . . like Torfrida and Maid Marian; Then called they themselves "merry men"; and the forest the "merry greenwood"; and sang, with Robin Hood,

"A merrier man than I, bdyve
There lives not in Christentie."

Hereward's luck ran out in the end. According to some chronicles, he finally conceded defeat, and slipped back into exile. According to others, he was ambushed by a band of Norman knights, and slaughtered on the spot. But the bitterest tale is that told by Charles Kingsley—in his novel, Hereward finally made peace with the king, only to be murdered in his bed. Torfrida is left alone to howl her grief.

He writes a happy ending, however. After a fashion.

And after that things waxed even worse and worse, for sixty years and more; all through the reigns of the two Williams, and of Henry Beauclerc, and of Stephen; till men saw visions and portents, and thought that the foul fiend was broken loose on earth. And they whispered oftener and oftener that the soul of Hereward haunted the Bruneswald . . . many hunters hunting, black, and tall, and loathly, and their hounds were black and ugly with wide eyes, and they rode on black horses and black bucks.

. . . the French monks of Peterborough said how it was The Wake, doomed to wake for ever . . . but the poor folk knew better, and said that the mighty outlaw was rejoicing in the chase, blowing his horn for Englishmen to rise against the French.

. . . and those who had the spirit of Hereward in them, fled to the merry greenwood, and became bold outlaws, with Robin Hood, Scarlet, and John.

What Did Robin Have Against the French?

Apart From the Fact That They Killed the Rightful King of England, Subjugated the Land Beneath a Totalitarian Yoke, and Insisted on Speaking a Foreign Language, That Is.

For confirmed forest dwellers, Robin and his men certainly got around. A lengthy verse published in the eighteenth century collection *The English Archer: Or Robin Hood's Garland*, and titled "The Noble Fisherman or Robin Hood's Preferment," finds our hero tiring of foraging for food and poaching deer in the woods, and resolving instead to take up an alternative, better-paying occupation.

> Therefore I will to Scarborough go
> A merry fisherman I will be

And so he does. Disguising himself as a simple, poor fisherman named Simon, Robin made his way to what was then one of England's premier fishing ports, and signed on as a fisherman.

Unfortunately, he is useless. He does not have a clue how to perform the simplest task, and one could almost imagine his shipmates cursing the day he ever set foot on their vessel—until, that is, the day that a French warship hove into view and launched an attack on the fishing boat.

Now Robin could show what he could do. The moment danger threatened, he became a changed man, casting off his lowly demeanor and proceeding to slaughter the entire French crew.

For give me my bent bow in my hand
And never a Frenchman will I spare
Then straight they boarded the French ship
They laying dead all in their fight

Barry Ingham was Robin in 1967's *Challenge for Robin Hood.*   *Photofest*

Of course, this all occurred to the unbridled delight of Robin's new-found companions. For not one of them had any love for the Frenchman, and it wasn't only because the Normans had conquered England a century or so before.

In fact, much the reverse was now true—French by descent, William's successors weren't only becoming increasingly Anglicized. They were also acquiring ever greater swaths of France for the English crown, either by war or by marriage.

A near permanent state of distrust now existed between the two nations, an enmity that only flared further when King Henry II, the Conqueror's grandson, ascended to the English throne, and added the French duchy of Aquitaine and the county of Poitou to his realm following his marriage to Eleanor, the Duchess of Aquitaine.

Eleanor herself had previously been married to France's King Louis VII. When he, rather foolishly, had the marriage annulled after Eleanor failed to produce any male heirs, he not only lost an influential wife, he also lost what had been a substantial dowry—Aquitaine at that time stretched from Loire to the Pyrenees, and the doorstep of the counts of Toulouse, and Louis had believed (or had been led to believe) that the territory would now pass to the two daughters he and Eleanor had produced.

Instead, Eleanor gave it to the hated English, an action which many historians have credited with ensuring the appalling relations England and France were to endure throughout the medieval period.

Aquitaine itself was outraged over this sudden change of sovereign, and Henry II spent much of his reign watchful against rebellion. This finally erupted during the mid-1160s, a minor affair compared with the mischief which subsequent French peasants would ferment, but still troublesome enough that the king's intention of passing the provinces along to his son Richard (the future Lionheart) had to be postponed until the uprising was quashed. This finally accomplished, Richard became ruler of Aquitaine and Poitou in 1168.

But still the province simmered, and Richard would find much of his own reign bedeviled by the French, both within Aquitaine and beyond. The new French king, Philip II, was obsessed with reclaiming what he believed to be his national birthright, and he would prove a tenacious adversary.

Richard became king of England in 1189, and promptly relinquished Aquitaine to his mother, Eleanor, while retaining Poitou for the crown. This did not, however, quell the unrest—it would be 1226 before a new English king, Henry III, and the likewise newly crowned eleven-year-old French

Released to coincide with Disney's 1952 movie version of the legend, this 45 depicts Richard Todd in a classic pose, but raises one question. Robin did lots of things in the forest, but did he ever sing "Riddle-de-diddle-de-Day"?

monarch Louis IX, concluded a treaty which saw the English finally relinquish their claims on Poitou (together with Normandy and Anjou) in return for a new territory in the south, the so-called Duchy of Guienne.

As it turned out, no such Duchy was ever actually passed to the English, and so the squabbling and warring continued, both in the disputed territory of Aquitane and elsewhere.

Neither side, however, relinquished an inch. When the future King Edward I married Eleanor of Castile, he received the province of Gascony as part of her dowry, much to the dismay of its inhabitants; and by 1337, a new English king, Edward III, was not only claiming to be the rightful king of France, he was even issuing coinage that described him as such! Edward would not relinquish this claim until 1360, when the Treaty of Bretigny persuaded him to exchange it for an unchallenged claim upon Aquitaine.

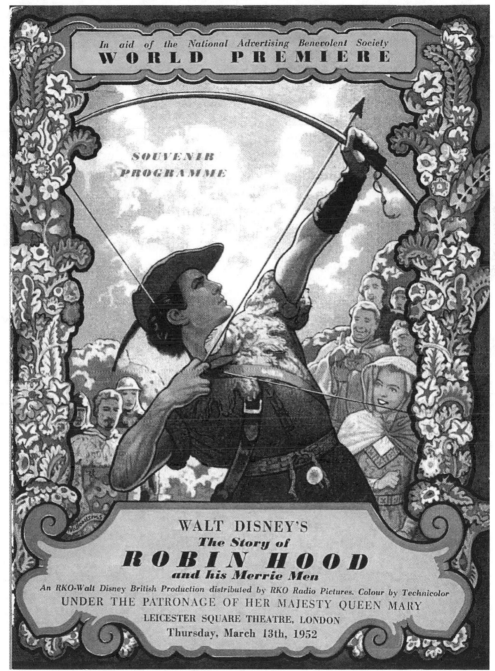

"Richard Todd, Richard Todd, riding through the glen . . ."

Now, however, the English hold on the land began to slip. In 1362, Edward's son, the Black Prince, Edward, was raised to Prince of Aquitaine, before his failing health forced him to return it to his father in 1372.

Edward then elevated the Duke of Lancaster to the lordship, but it was an ill-starred decision. By the end of the year, a series of often embarrassing reverses ensured that Bordeaux remained the only sizable town left in English hands throughout the entire province!

But France was in no fit state to take advantage of the fact. Throughout the first decades of the fifteenth century, the country was in a state of virtual anarchy, as the insane King Charles VI bumbled and blustered the country to a political—and therefore military—standstill. By early 1419, England had reclaimed Normandy, and now it was King Henry V whose coinage was styling him King of France.

By the end of the year, Henry had won the hand of Princess Catherine of France; was claiming powers of Regency for the remainder of the mad king's reign; and had guaranteed for his son, Henry VI, the succession of the French throne.

Sadly, his triumph was to prove short-lived.

Although much of France did accept Henry's right to the throne, to the south and west, isolated pockets of resistance rallied to the cause of the country's independence.

Between 1429, when Joan of Arc inspired a ragtag French army to win Orleans back from the English, and 1451, virtually the entire country was clawed back by the perfidious French. Only one "English" town remained, the channel port of Calais, and this foothold England would retain until the reign of Mary Tudor, a century later.

But that's why Robin Hood hated the French, and so many of their number met sticky ends at his hands. No matter which period of medieval history in which one chooses to set his stories, and different interpretations give us some two hundred years to play with, one thing remained constant—the French were the enemy. Except, of course, when somebody else was.

7

Robin Hood and the Holiest War

A Brief History of the Crusades

The problem with history is that it was all such a long time ago. We read, for example, of a war that lasted for three hundred years, and it feels like the blinking of an eye, been and gone in as much time as it takes to read the sentence.

Put it into perspective, however. Imagine if the American revolution, sparking into life in 1775, was *still* being fought today; if the English crown still ruled the land, and would continue to do so until somewhere in the region of another few decades to come. Reflect upon the entire history of an independent United States of America, and effectively wipe it all out.

That is how long the Crusades lasted, from 1095, when Pope Urban II first rallied Christendom to reclaim the Holy Land from the Saracen hoardes (as Moslems and Arabs alike were termed at the time), until well into the 1300s, and beyond that if one wants to consider sundry expeditions against the expanding Ottoman empire of what is now Turkey.

The wars were not constant. The first crusade, which launched in 1096, was initially fought by twenty thousand religiously inspired peasants who flocked from their western homelands to fight, only to be slaughtered in an ambush in northern Turkey.

More conventional armies followed, however, and these troops succeeded in taking the city of Antioch, also in modern Turkey, before heading south to besiege Jerusalem—the center, insisted the pope, of Christian worship.

The city fell to the western invaders in 1099, and the region was divided into four so-called Crusader states: the Kingdom of Jerusalem, the County of Edessa, the Principality of Antioch, and the County of Tripoli.

Thus ended the First Crusade, although of course, the fighting did not stop. Moslems and Jews alike continued to battle the Crusader garrisons,

PLAYER'S CIGARETTES

RICHARD I

The Lionhearted King of twelfth-century England is at the center of most retellings of the Robin Hood legend.   *Photofest*

their resistance building in strength over the next fifty years until finally, in 1145, the Second Crusade was launched to suppress the multitudinous mutinies.

But while a certain stability was created, a most fearsome enemy was gathering strength.

King Richard and Saladin

An-Nasir Salah ad-Din Yusuf ibn Ayyub—Saladin to the westerners—was Sultan of Egypt and Syria, the founder of the Ayyubid dynasty, a master tactician, and an inspiring warrior.

Under his leadership, the Crusader states came in for more punishment than ever before, and in 1187, Saladin retook the city of Jerusalem, while dealing the occupying Crusaders an utterly humiliating defeat at the battle of Hattin.

The Third Crusade launched less than two years later, and this is the one that intrigues Robin Hood's supporters, both those who flock to the familiar tellings of the tale, and those who support the Earl of Huntingdon's claims.

In a rare moment of agreement, it was kings Henry II of England and Philip II of France who led the outing, suspending their own warring to battle with what they perceived as a greater foe. Modern historians disdain their zeal, pointing out that Jerusalem is as holy to Moslems and Jews as it is to Christians. At the time, however, no such distinctions were made, or even considered.

Again, the populace was rallied, with thousands of men from the lowest peasant to the highest aristocrat flocking to the banner, and as they made their way across Europe, some by sea, many more by land, so more people joined them. By the time the various forces landed in the Holy Land, it was one of the greatest invasion forces history had ever seen.

England's King Henry II was not among them, however. On July 6, 1189, he finally succumbed to the bleeding ulcer that had long been tormenting him. His son Richard, already a skilled military man, succeeded him to the throne.

Already, Richard had a reputation for religious zealotry; barely had he taken the throne than a rumor spread that he was planning to massacre London's Jews. He probably wasn't (although he did ban Jews from attending his coronation on September 3), but the city's Christians were nothing if not loyal. *They* rose up against the Jews, destroying Jewish-owned property, and even forcibly baptizing anybody unfortunate enough to fall into their hands. Richard responded not only by quelling the mob, but also executing many of its ringleaders.

Although he had frequently disagreed with, and even risen up against, his father, Richard was wholly in agreement with the need for a new Crusade. Early into the following summer of 1190, Richard departed for the Holy Land. He would be gone much of the next four years.

One of the key ingredients of the Robin Hood legend is that Prince John, Richard's younger brother, took advantage of his sibling's absence to raise taxes, and then to keep on raising them.

This is true, but Richard himself was no weakling when it came to bleeding the poor. A crusade was a costly business, and having drained the country's treasury, Richard set about raising further finances through taxation.

It was not a popular move, and not only for financial reasons. Although the general populace supported the idea of restoring the Holy Land to Christian rule, there was nevertheless a strong belief in the fact that the war was Rome's, not England's or even France's. Should not Rome, therefore, be bearing the brunt of the cost? (The Sheriff of Nottingham raises a similar point in the 2006 *Robin Hood* television series.)

To believe that, however, is to overlook not only the sheer power of the Church at that time, but also the deeply held faith of the people. Kings were powerful men, of course, but their powers were limited to this life, this earth. Please your king, and at best he could reward you with property, titles, money.

The pope, and the hierarchy of bishops and abbots that were arrayed beneath him, on the other hand, held eternity in their hands. Please them, and all the riches of heaven were yours. Displease them and only hell awaited—and hell, to the medieval mind, was as real as London, Rome or Jerusalem.

That, if we want to be cynical about it, was why kings paid for papal wars; that was why peasants fought in foreign wars. They were purchasing salvation.

It was June 1191 before Richard arrived in the Holy Land, having wintered in Sicily and conquered Cyprus *en route*. Now the real crusading could begin, with the capture of the city of Acre, and the defeat of Saladin's armies at the battle of Arsuf. And the first legends began swirling around

Robin Derek was Robin in 1950's *Rogues of Sherwood*.

the king—how, though the long sea journey had seen him laid low by scurvy (a common illness among seamen, brought on by a lack of fresh fruit and vegetables . . . its cure is the reason the English are still sometimes referred to as "limeys"), he was still able to fight, picking off enemy soldiers with his crossbow while being borne across the battlefield on a stretcher.

The city of Jaffa was the next to fall, and by November, Richard and his army were marching on Jerusalem, the enemy fleeing in absolute disarray before them. But twelve miles from the city, the weather turned against the invaders.

Biting cold and torrential rains bogged the army down, and the prospect of successfully besieging the city under such conditions grew less and less palatable. Finally, Richard ordered his troops to withdraw to the coast, while he attempted to arrange a truce with Saladin.

The sultan rejected his overtures. Though his Saracen armies had taken a heavy beating at Arsuf, they were by no means defeated. Had Richard plowed on through the bad weather, Jerusalem would probably have fallen without too much of a fight. But the decision to back away gave Saladin the chance to regroup his armies and rebuild their morale.

Richard was not idle throughout this period. He refortified the city of Ascalon, and was kept further occupied by the politics of the Crusader states, striking deals within deals with their leaders.

The Saracens remained a threat, too; no sooner had Conrad of Montferrat been acclaimed the rightful King of Jerusalem than he was struck down by the most feared fighters in Saladin's entire arsenal, the Hashashin, from whom we take the modern word "assassin."

Or was he? Richard had personally opposed Conrad's crowning, favoring instead his own nephew, Henry II of Champagne. Barely had the unfortunate Conrad been laid to rest than his widow, Isabella, was being married to Henry, and he was being prepared for the kingship. It was all, whispered rumor insisted, very convenient indeed.

In June 1192, Richard marched again against Jerusalem, but those tiresome politics continued to niggle, and the army turned around again.

This time it was a matter of strategy; Richard, at the head of the English army, believed the best way to defeat Saladin was to ignore Jerusalem and instead attack the sultan's home base in Egypt. The Duke of Burgundy, commanding the French, wanted only to secure Jerusalem. In fact, the only point they could agree upon was that there were not enough men to undertake both missions. So they ultimately chose to do neither.

Saladin, in the meantime, was growing stronger. The Crusaders were under constant attack now, skirmish after skirmish keeping them on their toes. The one time a Saracen army did confront them in the field, it was soundly defeated, but the war of attrition continued. And now, Richard began hearing disquieting rumors from his own far-off kingdom—how Prince John had struck an alliance with the French King Philip (who, rather sensibly, had already returned home), and was now plotting to usurp the throne of England.

It was time to go home.

According to the most popular modern retellings of the legends—the Richard Greene and Jonas Armstrong television series, and movies starring Douglas Fairbanks and Kevin Costner—the man who would become Robin Hood was alongside the king throughout this entire period, a brave warrior who might even, according to some variations, have ascended to the king's personal guard.

Indeed, the 2006 television series even claims that Robin saved Richard's life when another band of Hashashin descended upon the Crusaders camp and came within an inch of murdering the king—a plot line that also permitted the writers to illustrate the growing strength of Prince John's position back home.

Just as contemporary rumor insisted that Conrad of Montferrat's killers, far from being trained Saracen assassins, were in reality Englishmen in heavy disguise, so this televisual assault upon Richard is revealed to have been designed and carried out by Prince John's most fervent supporters, under the leadership of the man destined to become one of Robin's most resolute foes, the wicked Sir Guy of Gisborne.

This particular incident is pure fiction. But Robin's return from the Holy Land would have followed regardless; in September 1192, Richard and Saladin finally arranged a truce and the king and his armies set out for home.

Eighteen months of captivity, ransom, intrigue and plotting later, Richard finally set foot once again on English soil. He had been King of England for five years, but had spent less than one-fifth of his reign in the country.

The King Comes Home

It was just before Christmas 1192 that Richard realized he wouldn't be seeing his home any time soon. Shipwrecked off the Italian coast, near

Aquilea, he decided to continue his journey by land. Just outside Vienna, however, he was captured by the Duke of Austria, Leopold V—cousin to the unfortunate Conrad of Montferrat.

Leopold was among those who firmly believed Richard had been behind the assassination, and imprisoned him. However, when word of the capture reached the pope, Leopold found himself excommunicated by the Church—it was illegal to imprison Crusaders.

Unwilling to meekly give in, Leopold instead handed Richard over to the Holy Roman Emperor Henry VI, who had his own reasons to dislike the English king—mostly for his meddling in continental affairs on his way out to the Holy Land.

Henry, too, was excommunicated, but seems not to have cared. Instead, he demanded a ransom of 100,000 pounds of silver, a sum in the region of three times the English crown's annual income. Prince John, upon receiving the demand, instead offered around half that amount—if Henry would *keep* Richard.

Richard's mother, Eleanor, was more loyal. Taxes, high under Richard, even higher in those regions that were under John, were raised again, this time to raise the required ransom, although Eleanor also recognized that the Church had some responsibility for the situation. Not only was the clergy taxed at the same rate as laymen (25 percent of the value of any property they held), she also set about confiscating the Church's treasures.

Robin Hood, too, did what he could—according to the Errol Flynn movie, he set about robbing the rich with even greater vigor, to raise the necessary money. And finally, on February 4, 1194, Richard was freed. A few days later, Prince John received a note from the King of France: "Look to yourself; the devil is loose."

Richard would not be taking things easy once he arrived home. First he needed to reestablish his control over his own kingdom, pushing his brother's supporters out of the positions of power to which they had been unlawfully raised; restoring the rightful landowners (or, at least, men that he could trust) to the newly liberated estates; and where the law, or politics, failed to budge a particular incumbent, he turned to military might.

The siege and eventual capture of Nottingham Castle was just one of the actions that Richard was forced to fight once he returned to England, and the tradition that Robin Hood was a part of the besieging army is one that is too good to ignore. Because David, Earl of Huntingdon, was certainly there.

The Siege of Nottingham Castle

Prince John had seized Nottingham Castle (together with that at nearby Tickhill) in 1191. It was a sturdy, imposing edifice, erected upon a narrow ridge of sandstone that, at its highest point, soared some two hundred feet above the city.

Both natural and man-made defenses safeguarded it and the castle's defenders, under the guidance of the Sheriff of Nottinghamshire, had had plenty of time in which to prepare for a siege—in fact, they'd been expecting one almost since the castle was first taken.

Prince John himself was in France when Richard finally landed in England on March 13, 1194, and less than two weeks later, on March 25, the Lionheart's armies were camped not only at the gates of Nottingham Castle, but also those others that John had taken over: Tickhill, where the Bishop of Durham, Hugh de Puiset, commanded the armies of Yorkshire and Northumberland; Marlborough, where the Archbishop of Canterbury led the attack, and Lancaster Castle, besieged by Canterbury's brother, Theobald.

The siege of Nottingham Castle was placed in the hands of Ranulph, Earl of Chester; William, Earl Ferrers; and David, Earl of Huntingdon. (One other castle was to be attacked, Mont St. Michel in Cornwall, only for the siege to be canceled when it was discovered that its commander, Henry de Pumerai, had died of fright the moment he heard that the king had been freed.)

In each of these instances, the defenders were actually in a rather awkward position. The power that Prince John had managed to garner for himself, while irresistible, was not necessarily legal—the regency which had been appointed to rule England during Richard's absence had furiously and regularly denounced the prince's ambitions. It was *their* armies that the castles' occupants had been expecting to fight.

Word that it was actually the king's troops who were outside was not slow in reaching them. But could that word be believed? After all, anybody could say they were the king, and it wasn't as though there were stamps or coins in those days that bore anything remotely approaching a lifelike portrait of him. (In fact, there were no stamps, period. It would be another seven hundred years before they came along.)

So the defenders sat tight—or as tight as they could under the circumstances, intending to hold out for as long as they were able, or at least until the attackers could offer them some proof that they were actually fighting in the name of the king, and not just his government. And in the meantime,

The Prospect of Kirkleys Abbry, where Robin Hood dyed from the Footway leading to Hearyshead Church, at a quarter of
a mile distance. A. The New Hall. B. The Gatehouse of the Nunnery C. The Trees among which Robin Hood was bury
D. The way up the Hill where this was drawn. E. Bradley Wood. F. Almondbury hill. G. Casle Field.
Drawn by Dr Johnston among his Yorkshire Antiquitys. P. 54 of the Drawings.

From an old print, Kirklees Abbey, where Robin is said to have met his end.

An old engraving reconstructs Nottingham Castle as it might have been in Robin's time.

they suffered through what, for many of them, would have been their first-ever taste of modern warfare.

Richard was not playing, after all, and his experiences in the Holy Land had taught both him and his men a lot of new tricks; garnered them new weapons; taught them new tactics.

According to the near-contemporary historical chronicles of Roger of Howden, *Gesta Henrici II et Gesta Regis Ricardi*, the defenders at Tickhill Castle sent messengers out to meet with the king the moment they heard of his return; then, once they returned with the news, the castle surrendered. Richard, apparently, expected the Nottingham defenders to show similar common sense.

> But those who were in the castle of Nottingham did not send anyone to meet the king. Whereof, the king, angry, came to Nottingham on 25th March with so great a multitude of men and the sound of horns and trumpets, that those who were in the castle, hearing and seeing this, were astonished, perturbed [*and*] upset; fear overcame them and yet they were unable to believe that the king had come but hoped that all this [*noise*] was being made by the principles of the army to have sport with them.

The castle's outer gates were burned, and the king's men poured into the outer enclosure of the castle. They withdrew when night fell, but the fighting recommenced the following morning, with great siege engines, mangonels, and petraries, designed to hurl vast stones against the walls in a bid to shatter them, being brought into play against the defenses that confronted them. The king also had a gallows erected in sight of the castle, and started executing prisoners.

Still the defenders held out, convinced that they were being tricked. By day three of the siege, however, the flow of high-profile visitors to the battlefield, a constant stream of bishops, earls, abbots, and so forth, all of them accompanied by their own armies, appears to have provided the proof that the castle's occupants required.

That day, as the king sat at dinner, the castle's constables dispatched a couple of emissaries to find out whether the rumors were correct. They returned to say they had indeed met the king, and the castle promptly surrendered.

The following day, while the carnage of the battle was cleared away, the king went sightseeing in Sherwood Forest; the day after that, he convened a four-day council designed to bring the entire region back under his own control.

Ironically, in view of all the legends that have been told about Robin and the Sheriff of Nottingham, he also introduced a new tax, a carucage, or a forerunner of modern property tax.

The more things change . . .

The Death of a King

As for John, Richard forgave him. It was sheer happenstance, after all, that either brother found himself in their present situation—their father's first son, William, had died in infancy, and so the line of succession passed to Richard and John's elder brother Henry.

But he, too, was dead now, laid low by dysentery after a short life spent battling with both his father and his family, while a third brother, Geoffrey, younger than Richard but older than John, was trampled to death at a jousting tournament in 1186. Of such tragedies is any royal line of succession made.

As the youngest child, John also appears to have been the most unfortunate. Contemporary chronicles often nickname him "Lackland," which means precisely what it says. When Henry II divided his lands between his children, John received none.

However, family attrition saw his situation improve; Lord of Ireland (at that time, regarded as a part of England), Earl of Gloucester, and Count of Mortain, he was also given sway over a number of other English counties when Richard departed for the Crusades—including Nottinghamshire.

But his plotting with the French king saw him lose territory as well, including—ironically—Normandy. A fresh war with France, then, was the next item on the returning Richard's agenda, and he was still fighting it when he died in 1199. A crossbow arrow hit him in the shoulder, and having failed in his attempts to remove it himself, the king placed himself in the hands of a surgeon named Howden, who just happened to be nicknamed the Butcher.

Howden's attempts to remove the arrow were even worse than Richard's. Swiftly, gangrene set into the wound and it was clear the king was dying. As a last act of mercy, he had the crossbowman who fired the fatal shot brought to him, offered the man his forgiveness, and then died—only for one of his mercenaries to then have the wretch flayed alive and hanged the moment Richard breathed his last.

Prince John, who had brought so much hardship to the land during Richard's absence, succeeded him. He had been the model of the loyal supporter and advisor since Richard returned home. But, of course, he was merely biding his time.

Barely had John settled onto the throne than he was proving that time had not lessened his avarice—and the British Royal Family remembers him for that. There has never been another king, or even prince, John placed anywhere close to the line of succession.

8

Robin Hood and the Band of Brothers (Part One)

Introducing The Merry Men— the Big Three

"Now wend we together, my merry men all,
To the green wood to take up our stand"
These archers were ready at Robin Hoods call,
With their bent bows all in their hand.
"Come, merrily let us now valiantly go
With speed unto the green wood,
And there let us kill a stout buck or a do,
For our master, Robin Hood."

from "Robin Hood and Queen Katharine" (traditional ballad)

Robin Hood did not fight alone. From the beginning, and throughout the stories that are told of his life, he is accompanied by a seething assemblage of accomplices—sometimes as few as a dozen; sometimes as many as 140. Which is a lot of people to hide in a forest when the danger of discovery is an everyday risk, but it was a very large forest. He could have done it.

Despite such numbers, however, legend has passed down the names of a mere handful of Robin's accomplices, the earliest tales offering immortality to just three of them. Others, however, would be added as the tales expanded, and that is a process that is still underway today.

Just a decade ago, in the BBC's most recent retelling of the legend, *Robin Hood* (how *do* they think of these titles?), we were introduced to a generally unpleasant and uncommonly loutish merry man named Roy.

He lasted just five episodes, however, before being hacked to pieces by the sheriff's soldiers—and that is the traditional fate of many of these latter-day arrivals; sacrificial lambs to the greater story, and generally forgotten before the next tale is told.

Others, though, were made for the long haul.

Barrie Ingham and Gay Hamilton, as Robin and Marian, in the 1967 British film, *A Challenge for Robin Hood*.
Photofest

Little John

He's not little, but his name is John. A giant of a man, in fact, which is why his real name, John Little, was flipped for a nickname.

Generally regarded as Robin's second-in-command, Little John was the first of the named Merry Men to appear in any of the stories (at least among those that have survived); in fact, he all but received equal billing with Robin in the earliest ballads, and later, once the rest of the gang was in place, he frequently took the lead when Robin was otherwise engaged. Or when he needed to be rescued from his latest scrape.

Little John was, then, already firmly installed into the story by the time readers learned how he and Robin first met, in a ballad written in the seventeenth century.

Contrary to earlier verses, Robin already commanded a small army, no less than sixty-nine bowmen. And his standard practice, whenever he went out alone, was to remind them that, should he be in need of their assistance, he would blow his distinctive hunting horn.

On this particular day, it was fortunate that he did.

> When Robin Hood was about twenty years old,
> With a hey down, down, and a down.
> He happened to meet Little John.

Abroad in the forest, Robin was about to cross a bridge when a towering figure appeared before him, refusing to let him pass.

> Though he was called Little, his limbs were large,
> and his stature was seven feet high;
> Where-ever he came, they quaked at his Name,
> for soon he would make them to fly.

The two men fought with cross staves, lengthy wooden sticks that could deal a dreadful blow, and the giant prevailed. Robin was knocked off his feet and into the water.

> O then in a fury the stranger he grew;
> and gave him a damnable Look,
> And with it a Blow which laid him full low,
> and tumbled him into the brook.

At which point, Robin sounded his horn, and his men rushed to his aid. Rather than permit them to exact revenge, however, Robin could only

The eighteenth-century engraver Thomas Bewick reimagined Robin's first encounter with Little John.

marvel at the giant's strength. He asked John Little to join his merry men, and John agreed.

No less than with Robin, researchers have tied themselves in knots attempting to link Little John to a historical character, with the best known of them all now lying in a grave in a pretty little churchyard in Hathersage in Derbyshire.

Of course, there is no way of telling if it really is he; just a tradition that dates back to the sixteenth century and, once upon a time, a longbow, also said to be John's, which was on display in the church.

Elsewhere, the records have been combed for any other men who might have fit John's description, a litany of possibilities that range from a Yorkshire poacher named Littel John, who was active during the 1310s, to a former sheriff of London, John Litel, around forty years later. In neither case, nor any of the others, however, do the chroniclers appear to have thought to have recorded their subject's height.

Where history lets us down, the storytellers slip in. In the 1975 television series *The Legend of Robin Hood*, Little John is the leader of a rival outlaw gang, defending himself against what he believes to be a planned takeover by Robin; a decade later, in the series *Robin of Sherwood*, he is the servant of the Baron Simon de Belleme, an evil magician who has bewitched John by painting an inverted pentagram over his heart, and who sends him out into the forest to kill Robin Hood.

In both shows, Robin has already accumulated the beginning of a band; in both, his first encounter with Little John is on a bridge that the man-mountain will not allow him to cross; and in both, he takes a dunking before John topples in after him. And, in the latter show, when Robin washes the magical symbol away with a few handfuls of water, the wizard's enchantment is lifted—which certainly doesn't say much for period hygiene.

It's not exactly a traditional story, with the magician himself being created wholly for, and by, the television series, but so what? It's as good an origin as any other.

Although Robin and John were unquestionably devoted to each other, however, there remained an element of rivalry between the two men, with John in particular often portrayed as somewhat temperamental. Several old ballads feature squabbles between John and Robin, usually brought on by the latter's superior skills as an archer or swordsman, but, of course, they always reconcile before the end of the song.

But John is also capable of having his own adventures, such as another ballad, "Little John and the Four Beggars," in which he disguises himself indeed as a beggar, and then inveigles himself into the company of four more, whom he suspects of not quite being all they seem.

As word of Robin Hood's reputation spread, a number of wealthy travelers seem to have taken to dressing in rags, hoping that Robin and his men would let them pass unscathed. So it is with this quartet, but John is not taken in. Rather, he hits them all on the head, steals their riches, and then makes his way back to camp.

Another ballad, meanwhile, introduces us to one of Little John's (unspecified) relatives, Arthur a Bland. According to the sixteenth century ballad "Robin Hood and the Tanner," Arthur was inspecting the deer in the forest when Robin—claiming to be a forester—challenged him to a fight.

For two hours they battled, armed with great wooden staves, until finally Robin halted the proceedings (this story is going to get very old, very quickly! There must have been easier ways to meet people than this) and invited his adversary to join him in the forest.

Arthur agreed, and then revealed that Little John was his kinsman. Robin blew his horn to summon John, and the ballad ended, quite peculiarly, with the three of them holding hands and dancing around a tree.

> Then Robin Hood took them both by the hand,
> And danc'd round about the oke tree;
> "For three merry men, and three merry men,
> And three merry men we be.
>
> "And ever hereafter, as long as I live,
> We three will be all one;
> The wood shall ring, and the old wife sing,
> Of Robin Hood, Arthur, and John."

In fact, we rarely hear of Arthur ever again.

Will Scarlet

In terms of appearing in ballads and stories, the character of Will Scarlet is almost as old as Little John. He is also, potentially, even more mysterious than Robin.

Modern scholars tend to believe that the man whom we know as Scarlet is no different to those other Wills whom past historians, balladeers, and storytellers named Scarlett, Scarlock, Scadlock, Scatheloke, Stutly, and Stutely, and given the similarity between all of these names, it is quite possible that they are correct.

But are they *certain* of the fact? How long is an uncut bow string?

The Elizabethan author Anthony Munday certainly differentiated between Wills Scarlet and Scathlocke when he wrote his play *The Downfall of Robert, Earl of Huntington*; according to him, they were half brothers. And three centuries later, Howard Pyle's *Merry Adventures of Robin Hood* likewise features both Will Scarlet and Will Scathelock, *plus* Will Stutely.

Whoever he was, and whatever his name, he had a long and glorious life behind him by the time the seventeenth century ballad "Robin Hood Newly Revived" detailed how he came to join the Merry Men.

> As Robin Hood walked the forest along,
> It was in the mid of the day,
> There was he met [with] a deft young man
> As ever walked on the way.
> His doublet it was of silk, he said,

His stockings like scarlet shone,
And he walked on along the way,
To Robin Hood then unknown.

Falling into conversation, the pair then decided to have an archery contest. The stranger proved to be an excellent shot, so Robin offered him a place in the gang.

A nineteenth-century "penny dreadful," retelling the adventures of Little John.

The stranger refused. Indeed, he seemed positively insulted by the suggestion.

> "Go play the chiven," the stranger said,
> "Make haste and quickly go,
> Or with my fist, be sure of this,
> I'le give thee buffets store."

They fought, and again Robin was defeated—at which point he asked his assailant's identity, and the story came tumbling out.

> The stranger then answered bold Robin Hood,
> "I'll tell thee where I did dwell;
> In Maxfield was I bred and born,
> My name is Young Gamwell.
> For killing of my own father's steward,
> I am forced to this English wood,
> And for to seek an uncle of mine;
> Some call him Robin Hood.

We have met this man before, in the ballad "Robin Hood's Birth, Breeding, Valor and Marriage," although the family connection has changed slightly. In the earlier text, and in another ballad, "Gamble Gold and Robin Hood," Robin's uncle was the squire of Gamwell Hall, making Young Gamwell his cousin. Here, the youth's mother is Robin's own sister, making him his nephew.

Either way, with all their differences forgotten, and all their blows forgiven (Robin took a nasty crack to the skull in an earlier verse), the family is reunited. Young Gamwell accepts the invitation into the gang, and Robin ends the ballad in celebratory mood, informing Little John:

> ". . . he shall be a bold yeoman of mine,
> My chief man next to thee,
> And I Robin Hood and thou Little John,
> And Scarlet he shall be,
> "And wee'l be three of the bravest outlaws
> That is in the North Country." . . .

Full marks to the ballad's anonymous author, by the way, for having done his historical research. Scarlet was indeed first referenced in song at a time when the gang comprised Robin and Little John alone, since when he had grown to become one of the band's most visible members.

He was not necessarily its luckiest, however. The ballad "Robin Hood Rescuing Will Stutly" is only the first of a long line of adventures in which Robin was forced to lead his men into combat to retrieve the hapless lad from the clutches of the Sheriff of Nottingham.

Similarly, most of the legends agree that Scarlet was as quick with his sword as Robin was with the bow, able even to fight two men with two swords simultaneously. But this admittedly magnificent talent did not help him when, according to some traditions, an entire band of Norman soldiers fell upon him, and the churchyard of the Church of St. Mary of the Purification, in the Nottinghamshire village of Blidworth, is said to contain Will Scarlet's final resting place.

Other stories, however, have a happier ending. Having joined Robin and Little John in rescuing a princess for the terrifying clutches of a Saracen suitor (in the ballad "Robin Hood and the Prince of Aragon"), Scarlet (or Scadlock, as he is called here) is rewarded not only with the love of the maiden, but also with a touching family reunion.

Watching the battle, the Earl of Maxfield (a new name for us, but we will let it pass) remarks upon the soon-to-be groom's remarkable resemblance to his own long-lost son, Young Gamwell. Scadlock reveals himself and falls at his father's feet.

Much Miller

The son of a miller, hence his name, Much (or, according to author Howard Pyle, Midge) was the third and last of Robin's original Merry Men, and one who generally serves as simply an extra pair of hands (and a constantly flapping tongue) in the majority of the modern adventures.

In earlier times, however, Much was as powerful as any man in the band, and a lot more useful too. As befits the son of a miller, he was originally seen as an incredibly strong young man, his muscles built up by years of carrying weighty bags of flour for his father.

It is traditional in modern retellings for Much's father to have effectively raised Robin as a boy, meaning he and Much grew up together. That explains the bond which binds the pair together.

In earlier times, however, they were strangers the first time they met, with the outlaw convinced that boy was carrying gold, so heavy were the bags that he had slung across his back. So he forced Much to halt, and demanded that the bags be opened—the cue for what is already a wearily familiar tale.

First Much threw a handful of flour in Robin' face; then, while the outlaw was still spluttering and blinking, he administered a sound thrashing.

Of course, Robin responded by inviting Much to join the Merry Men, an offer which was gratefully accepted. And, in the earliest surviving stories, a bloodthirsty little soul he turned out to be, one who thought nothing of

Another of Little John's "penny dreadful" adventures, this one penned by the master Pierce Egan.

beheading a page boy in the ballad "Robin Hood and the Monk," and wreaking plenty more carnage besides.

Unfortunately, his role was destined to diminish from there and, by the twentieth century, Much was usually characterized as either a hot-headed brat who is constantly whining, or a dimwitted buffoon . . . who is constantly whining. It is in this latter guise that actor Sam Troughton delivered what is surely Much's most resonant portrayal, in the 2006 *Robin Hood* series.

Robin's squire throughout his years as a nobleman, this version of Much then traveled to the Holy Land with him to fight in the Crusades, and there they forged such a bond that nothing, not even his sonic resemblance to a flock of gannets gathered around a candy wrapper, could shatter their propinquity.

Which is lucky for Much. Because anybody else would have slapped him silly.

9

Robin Hood and the Band of Brothers (Part Two)

Merrier and Merrier Still

I'll give thee, good fellow, a twelvemonth or twain,
To search Europe through, from Byzantium to Spain;
But ne'er shall you find, should you search till you tire,
So happy a man as the Barefooted Friar.
Your knight for his lady pricks forth in career,
And is brought home at even-song prick'd through with a spear;
I confess him in haste—for his lady desires
No comfort on earth save the Barefooted Friar's.
Your monarch?—Pshaw! many a prince has been known
To barter his robes for our cowl and our gown,
But which of us e'er felt the idle desire
To exchange for a crown the grey hood of a Friar!
The Friar has walk'd out, and where'er he has gone,
The land and its fatness is mark'd for his own;
He can roam where he lists, he can stop when he tires,
For every man's house is the Barefooted Friar's.
He's expected at noon, and no wight till he comes
May profane the great chair, or the porridge of plums
For the best of the cheer, and the seat by the fire,
Is the undenied right of the Barefooted Friar.
He's expected at night, and the pasty's made hot,
They broach the brown ale, and they fill the black pot,
And the goodwife would wish the goodman in the mire,
Ere he lack'd a soft pillow, the Barefooted Friar.
Long flourish the sandal, the cord, and the cope,
The dread of the devil and trust of the Pope;
For to gather life's roses, unscathed by the briar,
Is granted alone to the Barefooted Friar.

—*Sir Walter Scott, Ivanhoe*

Little John, Will Scarlet and Much Miller were Robin's first accredited followers. Others, however, swiftly followed them into Sherwood Forest, there to make merry and torment authority.

Some were (or would become) renowned fighters, some were destined for other fates. But only one was a man of God, and a figure of fun as well. Which says a lot, despite the piety of the age, for the opinion of the common man when it came to respecting the clergy.

Friar Tuck

It is strange, when one considers the renown of Friar Tuck, to discover that his arrival in the legend came somewhat late in the day. Absent from any of the earliest ballads, the first-known appearances of the paunchy priest date from the sixteenth century.

Medieval village life at that time was often highlighted by a fair, usually taking place around the traditional May Day festivities, and inevitably featuring some kind of play about Robin Hood—such tales of heroism not only appealed from a storytelling point of view, after all. As we shall see

These one-seventy-second-scale Merry Men were a staple ingredient in any 1960s English child's toy box.

shortly, they were also a grand vehicle for satirical comment on the lives of the villagers, too.

Why May Day? According to Mary I. Curtis, author of *England of Song and Story*, a positively shimmering history of the country's traditions that was first published in 1932, it was because May 1 "was supposed to be the anniversary of [Robin's] death."

Often, the games served not only as an entertainment; they were also a charity drive, with Robin and his men collecting money for the poor. Neither did their ministrations always pass off peaceably. In 1497 in Staffordshire, Robin Hood rode into a neighboring town at the head of some one hundred followers, and proceeded to beat up anybody who would not give them money. And this was not the only example of that.

Nevertheless, the popularity of these celebrations could never be questioned, outweighing even the power of the Church in the mind of the populace. As the sixteenth century Bishop Latimer discovered to his chagrin. Preaching a sermon on the decline of religion in 1549, and recalling an event from perhaps ten years earlier, the notoriously antithalian prelate grumbled bitterly,

> I came myself once to a place, riding on a journey homeward from London, and I sent word over night into the town that I would preach there in the morning, because it was a holiday, and methought it was an holiday's work. The church stood in my way, and I took my horse and my company and went thither. I thought I should have found a great company in the church, and when I came there the church door was fast locked. I tarried there half an hour and more; at last the key was found, and one of the parish comes to me and says "Sir, this is a busy day with us, we cannot hear you; it is Robin Hood's day. The parish are gone abroad to gather for Robin Hood . . . " I was fain there to give place to Robin Hood.

Perhaps somebody in the congregation, which included the young King Edward VI, smiled at this thought, but Latimer did not share the joke.

> It is no laughing matter . . . it is a weeping matter, a heavy matter, under the pretense of gathering for Robin Hood, a traitor and a thief, to put out a preacher, to have his office less esteemed; to prefer Robin Hood before the ministrations of God's word. . . . This realm has been ill provided for, ere it hath had such corrupt judgments in it to prefer Robin Hood to God's word.

The disapproval of the Church notwithstanding, these plays were riotously successful; and, of course, every aspiring thespian in the village would demand a role. It is likely here, in fact, that the numbers of the Merry Men first began to swell, as fresh roles were invented to accommodate every would-be player.

Friar Tuck was paramount among these new inclusions, and clearly a popular one, too. Soon, he was as permanent a member of the gang as any of his longer-established comrades, and though he seems to have had little purpose beyond providing a little light relief (usually revolving either around his girth, or his gluttony), such qualities were welcomed into the legend.

All of which makes it seem somehow remarkable that Friar Tuck *was* based upon a real-life, and historically recorded character.

The first surviving mention of a "Frere Tuk" in the Robin Hood legends dates from around 1475, and a fragment of a contemporary play. Around fifty years earlier, however, it was not the stage that the Friar graced with his corpulent presence, it was the annals of English crime.

For over a decade in the early fifteenth century, southern England was blighted by an outlaw gang led by a former holy man, Richard Stafford, once the chaplain at the church in Lindfield in Sussex—although he was better known to his pursuers by his chosen nom-de-nasty, Frere Tuk.

We know next to nothing about his actual felonies, and can only guess at what foul calumnies were enacted by this fallen priest. But the concept of a man of God turning to crime was one that would surely have thrilled and intrigued all who heard it. The public's insatiable appetite for salacity and scandal is not, after all, a recent development, and where there is an appetite, there is usually somebody willing to assuage it— today, in the form of newspapers and television; back then, via ballad and storytelling.

Tuck's transition from fact to fable is not itself unusual. Paul Clifford and Dick Turpin, the notorious eighteenth century highwaymen whose respective adventures fired novelists Edward Bulwer-Lytton and Harrison Ainsworth's imaginations, both existed (the former as an archetype, if not an actual person), and the legend and renown in which Turpin continues to revel today is derived wholly from the text of Ainsworth's *Rookwood*.

Drawn from life, too, were those other heroes of Victorian literature— the housebreaker Jack Sheppard, the murderous scholar Eugene Aram, and the killer poet Richard Savage. Likewise Fagin, the wily old crook who engineers Oliver Twist's downfall in the greatest of Dickens's earliest novels; and Charlie Peace, the nineteenth century murderer who became the hero of twentieth century movies and comic strips alike.

They existed, and in so doing, they became the stuff of legend. The authors who grasped those lives and wove them into fiction were simply embellishing those legends, furnishing them with new attractions.

These men became role models, *not* because they broke the law and caused untold hardship and pain to their victims (one of the less noble legends of Dick Turpin, for example, has him sitting an old lady on her own fire until she told him where she had hidden her money), but because they spent their lives living life as they wanted to, bucking the system, thumbing a nose at authority, and kicking out at each and every constraint that attempted to govern their lives. And while imaginary villains could have given a similar impression, how much more exciting it was to know that these people really *had* lived, and really *had* done so much of that with which they were credited.

At a time when men were fighting, and sometimes dying, to break out of society's bondage for the common good, few readers caught up in these adventures cared that the heroes of whom they read, who fought those same bonds just as valiantly, did so out of selfish gain. It was enough that they fought. And not even the disdain of those people who had sighted the contradiction (primarily elitist critics, disapproving politicians, and killjoy do-gooders) could sway them from their judgment.

That is the company into which Frere Tuk slipped, four hundred years before the heyday of the Victorian criminal novel, and he never lost his taste for brigandry.

He did, however, change his name a little. *Frere*, French for brother, suggests he was a monk; *Friar* singles him out as a mendicant—that is, a monk who was not bound to any particular monastery, but who was free to travel and preach. Although, that said, this explanation is distinctly at odds with the ballad "Robin Hood and the Curtal Friar," in which Tuck is housed at Fountain's Abbey in Yorkshire. Mendicants followed the teachings of St. Francis of Assisi (Franciscans) or St. Dominic (Dominicans), which bade them go out among the people; Fountains was owned by the Cistercian order, whose contact with the outside world was considerably more limited.

Nevertheless, the tradition has held, and this most beautiful abbey, which is now a most beautiful ruin, is firmly affixed to Robin's legend, with Tuck ranking high among its best-known occupants.

It was in 1560 that the Friar first took center stage in the legends (at least so far as the surviving evidence goes), when the London printer William Copland published a new play, titled *A mery geste of Robyn Hoode and of hys lyfe, wyth a new playe for to be played in Maye games very pleasaunte and full of pastyme.*

The action opens with Robin setting off in angry pursuit of the Friar, for not only did he add his name to the lengthening list of passing strangers who bettered Robin on the battlefield, he compounded his triumph by stealing Robin's purse.

Again they meet, again they fight, and again the Friar has the upper hand. He prepares to strike the death blow, and Robin, knowing his end is nigh, begs to be allowed to call for his faithful dogs, so that he might bid them farewell.

The Friar agrees, and Robin blows his hunting horn—the same horn that earlier ballads assured us would bring the Merry Men hotfoot to their leader's aid. And down they come, disarming the Friar and now contemplating the manifold ends to which he might be put.

But Robin, of course, is magnanimous in victory, not only offering the Friar a role in the gang, but sweetening the pot with sundry other gifts—gold and coin, and even a woman.

The Friar accepts the offer. More than that, he then embarks upon a soliloquy that still astounds with its unbridled lustfulness:

> Here is an huckle duckle,
> An inch above the buckle.
> She is a trul of trust,
> To serue a frier at his lust,
> A prycker, a prauncer, a terer of shetes,
> A wagger of ballockes when other men slepes.
> Go home, ye knaues, and lay crabbes in the fyre,
> For my lady & I will daunce in the myre,
> For veri pure joye.

Not surprisingly, this side of the Friar's nature would be seriously constrained in subsequent retellings, although his lusts would occasionally resurface.

Sir Walter Scott's *Ivanhoe*, for instance, reveals Tuck to be a hermit, the barefooted friar, the Clerk of Companhurst, living alone with no more company than his dogs, his wine, and his venison—the latter of which he consumes with glorious gluttony. But he lives a double life.

Red-cheeked and jovial, as a holy man, he wears drab gray robes. As a brigand, he dons Lincoln green and declares, "When I am cased in my green cassock, I will drink, swear, and woo a lass with any blythe forester in the West Riding."

And he reconciles the two lifestyles by promising that he always confesses his sins to the first priest he should meet . . . in other words, to himself.

The aforementioned "Robin Hood and the Curtal Friar" proposes an alternate version of the two men's first encounter. (The word "curtal," incidentally, suggests that Tuck tended the abbey's gardens, and would also have been skilled with herbal medicine.)

It begins, as so many do, with the Merry Men having a little sport together.

> Will Scadlock he killed a buck,
> And Midge [Much] he killed a doe,
> And Little John killed a hart of geese,
> Five hundred foot him fro'
> "God's blessing on thy heart," said Robin Hood,
> "That hath such a shot for me;
> I would ride my horse a hundred miles,
> To find one could match with thee."
> That caused Will Scadlock to laugh,
> He laughed full heartily:
> "There lives a curtal frier in Fountains Abby
> Will beat both him and thee."

Robin immediately sets out to meet this alleged superman,

> And coming unto Fountain's Dale,
> No further would he ride;
> There was he aware of a curtal frier,
> Walking by the water-side.

Although his mission would appear to have been peaceable, Robin cannot resist taunting the friar, demanding that the holy man "carry me over the water . . . or else thy life's forlorn."

Neither does the friar protest. He simply takes Robin upon his broad back and transports him to the other side of the river; then, once safely on the bank, he demands that Robin carry *him* back to where they came from. "Or it shall breed thy pain."

Robin agrees; then, not to be outdone, he demands the friar carry him back again, and it appears that Tuck will obey.

> [*But*] coming to the middle stream,
> There he threw Robin in:
> "And choose thee, choose thee, fine fellow,
> Whether thou wilt sink or swim."

Robin swims, and now the two do battle, first with arrows, then with swords.

It's a long contest, some six hours in duration, but finally the Friar gets the upper hand. Just as in the aforementioned play, Robin is on his knees and begging one final request.

> "A boon, a boon, thou curtal frier,
> I beg it on my knee;
> Give me leave to set my horn to my mouth,
> And to blow blasts three."
> "That will I do," said the curtal frier,
> "Of thy blasts I have no doubt;
> I hope thou'll blow so passing well
> Till both thy eyes fall out."

(Which has to be one of the finest curses ever spoken by a holy man.)

Of course we know what happens next: "Half a hundred yeomen, with bows bent, came raking over the lee." The friar is captured, and now it is his turn to beg one final boon: "[T]he like I gave to thee; give me leave to set my fist to my mouth, and to whistle whistles three."

Robin agrees, the friar whistles, "and half a hundred good ban-dogs came running the frier unto."

Now ensues a fearful fight, well-trained bowmen versus highly trained dogs, who simply leapt up at every speeding arrow and caught it in their mouths. Not until Little John steps forward and shoots down half a dozen of the hounds does the friar agree to call off the dogs, if Robin will call off his men.

Robin agrees, and now they strike their bargain. Tuck joins the Merry Men, and Robin has another ferocious warrior in his camp—although, once again, the friar's services do not come cheap, and it is clear he has not made this alliance out of the goodness of his heart, or for a love of his fellow man.

"If thou wilt forsake fair Fountains Dale, and Fountains Abbey free," Robin swears, the Friar will receive one noble—a gold coin valued at one-third of a pound—a week. To be paid out, of course, on a Sunday.

Allen a Dale

Allen a Dale . . . Alan of the Dale . . . is an even later addition to the legend than the Friar; indeed, he would be the very last of what we might now call the traditional Merry Men to join the band, and perhaps this is why he has also struggled to truly assert himself in the legend.

He rarely takes the lead in any adventure, being content to remain in the shadows and simply throw in his weight when it is required; more often, he appears as the Merry Men's personal minstrel, accompanying their revelries with music and jokes, and composing his own ballads about the bold outlaw Robin Hood, which he then takes and performs at village fairs and the like.

Today, we'd call him their PR guy.

Neither is his so-called "origin" story especially heroic. Making his first published bow back in 1723, in a book entitled *A Collectyion of Old Ballads*, he first comes to Robin Hood's attention as a potential victim.

The nineteenth century ballad collector Francis James Child summarizes "Robin Hood and Allen a Dale" thus:

> A young man . . . whom Robin Hood has seen passing, one day singing and the next morning sighing, is stopped by Little John and the Miller's Son, and brought before their master, who asks him if he has any money.
>
> He has five shillings and a ring, and was to have been married the day before, but his bride [*usually known as Ellen*] has been given to an old knight. Robin asks what he will give to get his true-love. All that he can give is his faithful service.
>
> Robin goes to the church and declares the match not fit: the bride shall choose for herself. He blows his horn, and four-and-twenty of his men appear, the foremost of whom is Allen a Dale. Robin tells Allen that he shall be married on the spot. Robin gives Allen the maid, and bids the man take her away that dare.

In the original ballad, the marriage ceremony itself is performed by Little John, whom Robin has draped in the bishop's own robes.

Later variations on the tale, however, perhaps more mindful of the legal requirements of marriage, see Friar Tuck officiate.

The Jolly Pinder of Wakefield

Another especially ancient ballad, "A ballett of Wakefylde and a grene," (better known today as "The Jolly Pinder of Wakefield") was published on the Stationers' Registers in 1557–1558, and appears in both the Sloane Manuscript and (partially) in Anthony Munday's two plays.

The pinder was a part of the medieval town administration, a man largely responsible for rounding up any animals that should stray onto the landowner's property, but also with a degree of peace keeping. The Jolly Pinder with whom this ballad is concerned, for instance, has pledged that no man shall trespass upon his domain of Wakefield, in Yorkshire, without his say-so—a vainglorious boast that Robin, Scarlet, and John are determined to challenge.

The pinder, however, is made of sterner stuff than ever they imagined, fighting them to a standstill and breaking all three of their swords in the process. At which point, Robin calls a halt to the combat and asks the pinder, instead, to join his band of men.

The pinder agrees to do so, but not until the feast of Michaelmas (September 29—the feast day of St. Michael), when his contracted term of service is over. So the quartet share a meal and part, best of friends.

The theme from Reginald De Koven and Harry B. Smith's acclaimed operetta.

This same story is retold with a little more detail in the works of another Elizabethan playwright, Robert Greene. First printed in 1599, the play *George a Greene* largely involves Robin in an uprising led by the Earl of Kendall. However, several traditional stories are woven into its framework, with Greene's version of the Pinder of Wakefield replacing Little John with Much, although the outcome of the skirmish remains the same. The outlaws are soundly defeated and Robin declares:

> George, wilt thou forsake Wakefield
> And go with me?
> Two liveries will I give thee every year,
> And forty crowns shall be thy fee.

The story appears again in a prose history of *George a Green*, which dates from around 1632, only here, the pinder takes down "Slathbatch" (another of Will Scarlet's inadvertent aliases), Little John *and* Friar Tuck, before commencing his duel with Robin.

The popularity of this particular tale suggests that there really was a particularly powerful pinder at large in Wakefield, sometime during the sixteenth century; and that, like Friar Tuck, his adventures were woven into Robin's legend in a manner not unlike modern comic book crossovers.

Sadly, few of these have survived and even fewer are being told today, a fate that befalls several other of the characters whom various old ballads paint as worthy additions to the troupe—an unnamed Scotsman (in the ballad "Robin Hood and the Scotchman"), an anonymous forester ("Robin Hood and the Ranger"), and Little John's aforementioned kinsman, Arthur a Bland. Like them, the plucky pinder simply vanishes into the vast corpus of otherwise unnamed merry men who are the background noise in so many other stories.

The Three Squires

Three more of these unnamed characters appear in the ballad "Robin Hood Rescuing the Widow's Three Sons from the Sheriff, when Going to be Executed," in which Robin learns, from a weeping widow, that three of his men, who happen also to be brothers, have been captured while poaching deer. All three have been sentenced to hang that same day.

This is truly one of the great heroic tales, albeit one that might also be described as one of the most poorly executed, more akin to modern television sensationalism than any shimmering paragon of the balladeer's art.

First, Robin disguises himself as a beggar; then he presents himself to the sheriff, offering to act as the hangman.

Taken in by the disguise, the sheriff agrees, offering him coin and clothing as payment for the job—at which point Robin blows his horn, and 150 of his men descend upon the town. He blows it again, and sixty more appear. The sheriff is surrounded and led to his own scaffold. And there he is hanged.

The end.

The Saracen

The last decades of the twentieth century added one further regular to the gang—a Saracen.

It is never the same one. In the 1980s TV series *Robin of Sherwood*, he is the impressively named Nasir Malik Kamal Inal Ibrahin Shams ad Duala Watthab ibn Mahmud, a member of the Hashashin who, like Little John, was originally a servant of the wicked Baron de Belleme, captured and bewitched while the baron was fighting in the crusades.

The enchantment is lifted when the baron is finally killed by Robin Hood. Nasir, impressed by the outlaw's fighting skills, agrees to join him in Sherwood Forest.

In terms of the original Robin Hood legend, the recruitment of what had traditionally been an enemy warrior to the Merry Men might be seen as an audacious decision (one of several that writer Richard Carpenter offered up as the series progressed), and one that was fraught with difficulty—cultural and linguistic, not least of all.

However, it quickly proved to be a popular one.

With its historical backdrop of the Crusades, Saracens are no strangers to the legends of Robin Hood. In the past, however, all had been cut from the darkest cloth—the titular nobleman in the eighteenth century ballad "Robin Hood and the Prince of Aragon," for example, in which the Prince of Aragon, a Turk, has insinuated himself into London society and has vowed to marry a royal princess, despite the protestations of her family and friends.

Only if he and his bodyguards, a pair of giants, can be defeated in combat will the prince relinquish his claim, and so Robin Hood, Scadlock, and Little John step forward, in disguise, and kill all three of them.

The grateful king, on learning their identities, offers them each a free pardon, while the princess and Scadlock fall in love and marry.

The introduction of a "good" Saracen would not change the overall historical backdrop to the tales; Robin is still a loyal and devout Christian and Crusader, and there remains plenty of blood on his blade.

But he is also smart enough to realize that his enemy was a concept, not a people; that, just as not every Englishman drinks tea from dawn to dusk and precedes every sentence with a nasal "I say . . . ", so not every Saracen was born to bathe in the blood of slaughtered infidels.

There is good and bad in every race, and just as Robin would not expect to be held accountable for the misdeeds of another Englishman just because he was English, so he extended the same understanding to the Saracen. (But not, interestingly, to the Normans. Robin never once met a Norman whom he did not try to kill.)

Of course such a notion flies in the face of many political norms, both past and present, and perhaps that is why the addition of a Saracen proved so popular with television audiences. It reminded them once again that Robin represents a challenge to the establishment, both in thought and deed.

Plus, it opened the door for some remarkable variations. Within just a couple of years of the Saracen's introduction, he was being parodied in the late 1980s comedy *Maid Marian and her Merry Men*, in which writer Tony Robinson (Baldric of *Blackadder* fame) conjured a Rastafarian outlaw named Barrington.

It was echoed in the *Prince of Thieves* movie by the inclusion of a Moor named Azeem, who, in turn, was parodied as Achoo and Asneeze in Mel Brooks's *Robin Hood: Men in Tights* (1993).

The New Adventures of Robin Hood upped the absurdity quotient a little further with the introduction of Kemal, who also happened to be a martial arts expert; and it was left to the 2006 *Robin Hood* series to restore a semblance of sanity to the character with the arrival of Djaq. Rescued from a slave trader who was taking Saracen prisoners to Nottingham, Djaq combines the roles of fearless warrior, astute herbalist, competent scientist—and a love interest for Will Scarlet.

In keeping with any number of traditional (non–Robin Hood) ballads, Djaq is actually a woman who disguised herself as a man in order to go and fight. Only by accident is her true identity discovered, teased out to both audience and the Merry Men over the course of a couple of episodes, and Djaq emerges as one of that particular series' most successful innovations— even if she does ensure that the character of the Saracen might never be permitted to settle down to a single person.

But, maybe, that is not such a terrible thing. As we've already seen, it took a long time for his/her comrades to do so.

A Maid Called Marian

The Fairest Flower of the Forest

T he fact that it's a cliché doesn't mean it isn't true. Behind every great man, blah blah blah. From Napoleon's Josephine to King Arthur's Guinevere, from Hereward's Torfrida to Emperor Maximilian I's beloved Charlotte, that is one subject upon which both fact and fiction (almost) always agree.

Sometimes, it just takes them a while.

Maid Marian, universally known as Robin Hood's consort (some say wife, some say lover) was not among his earliest companions.

Indeed, like Friar Tuck, it is generally believed that she did not enter the fables until the age of the May games, when (those same ubiquitous

Maid Marian in 2006, played to perfection by Lucy Griffiths. *Photofest*

"some" say) the role was given to the current Lady of the May—that is, the local maiden who had been crowned during the Mayday celebrations as a personification of the upcoming summer. Utilizing that same logic, we might then assume that the role of Robin was given to the Lord of the May.

On other occasions, however, her role was given to a man, often at the behest of the Church, which regarded the stage as a most improper place for a woman. It would be 1660 before the newly crowned King Charles II finally did away with this prohibition, but old habits died hard, as connoisseurs of the British tradition of pantomime will swiftly aver. "Panto" continues to offer men a number of feminine roles, even if they are usually no more glamorous than Cinderella's ugly sisters.

No matter who was playing the role, however, Marian does not appear to have been an English creation.

Researchers pursuing her lineage through the literature of the age fall time and again upon a popular *French* romance, dating from the end of the thirteenth century.

Eva Moore, Anita Louise, and Cornel Wilde in 1946's *The Bandit of Sherwood Forest.*   *Photofest*

Adam de la Halle's *Le Jeu de Robin et Marian* is the story of the love between a humble shepherdess and a high-born knight, and though it is unclear precisely how and when the story arrived in England, a collection of ballads published in 1723 includes one, the aforementioned "Robin Hood's Birth, Breeding, Valor and Marriage," in which he does indeed fall in love with "the queen of the shepherds."

Furthermore (again, as aforementioned), it is described by the volume's author as "the most beautiful and one of the oldest extant," and while the ballad names the shepherdess as Clorinda, still two separate strands of literary tradition would appear to have become entwined. Maybe sundry balladeers simply assumed the French romance concerned *our* Robin; maybe they just took the name because it was so familiar (if less lovely); maybe, they valued it for its alliterative value. "Maid Clorinda" scarcely trips off the tongue.

Either way, all agreed that Robin and Marian should forever be one.

Or did they? Other early writers have named her both Maud and Matilda, sometimes as an absolute alternative, sometimes as her true name, with Marian merely an alias that she adopted to disguise her origins. Which, it seems, were considerably loftier than those of a simple shepherdess.

One of the most popular beliefs surrounding Marian's "real-life" self is that coined by the antiquarian Joseph Hunter, whose investigations unearthed the previously discussed tale of Robert Hood of Wakefield, and in which she is described as a cousin of Elizabeth de Staynton, the Prioress of Kirklees Priory.

Our old friend Anthony Munday, the Elizabethan playwright, also assigns Marian a noble birth, insisting that she was born Matilda Fitzwalter, the daughter of Baron Robert Fitzwalter—who was forced into exile in France following an ill-fated attempt to assassinate King John. (He later received a full pardon and went to become one of the signatories to the Magna Carta.)

As for *why* he wanted to commit regicide, he said it was because the king had tried to seduce Matilda, a relationship that is echoed in various later versions of the Robin Hood legend, in which Guy of Gisborne is frequently depicted as Robin's premier rival for Marian's love.

Whether Munday believed this theory any more than sundry subsequent researchers is doubtful, however. In 1615, he penned a pageant to celebrate Lord Mayor's Day in London, in which that same Matilda Fitzwalter was married off to Sir Henry FitzAilwyn, a draper and the city's first-ever lord mayor, from 1189–1212. Maybe he just liked the name.

Robin's Last Romp

Of course, all of this is mere supposition, and as fogged by the passage of time as all attempts to unravel Robin Hood's "true" identity have proven to be.

No matter how many possibilities are unearthed by researchers, the fact remains that no single candidate has ever met every one of the criteria that a positive identification would demand. Maid Marian, quite simply, is Maid Marian, and that is how she will remain.

Certainly her place alongside Robin is inviolate, and according to one legend, hers was even the very last face he saw.

Joan Rice was Maid Marian in 1952's *The Story of Robin Hood and His Merrie Men.*
Photofest

Well, we call it a legend. In fact it was a newspaper story, albeit from a publication that placed a somewhat tenuous definition on the word "news"— the English *Sunday Sport*, a scandal-and-gossip–filled tabloid that flourished during the 1980s and 1990s.

According to the July 19, 1992, issue, "[H]istorians were staggered . . . after the body of Robin Hood was found in a shallow woodland grave— clutching Maid Marian's panties."

Both corpse and clothing were, apparently, perfectly preserved in a "peaty pit deep within Sherwood Forest," with further evidence as to its identity provided by the bow and arrows that also lay alongside the body.

The newspaper's assumption is that Robin and Marian had been enjoy- ing one final round of conjugal bliss before he fled this mortal coil, pointing out that "the last recorded sighting" of "a fit and active" Robin was at a celebration marking his eighty-seventh birthday . . . "fuelling the myth that he was fit enough to have been on the job [an English colloquialism for having sex] at the time of his death."

We will ignore the very dubious veracity, or even existence, of that "last recorded sighting."

The question is, how old must Marian have been at the time? And why did she leave her panties behind?

A Foolish Ditty

Perhaps the most romantic of all the Marianic legends is one that does not even try to identify her. The ballad "Robin Hood and Maid Marian," was first published in antiquarian Joseph Ritson's *Robin Hood: A Collection of All the Ancient Poems, Songs, and Ballads, Now Extant, Relative to that Celebrated English Outlaw: to which are Prefixed Historical Anecdotes of His Life* in 1795.

The great collector Francis James Child describes it as "a foolish ditty," but his standards, as we shall discover later, were especially high. So far as the rest of us go, no less than the populace to whom an author known only as "S. S." addressed his ballad, "Robin Hood and Maid Marian," as the foundation for one of the greatest of all love stories.

And that despite Robin introducing himself to the girl in exactly the same manner as he met the majority of his Merry Men—by challenging her to a fight.

He really did have a peculiar way of making friends.

The pair had, in fact, met once before, during Robin's tenure as the Earl of Huntingdon, and things apparently went very well between them:

A bonny fine maid of a noble degree,
With a hey down down a down down
Maid Marian calld by name,
Did live in the North, of excellent worth,
For she was a gallant dame.

For favour and face, and beauty most rare,
Queen Hellen shee did excell;
For Marian then was praisd of all men
That did in the country dwell.

'Twas neither Rosamond nor Jane Shore,
Whose beauty was clear and bright,
That could surpass this country lass,
Beloved of lord and knight.

The Earl of Huntington, nobly born,
That came of noble blood,
To Marian went, with a good intent,
By the name of Robin Hood.

With kisses sweet their red lips meet,
For shee and the earl did agree;
In every place, they kindly embrace,
With love and sweet unity.

However, dark forces were moving in the land, and soon Robin was stripped of both his status and his lands. He fled into the woods to live as an outlaw, and Marian was left alone.

Time could not repair their broken hearts. In the greenwood, we are told, Robin sat and mourned his lost love; and at home, Marian all but pined away.

Finally she resolved to seek out her lost love, no matter where he might now be. But aware that Sherwood Forest was no place for an unaccompanied woman, she first took the precaution of disguising herself as a man, in the costume of a page, and heavily armed as well, with a bow and a quiver full of arrows, and a sword.

But Robin Hood, he himself had disguised,
And Marian was strangly attired,
That they proved foes, and so fell to blows,
Whose valor bold Robin admired.

The fight was long and fierce, "at least an hour or more" says the ballad, reminding us that neither Marian (nor, indeed, the shepherdess Clorinda) has ever been a mere adornment in the legends.

Whether operating as Robin's eyes and ears inside the sheriff's castle, or fighting alongside the other Merry Men, Marian has seldom been portrayed as anything less than one of the gang, while she has even been known to step outside of both Robin and the sheriff's jurisdiction, to combat injustice alone.

In 1784, playwright Leonard McNally depicted Clorinda as a veritable warrioress, arriving in the outlaws' camp spoiling for a fight.

> But 'tis not you; bold Robin Hood
> I come to seek with bended bow,
> That man of might
> I fain would fight,
> And conquer with my oh, ho, ho!
> Through frost and snow,
> Though cold winds blow,
> I never fail,
> In rain or hail,
> Though thunders roll
> From pole to pole,
> To conquer with my oh, ho, ho!
> With bended bow,
> The buck or doe,
> I never fail,
> Through rain or hail,
> Though thunders roll
> From pole to pole,
> To conquer with my oh, ho, ho!

Two hundred years later, in the late eighties, British series *Maid Marian and her Merry Men*, Marian doesn't simply remain a force to be reckoned with, she is portrayed as the actual leader of the gang; while the 2006 *Robin Hood* series reveals Marian to have led a secret life as the Nightwatchman, feeding and helping the poor of the region long before Robin returned from the Holy Land.

In this guise she not only defeats both Robin and Guy of Gisborne in hand-to-hand combat, she also sees off sundry other ruffians, soldiers, and foes.

She is equally ferocious in the ballad, dealing Robin at least one serious injury before, finally, he called a halt to the battling and offered his mysterious adversary a place in his band, "to range in the wood with bold Robin Hood, to hear the sweet nightingale sing."

At which point Marian recognized his voice (and, presumably, his name), flung off her disguise and threw herself upon him.

> ... And with kisses sweet she did him greet,
> Like to a most loyal lover.
> When bold Robin Hood his Marian did see,
> Good lord, what clipping was there!
> With kind embraces, and jobbing of faces,
> Providing of gallant cheer.

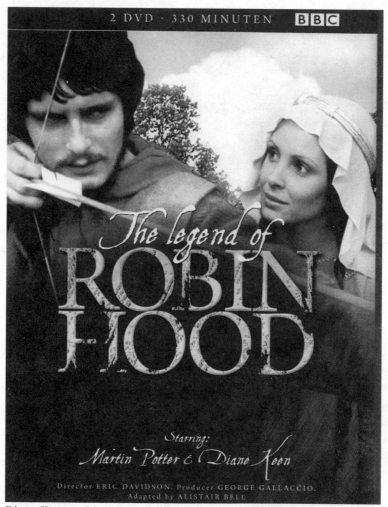

Diane Keen as Marian, and Martin Potter as Robin, in the BBC's 1975 mini-series.

Back to Robin's hideout they sped, to celebrate Marian's return with a positively Lucullan feast, and . . . well, they all lived happily ever after.

> In solid content together they lived,
> With all their yeomen gay;
> They livd by their hands, without any lands,
> And so they did many a day.
>
> But now to conclude, an end I will make
> In time, as I think it good,
> For the people that dwell in the North can tell
> Of Marian and bold Robin Hood.

Into this ballad, "S. S." poured every ingredient that we demand of Marian, including the observation that her beauty exceeded that of Helen of Troy and Rosamond Clifford (King Henry II's supposedly spectacular lover), and even Jane Shore, the legendarily stunning mistress of King Edward IV (among others).

Indeed, while the latter's reputation is all but forgotten today, throughout the medieval era and beyond, via the works of Shakespeare (*Richard the Third*) and Nicholas Rowe (*The Tragedy of Jane Shore*), she was adjudged one of the loveliest women ever to have walked the earth, and certainly sufficiently well known to merit mention in a popular song.

It is an attribute that subsequent Marians have shared—the Lady of the May was traditionally drawn from among the most beautiful maidens in the village, and neither Hollywood nor the television have ever considered a maid who is, as a medieval talent spotter might have put it, less than comely.

From Enid Bennett to Lucy Griffiths, from Olivia de Havilland to Diane Keen, from Cate Blanchett to that foxy little vixen . . . really, she *was* a vixen . . . in the 1973 Disney retelling, Maid Marian remains one of literature's most beautiful women.

If the "real" Marian surpassed all of them, then she truly made a fitting consort for Robin Hood.

Shooting at the Sheriff

Nottingham, Gisborne, and a Few Other Fiends

No less than there being a great woman behind every great man, there needs to be a great enemy in front of him. Superman has Lex Luthor, Sherlock Holmes has Moriarty, and Robin Hood has the Sheriff of Nottingham, a man so avaricious, so cruel and so self-serving that it is no surprise whatsoever that the greatest-ever portrayals of him should frequently drift into satire.

How many medieval squires and landowners, one wonders, must have squirmed at least a little uncomfortably as they watched their villagers performing a Robin Hood tale, and recognized their own selves peering out from beneath the sheriff's venal carapace?

As many, one hopes, as there were politicians and spin doctors watching the 2006 television series, who heard their own weasel-like aeolisms echoed by this latest sheriff—played with excoriating glibness by comedian Keith Allen, in whose honeyed tones the cultural climate of the post 9-11 world was bared with ruthless precision.

This unending battle between good and evil lies at the very heart of the Robin Hood legend, as English folk musician Grey Malkin explains.

> *Robin Hood* symbolizes a deep undercurrent and historical tradition in English society of distrust of authority and of dissent and political satire (not unlike the Irish, Scots or Welsh traditions, however Robin's was a particularly English rebelliousness).
>
> Robin Hood by his very existence defied the powerful and the rich (though was often portrayed as a fallen knight or lord himself). He took protective care of the land and the people and often made a mockery of the wealthy Sheriff and his noblemen. He represents

a sense of justice and equality; a revolt against power and wealth that is just as applicable in feudal times as in today's class ridden, capitalist society.

These tales are timeless because they represent something for every era. Indeed, they are in some respects as relevant now as they were in the 1500s, in this age of austerity and wealth divide. The stories of Robin Hood are also arguably so enduring because they are just damn good tales and they represent a number of different

Douglas Fairbanks, in all his glory. *Wikimedia Commons*

facets of what it is to be human; they incorporate aspects of being socially conscious, of defiance and rebellion, hardship, the joy and need for camaraderie, love and mortality.

The legends, both ancient and modern, leave us in no doubt as to just how vile the sheriff was; how sadistic, how heartless, how unrelentingly hateful he was. Take, for instance, his treatment of a condemned man in the ballad "Robin Hood Rescuing Will Stuteley."

Brought before the sheriff, with the gallows already prepared, Will makes his last request—that he die by the sword, in combat, as opposed to the rope.

The sheriff, ignoring all common etiquette, refuses.

Will tries again; can he at least be hanged with his hands untied?

Again the sheriff refuses. Stuteley will hang according to his, the sheriff's, stipulations, and had Robin and his men not been able to affect the titular rescue, no doubt he would have.

That is the kind of man the sheriff was.

But we might also look at him in a different light.

To the sheriff and his soldiers, to the kakistocracy of the day, Robin and his Merry Men were little more than terrorists, bent ruthlessly upon the total overthrow of the rule of law and order. They claimed they supported King Richard, but they might as well have been Saracens themselves.

To the people who supported and loved Robin, on the other hand, the people who lived beneath those laws and those orders, the outlaws were nothing less than freedom fighters, brave souls willing to give their lives in the name of liberty and equality.

This is how it is throughout history. To the Nazis occupying France during World War II; to the Romans ruling Gaul during the first century BC; to the British authorities in 1770s North America, to all of these, the forces that rose up against them . . . the Resistance, the Celts, the colonists . . . were simply an illegal, misguided, and treasonous rabble, and one that should be crushed by whatever means were necessary.

If they had grievances, there were courts to which they could appeal. If they had problems, there were officials to whom they could be taken. If they had demands, there were meeting halls in which to air them. But the moment they took up arms against the state, they lost all of those rights, all of those avenues.

They became the problem.

History sides with the winners. The British lost a colony, but the world gained a super power. The Nazis lost the war, but France regained its freedom. The ancient Gauls lost their rebellions, but Rome gained an empire (and France gained its own Robin Hood, the animated hero Asterix). And so forth.

Each and every struggle that has pitched a government against its people has eventually been resolved in one way or another, and history not only accepts the outcome, it defines it, as well. Either the freedom fighters win or the terrorists lose, and only the terminology changes; brave revolutionaries or lawless rebels, popular heroes or fraudulent messiahs.

Ask the Sheriff of Nottingham, and there is no doubt whatsoever which category Robin Hood fell into.

The Sheriff of Nottingham

There has always been one problem with Robin's long-standing feud with the Sheriff of Nottingham. At no point during the years in which any "real" Robin might have been active did the city of Nottingham actually have a sheriff—the first was appointed in 1449, by which time the legend of Robin Hood was already in full swing.

The county of Nottinghamshire, however, did have one, and he would likely have been headquartered in Nottingham Castle. Nottingham, Nottinghamshire, tom-ay-toe, tom-ah-to. He was a sheriff, and he lived in Nottingham, where his duties included the delivery of prisoners to the courts, the protection of the Royal Forests, the upholding of law and keeping the peace, and the gathering of local taxes, in amounts he set himself. Some of which went to the crown, some of which went to the county and some of which . . . oops! Some of which probably fell into his own private coffers.

Throughout the medieval period (and, of course, on either side of it as well), corruption among officials was high; so much so that even Prince John was moved to protest. Following his accession to the throne in 1199, he made it crystal clear that the local authorities were not entitled to keep any of the revenues they collected for their own personal use.

He did not, however, say anything about the bribes, blackmail, confiscations, and theft that were also a part of everyday life. So the sheriffs and so forth continued to live the high life, and the people whom they ruled over paid through the nose to ensure that situation never changed.

No less than twelve men held the position of High Sheriff of Nottinghamshire, Derbyshire, and the Royal Forests (to give the office its full title) throughout the years most commonly associated with Robin Hood.

From 1190–1191, the position was occupied by Roger de Lacy. William de Wendenal succeeded him until 1194, followed by the brief, seven-week tenure of William de Ferrers, 4th Earl of Derby; and then a five-year stint for William Brewer.

From 1200–1203, Hugh Bardulf held the office; and for the five years thereafter, Robert de Vieuxpont. The year 1208, however, brought the appointment of the man at whom the accusing finger of history never fails to point when the topic of the "real" sheriff of Nottingham arises, the Frenchman Philip Marc. And he would remain the lord of his domain for more than a decade.

A bully, a thief, an all-round bad egg, Marc ruled his sheriffdom with merciless avarice. If a debt was due, he gave debtors a choice—pay up, or see their property burned to the ground. He over-taxed the poor, he stole from the Church, he jailed or murdered all dissenters. And he did so with impunity.

Even when King John decided to crack down again on the growing plague of authoritarian abuse in 1213, and both dismiss and arrest the worst offenders in the land, Marc remained unscathed.

He survived, too, the signing of the Magna Carta, and that despite being personally singled out therein as a man who needed to be deprived of power. Item fifty of the document demanded that the king "entirely remove from their bailiwicks . . . (so that in future they shall have no bailiwick in England) . . . Philip Mar[c] with his brothers and his nephew Geoffrey, and the whole brood of the same."

If any man deserved a foe as tenacious as Robin Hood, then, it was Philip Marc, and television, on one occasion at least, would deal him his just desserts. The 1980s series *Robin of Sherwood* introduced Marc as a brutal former sheriff of Lincolnshire (his nickname there was "the Butcher of Lincoln"), appointed to Nottingham specifically to remove Robin Hood from the picture.

He fails, of course, and is killed for his troubles. The real Mark, on the other hand, went on to *become* sheriff of Lincolnshire, before retiring to live peacefully until his death in 1234.

Unfortunately, Marc did not hold the monopoly on abusing his position, even within Nottinghamshire. There were other, equally dubious officials at large, beginning with Marc's own deputy, Eustace of Lowdham.

The role of the deputy was effectively that of ensuring the actual sheriff's hands did not get too dirty, meaning it would have been Eustace who was responsible for enforcing the majority of his boss's orders.

He learned well, however. After leaving Nottingham, he was appointed sheriff of Yorkshire, in which role he would have pursued, captured, and finally executed one of the men we met in chapter one, Robert of Wetherby "outlaw and evildoer of our land" (and possibly "Robert Hod, fugitive" as well). And so well did he perform there that, before long, he was appointed Sheriff of Nottinghamshire in his own right.

Eustace, like Philip Marc, appears to have lived a happy life, despite his merciless depredations. But sundry successors who perhaps tried to follow in his footsteps were less fortunate.

Henry de Faucemberg, who held the office first between 1318–1319 and again from 1323 to 1325, was a renowned extortionist, as well as a debtor—at one point, he owed close to three hundred pounds to the crown, and that was his ultimate downfall. For those researchers who align Robin Hood with the former rebel and future porter Robert Hood, this particular sheriff makes both an ideal, and a deserving, arch-enemy.

Another sheriff, Sir Robert Ingham (1328–1332), was unmasked as a supporter and beneficiary of the notorious Coterel gang, four members of a reasonably well-off local family (opinions differ as to whether they were brothers, cousins or even a multi-generational concern) who had more or less free rein over Nottinghamshire and neighboring Derbyshire during that same period.

And, finally, there was Sheriff John de Oxenford (1334–1339), who himself was proclaimed an outlaw after failing to turn up in court to answer charges of "illegal purveyance, abusing his authority . . . as well as various extortions."

Again, any of these could have slipped out of the history books and into folk tradition as a suitable adversary for Robin Hood.

More likely, however, the sheriff whom we know and love to loathe was a composite not only of each of these men, but of every brutal, beastly, and bullying authority figure of the age, with his characteristics and crimes revised every time another balladeer or playwright turned his quill to the subject. A process, as Keith Allen has already shown us, that is still ongoing today.

Sir Guy of Gisborne

The sheriff of legend does not have a deputy per se. Rather, he has a chief henchman, a black-hearted knight known as Guy of Gisborne, and it is he who enforces the sheriff's wicked whims.

Or so 2006's *Robin Hood* would have it. In earlier movies and television shows, Guy has been portrayed as everything from the sheriff's cousin to a high-ranking nobleman; the chief enforcer for a duplicitous abbot, and even a common outlaw. Always, however, he is as black-hearted a scoundrel as ever stalked the leafy glades of Sherwood Forest.

Once again, Sir Guy was a relative latecomer to the annals of Robin Hood. In mere fragmentary form, there exists a tale, dating from around 1475, in which the sheriff hires an unnamed mercenary expressly to slay Robin Hood. Needless to say, he failed.

That, say sundry researchers and scholars, might have been Sir Guy of Gisborne, but the fact that he is unnamed means we will never know for sure. Besides, Robin fought, and sometimes killed, a lot of unnamed baddies.

Even if it was him, it doesn't really help, for we likewise have no idea when and why he was first identified as Sir Guy of Gisborne; sadly, no matter how many old ballads have survived into modern times, we are painfully aware that many, many more are lost.

However, the suspicion lingers that Sir Guy—like Maid Marian—was flown into the legends of Robin Hood from another source entirely.

This is not an unusual occurrence; according to Francis James Child, Robin Hood and Little John were similarly introduced into the old Scots ballad "Rose the Red and White Lilly" by reason of their popularity alone, there "to displace heroes of immemorial prescription."

In Gisborne's case, supporting evidence can be drawn from a verse penned circa 1500 by the English poet William Dunbar.

There, amid a host of names that doubtless resonated with the poet's audience, but mean little to us today, "Roger of Clekkinsklewch," "Simones sonnes of Quhynfell," "Schir Bewis, the Knight of Southe Hamptone" and many more, we are introduced to "Gy of Gysburne."

It is just a mention, but it must have had a purpose; some form of resonance to the period book lover. Just as a modern reader might leaf through an old gossip column, and wonder who its subjects might once have been, so we must read similar occurrences in the old ballads in similar ignorance, with even the Internet unable to satisfy our curiosity. The fact is, the people and deeds behind these names have been completely forgotten. The names alone live on, and so attempts to unearth a "real" Guy of Gisborne perish on the rocks of historical silence.

His background, however, would seem both fairly and tellingly clear— the Yorkshire town of Guisborough was once known as Gisburne, and was the home to the son-in-law of David, Earl of Huntingdon.

Nobody, not even those who believe David to have been the original
Robin Hood, have ever suggested that his own daughter's husband should
have turned against him in this manner. Nor do any of the ballads suggest
that Robin and Guy were in any way acquainted before they set out to
slaughter each other.

But it's an intriguing link, all the same.

Our own earliest surviving introduction to Sir Guy of Gisborne as one
of Robin's most fearsome foes thus comes via a ballad first published in the

The Sheriff (Keith Allen) and Guy (Richard Armitage) in the 2006 BBC series.
Photofest

book *Reliques of Ancient English Poetry* in 1765, although it is believed to be considerably older than that.

"Robin Hood and Guy of Gisborne" is a remarkable verse, not so much in terms of storytelling (it feels strangely scattered, suggesting that it might be incomplete), but because it marks one of the rare occasions when the sheriff receives his comeuppance.

The ballad opens with Robin reeling from a dream in which a pair of yeomen bound and beat him, and then steal his bow.

> Me thought they did mee beate and binde,
> And tooke my bow mee froe;
> If I bee Robin a-live in this lande,
> Ile be wrocken [avenged] on both them towe.

It's unclear whether what next transpires was also a part of the dream, or if Robin was now acting upon its warning, but soon enough he and Little John are out in the forest, searching for the pair.

However, they fall into an argument and John storms off, only to discover that the sheriff has launched an attack on the outlaws' hideout. Two of the Merry Men are already dead, and Will Scarlet is fighting for his life.

Little John kills one of the attackers, but his bow breaks. He is captured and tied to a tree.

> "Thou shalt be drawen by dale and downe,"
> quoth the sheriffe,
> "And hanged hye on a hill."
> "But thou may fayle," quoth Litle John,
> "If itt be Christs owne will."

Meanwhile, things are not going too well for Robin, either. Meeting a yeoman in the forest, Robin learns that the man is indeed seeking him.

> "Good morrow, good fellow," quoth Sir Guy;
> "Good morrow, good fellow," quoth hee,
> "Methinkes by this bow thou beares in thy hand,
> A good archer thou seems to be."
> "I am wilfull of my way," quoth Sir Guye,
> "And of my morning tyde."
> "Ile lead thee through the wood," quoth Robin,
> "Good fellow, Ile be thy guide."
> "I seeke an outlaw," quoth Sir Guye,
> "Men call him Robin Hood;
> I had rather meet with him upon a day,
> Then forty pound of golde."

Sir Guy of Gisbourne (Basil Rathbone) and Prince John (Claude Rains) were Robin's greatest enemies in *The Adventures of Robin Hood. Robin* (Errol Flynn) and Marian (Olivia de Havilland) share the scene from the 1938 film.   *Photofest*

Common sense insists that Robin should have promptly run the knave through with his sword; or at least made himself scarce. Or both.

But Robin being Robin, he decided instead to accompany the hunter on his search, and (of course) challenge him to some friendly sport, before finally asking his name.

> "I dwell by dale and downe," quoth Guye,
> "And I have done many a curst turne;
> And he that calles me by my right name
> Calles me Guye of good Gysborne."

Robin, who by now has firmly weighed up the fellow's abilities with sword and bow, then boldly responds:

> "My dwelling is in the wood," sayes Robin,
> "By thee I set right nought;
> My name is Robin Hood of Barnesdale,
> A fellow thou has long sought."

Sir Guy's friendly demeanor is cast aside. For two hours the two men fight, and the battle could go either way. But, at last, Robin strikes the fatal blow; then, having killed Sir Guy, he sets about so disfiguring him that he is unrecognizable.

> Robin pulled forth an Irish kniffe,
> And nicked Sir Guy in the face,
> That hee was neuer on a woman borne
> Cold tell who Sir Guy was.

This grisly task accomplished, Robin then switches clothing with the corpse, and sounds the dead man's horn—which he has guessed (for he has used the same ruse himself on occasion) is a signal to the sheriff. And, sure enough, that is who rides over to inspect the body.

At this point, suspicions that this particular ballad was forged from fragments of others is confirmed, simply because one of those other fragments, the aforementioned 1475 manuscript, has survived.

In this untitled piece, however, Robin does *not* disfigure the corpse before dressing it in his own clothing. Instead, he cuts off its head, and simply places that into his hood.

In both ballads, however, the sheriff is totally taken in by the deception. But while he gloats over the dead man, Robin releases Little John and hands him Sir Guy's own bow. Too late, the sheriff sees what is happening and tries to run for cover. But Little John shoots him down.

> John tooke Guyes bow in his hand —
> His arrowes were rawstye by the roote —;
> The sherriffe saw Litle John draw a bow
> And fettle him to shoote.
> Towards his house in Nottingam
> He fled full fast away,
> And soe did all his companye,
> Not one behind did stay.
>
> But he cold neither soe fast goe,
> Nor away soe fast runn,
> But Litle John, with an arrow broade,
> Did cleaue his heart in twinn.

So much, then, for Sir Guy, chopped down and then chopped up, the very first time he ever met Robin Hood. (And so much for the sheriff, too, on this occasion at least.)

Fairbanks in action in the 1922 silent movie.   *Photofest*

But of course, more recent retellings have allowed Sir Guy a far greater role in the saga, not only as a villain, but also as Robin's rival for Marian's affections. That was a principle plot line in the first-ever Robin Hood movie, back in 1912; it was a principal plot device in the 1975 *Legend of Robin Hood* TV series; and it was still going strong in 2006's *Robin Hood*.

Sir Guy, too, has undergone further change; a mercenary, an assassin, Robin's half brother (we'll get to that later) . . . in 1984, with the publication of Simon Hawke's novel *The Ivanhoe Gambit*, he was even portrayed as the Sheriff of Nottingham.

The role did not really behove him, however. Sir Guy is at his best when he is at the sheriff's beck and call, doing the deeds that need to be done; just as the sheriff himself should be forever twirling an imaginary moustache in true Snidely Whiplash fashion, while bemoaning his latest failed scheme, "I'd have got clean away with it if it wasn't for you pesky outlaws."

The Beggar

We are wearily familiar by now with the tale of Robin chancing upon a passing traveler, challenging him (or her) to a duel and then, having been sorely whipped, inviting his conqueror to become a Merry Man.

Considerably rarer are those occasions when the would-be victim not only triumphs over Robin, he takes out sundry companions as well, and then wanders out of the story altogether.

So it is in the case of "A pretty dialogue betwixt Robin Hood and a Beggar," a northern English (and perhaps even Scottish) ballad that first appeared in Joseph Ritson's 1795 *Collection of all the Ancient Poems, Songs and Ballads, Now Extant, Relative to That Celebrated English Outlaw Robin Hood.*

As usual, Robin is alone in the forest when he espies, and decides to rob, a passerby, in this case a beggar.

This in itself is unusual—Robin Hood was, after all, renowned for robbing the rich to give to the poor, and one cannot imagine many people poorer than beggars. Nevertheless Robin pounces, demanding that the beggar halt.

The beggar ignores him.

Robin speaks again, and is ignored again, at which point our swiftly tarnishing hero draws his bow and demands the beggar empty his pockets.

> "If thou have but a small farthing,
> I'll have it ere thou go.
>
> "Therefore, lay down thy clouted cloak,
> And do no longer stand,
> And loose the strings of all thy pocks:
> I'll ripe them with my hand.
>
> "And now to thee I make a vow,
> If thou make any din,
> I shall see if a broad arrow
> Can pierce a beggar's skin."

The beggar continues to stand firm, watching as Robin draws his bow, preparing to shoot, and then lashing out with his staff, shattering both the bow *and* the arrow.

Robin draws his sword; the beggar's staff swings again and Robin is once more disarmed, at which point the beggar sets about his assailant with such brutal zeal that soon, the outlaw is lying unconscious.

The beggar wanders off.

Three of Robin's men, passing by, find their leader still laid out, and revive him with water from a nearby stream. They listen as the still-dazed Robin details his encounter, and they resolve to capture the man and bring him back with them.

But there is further treachery afoot. The men ambush the beggar, and bind him, but he will not be held so easily. Rather, he offers them a huge amount of money if they only let him go, and a plan takes shape—they will stash the cash someplace safe, then return to Robin and claim simply to have killed the old man and concealed his body.

But the beggar is not finished yet. Laying his coat on the ground and pretending to rummage through its pockets, he instead takes a bag of meal from around his neck and throws it into his captors' faces. And while they stagger around blindly, wiping their stinging eyes, he sets about them with his staff, chases them away, and promptly disappears from sight and the song.

Which is a shame, because a man that powerful, and that cunning, could have become a great future adversary.

Robin Hood and Religion

A Real Love/Hate Relationship

Although there has never been any doubt that Robin Hood was a religious man (even if we overlook the ballads' references to his devotion to the Virgin Mary, his participation in the Crusades proves that), neither would anybody question the suggestion that he had a serious problem with the clergy.

Not all of them; not even most of them. But a lot of them. Throughout the ballads, and on into the modern age of novels, movies and television series, sundry abbots, bishops, and (of course) a prioress have crossed swords (figuratively, at least) with Robin, as he stands up against the medieval Church's greed for gold. And understandably so. Most of it was attained in the form of tithes paid by believers, ostensibly to aid the "good causes" for which the Church claimed to provide. Robin's redistribution of these funds simply made certain that the good causes were indeed good.

As he says in the eighteenth century ballad "The King's Disguise, and Friendship with Robin Hood":

> "I never hurt the husbandman,
> That use to till the ground,
> Nor spill their blood that range the wood
> To follow hawk and hound,
> My chiefest spite to clergy is,
> Who in these days bear sway;
> With friars and monks with their fine spunks,
> I make my chiefest prey."

As early as "A Lyttel Geste of Robyn Hode," he is at odds with the abbot of St. Mary's; and (as we have already seen), it is the Prioress of Kirklees, Maid Marian's own cousin, who bleeds him to death. In the 2006 TV series,

Robin even comes up against a fake abbess, although her lust for treasure is no less pronounced than if she had been the real thing.

The crucial point . . . in fact, the *only* point . . . is that Robin cared nothing for rank or status, in this life or in any other. In his eyes, there was no difference whatsoever between a sheriff demanding taxes, and threatening disfigurement or death to anyone who didn't pay them, and a priest demanding offerings, and threatening eternal damnation and hellfire to those who could not afford it.

Because if the king, or God, was that short of cash, then the sheriff, or the abbot, should hand over his own fortune first.

Particularly the latter, because the Church possessed more money and treasure than any number of kings put together, a seemingly boundless horde of gold and precious stones of which a mere fraction was actually on display in the churches. The bulk of it was concealed elsewhere on the premises, in places that no layman could ever venture.

With the exception of those religious souls who purposefully took a vow of poverty, or those who, for whatever reason, had somehow displeased their own earthly superiors, a successful churchman was a bloated one, financially if not physically.

It was not, after all, through any sense of loyalty that the monks of Ely betrayed Hereward the Wake, and it was not out of concern for the needy of Sherwood that Friar Tuck threw his lot in with Robin Hood. It was for money.

The Bishop of Hereford

Although he appears in just a couple of ballads, this particular beastly Balaamite is typical of Robin's religious adversaries.

First up is the smartly titled "Robin Hood and the Bishop of Hereford."

Knowing that the bishop is expected to pass through Sherwood Forest one day, Robin has one of the king's deer killed and then disguises himself and a half-dozen of his men as shepherds, and heads out to meet the bishop's retinue.

Of course the bishop demands to know why his journey has been interrupted, and Robin is happy to tell him—he intends making merry with the king's venison.

> "Then you are brave fellows!" then said the Bishop,
> "But the king of your doings shall know.
> Therefore make haste and come along with me
> And before the king you'll go."

Robin pleads for mercy.

> "O pardon, o pardon," said Robin Hood,
> "O pardon, I thee pray!
> For it becometh not your lordship's coat
> To take so many lives away."

The penalty for killing the king's deer was, invariably, death.

> "No pardon, no pardon," then said the Bishop,
> "No pardon I thee owe.
> Therefore make haste and come along with me
> And before the king you'll go."

Before the bishop can seize the shepherds, however, Robin blows on his trusty horn and out of the greenwood poured his Merry Men. The bishop is captured and taken back to their hideout; his belongings are ransacked and his gold is stolen. The outlaws even force the man to dance for them, before finally setting him free.

That's one version. In a variation on this same ballad, "Robin Hood and the Bishop," Robin lures his prey to his camp by exchanging clothes with an old woman, and allowing the bishop's men to capture her. He then reveals himself and, while the entourage are still reeling in amazement, he ties the bishop to a tree and robs him. He then agrees to free the poor man, only for Little John to demand one further favor. The bishop should sing a Mass for the Merry Men.

Whatever happened, the bishop is not the kind of man to forget his ill-treatment—or, one assumes, his gold. However, other events appear to have passed between the pair, perhaps in ballads that have long since been lost, for when we next encounter the bishop, it is in London, at an archery contest being arranged (pause here for a major chronological lurch) by King Henry and Queen Katherine—presumably the Tudor monarch Henry VIII (reigned 1509–1547) and either his first wife, Catherine of Aragon; his fifth, Catherine Howard; or his sixth, Catherine Parr.

This in itself speaks to the enduring popularity of the legend, that Robin's story should continue to be updated as though to give it contemporary relevance; and, more than that, that the outlaw and his men should now be able to count the King and Queen of England among their friends. At one point in the ballad, Henry even invites them to give up their life in the forest, and come reside at the Royal court with him.

The Bishop of Hereford, who is also present at the contest, is less pleased to see the outlaws, particularly after wagering heavily on the outcome of the archery contest.

> "Is this Robin Hood?" said the bishop then,
> "As I see well to be?
> Had I known that had been that bold outlaw,
> I would not have bet one penny.

> "He took me late one Saturday at night,
> And bound me fast to a tree,
> And made me sing a mass, God wot,
> To him and his yeomendree."

Robin is unrepentant.

> "What and if I did?" says Robin Hood,
> "Of that mass I was full fain;
> But for recompense to thee," he says,
> "Here's half thy gold again."

In other words, he pays the bishop for saying Mass by offering him back just half of the money he stole from him.

A cunning ruse, indeed.

Gilded Mice and Golden Hemorrhoids

The principal source of the Church's wealth in medieval times, once past the gifts of the wealthy and tithes paid by the poor, was the offerings made by pilgrims, seeking the blessings of whichever saint an individual church or abbey might be dedicated to, and whose remains (or, at least, a few pieces thereof) were to be found safely encased in a reliquary within.

At least a portion of the gold that Robin stole from the Bishop of Hereford, for example, would have been derived from the gifts made by the seekers who flocked to venerate the two sets of holy remains that were held at Hereford Cathedral—those of the Anglo-Saxon king, Ethelbert, who was beheaded by the Viking King Offa in 794, and who remained a major source of income until the fourteenth century; and the academic Thomas Cantilupe, a former bishop who died in 1282, having been both excommunicated by the Archbishop of Canterbury following a land dispute, and then absolved of his sins by Pope Martin IV.

Both men's tombs became the site of what were regarded as miracles (in England, only the martyred Thomas à Becket, in Canterbury, was said to have produced more miraculous happenings than Thomas Cantilupe), both were swiftly canonized.

The pilgrims flocked to worship there, but Hereford Cathedral could consider itself fortunate that it possessed the entire earthly remains of two saints. Other religious establishments were forced to purchase their relics from elsewhere, be it traveling salesmen with a suitcase (figuratively speaking) full of bones; from returning overseas travelers—Crusaders, for example—looking to offload their more osseous souvenirs; or from other churches and churchmen.

But they did so with abandon. For it is impossible to overstate the significance of holy relics to the world in which Robin Hood lived, nor the importance with which worshippers of the age regarded them.

Paramount among William the soon-to-be Conqueror's complaints against King Harold, for example, was the latter's willingness to take a holy oath—that is, one that was guaranteed by the involvement of what the Anglo-Norman historian Orderic Vitalis described as "the most sacred relics"—not to oppose the Norman's claim to the English throne. The chronicler does not reveal whose remains these ossified oddments were, but if, as seems likely, the oath was administered at Rouen Cathedral, that city's seventh century bishop Saint Romanus is a leading candidate.

WILLIAM I

William the Conqueror was certainly well named; he conquered England in 1066.

The value of, and quest for, holy relics is as old as Christianity itself. Most of the Romans who diced for Christ's clothing at the foot of the cross were simply hoping to win the cloak that the dying man had been wearing.

But one, Longinus, had converted to the new religion, and for him, the Holy Coat (or the Seamless Robe of Jesus, as it is more properly called) would have been of intense spiritual importance. And the fact that, today, there are at least two Holy Coats in existence—one in Trier, Germany; the other in Argenteuil, France—detracts little from that importance. History, after all, tells us that the distribution of Christendom's most sacred relics was seldom limited by simple numerical law, any more than their efficacy could be regulated by their mundanity.

If we were to believe surviving records of the relics that were scattered across the medieval world, we would be astonished to discover that Saint Mary Magdalene had *at least* six torsos; Saint Gregory the Great possessed four heads; and Saint Teilo, three entire bodies, created—his devotees insisted—"by a singular act of celestial diplomacy," to prevent bloodshed between the religious establishments which wanted a piece of him.

Teilo, a sixth century Welsh bishop, knew that his remains would be sought after; he simply provided enough that everyone could have some.

Throughout the first fifteen hundred years of English Christianity, where there was a church, there was a relic, and it mattered not whether it was the forty-third finger of Saint Brendan, or the umpteenth head of St. Sebastian; whether its provenance could be verified by consulting ancient writings, or if foul rumor insisted the monks had simply excavated it from their own graveyard and randomly assigned it to a favorite saint. Where there was a church, there was a relic; where there was a relic, there were worshippers; and where there were worshippers, there was cash.

Science long ago ensured that the cult of sacred relics has largely been relegated to museum collections and religious histories. Cathedrals and abbeys no longer beg, borrow and steal the fossilized fingers of princes and prelates; the pope no longer excommunicates kings on the grounds that they have mistreated the bones of a bishop; and the preserved remains of long-dead saints are no longer dispatched on fundraising tours by impoverished monks (although they do still make occasional visits—in June 2016, a small piece of elbow bone belonging to Saint Thomas à Becket spent a week on loan at Canterbury Cathedral, in England, from its home in Hungary).

Many of the relics were fakes. The controversy surrounding the authenticity of Jesus's winding cloth, the so-called Turin Shroud, is not a feud between modern skepticism and traditional belief. It is also based on prior experience. In Geneva, the long-revered arm of Saint Anthony was long ago proved to be a bone from a stag. In the same city, the brains of Saint Peter lost much of their allure when they were discovered to be a large pumice stone.

But the believers continue to believe. In Bruges, Belgium, a phial of Christ's blood is still paraded through the streets every Friday; in Naples,

Italy, the dried blood of Saint Janarius continues to liquify at regular intervals; in Glastonbury, England, tourists flock to see the thorn bush which sprouted on the spot where Joseph of Arimathea rested his staff; and in Calcata, Italy, Christ's foreskin is available for annual worship—one of five, incidentally, which are known to have existed.

The power of saintly relics to intercede in the lives of mortal men, too, has seemingly declined over the centuries. But Spanish dictator General Franco died clutching what he believed to be one of Saint Theresa of Avila's arms, confident that her intercession would ensure him everlasting peace; and to the medieval mind, the power and efficacy of relics was undeniable.

When Chaucer's pilgrims traveled to Canterbury to visit the shrine of the Saint Thomas à Becket, they did so in the hope of recommending their souls to heaven.

Other saints promised to heal sickness, discharge debt, end poverty, and cure disabilities, and maybe modern cynics should hold back their scorn for just a moment longer, for perhaps certain bones do retain their miraculous powers.

As recently as April 2016, no less an organ than the *Wall Street Journal* reported that the discovery (buried beneath a parking lot in the English city of Leicester) and subsequent re-entombment of the bones of England's King Richard III had had a remarkable affect on the fortunes of the local soccer team.

> [*the bones*] were reburied [*in Leicester Cathedral*] in March 2015 with fitting pomp and circumstance. Thousands of people turned out for the ceremony. Actor Benedict Cumberbatch, a distant relative of Richard, recited a poem. Then the impossible began to happen at King Power Stadium across town.

At the time of the bones' reburial, Leicester City had not won a single Premier League game in over two months and were red-hot favorites to be demoted to a lower division. Barely had the king's remains been laid to rest, however, than Leicester began winning. And winning and winning and winning. With nine games left in the season, Leicester rose from last place in the twenty-team table to fourteenth, and when the following year's competition began in August, they carried on from exactly where they had left off.

By the end of the season, the team that had been rated 5,000–1 outsiders were crowned deserved champions, and even the city's mayor, Peter Soulsby, admitted "there's a small part of me that feels it might not be a coincidence."

Richard III was not a saint. But for as long as miracles remain the grounds for sanctification, there are some thirty thousand Leicester City season ticket holders who will admit they witnessed one. As the *Wall Street Journal* continued, "[M]etaphysical logic seems to suggest that Richard, delighted with his new resting place, bestowed a supernatural blessing on the team."

There were no parking lots to excavate in medieval times, but still relics could be procured in some surprising, and surprisingly grisly, ways, themselves often dictated by the often gruesome manner in which their earthly owners . . . the saints themselves . . . left this life.

When Saint Ignatius ascended to heaven via the digestive tracts of the wild beasts in the Roman amphitheatre, it was those beasts' table leavings which were gathered up by his followers, for future veneration.

Neither was Ignatius's fate unusual. Few saints, martyred by tooth and claw, axe and sword, fire and water, survived the moment of death in one piece; and of those that did, fewer still survived the state of death intact.

Saint Willibrord was barely dead before she was being divided between the abbey of Echternach, in Luxembourg, Furnes in Flanders, and Aichstadt, Germany.

Friar Tuck and company, by Thomas Bewick (1795).

The patron saint of Scotland, Andrew, left nothing more than a shoulder blade in that country. His head was taken to Greece, a bone to Eton College in England, and his torso to the Church of Saint Sophia in Constantinople.

Then there was the case of Ireland's St. Oliver Plunket. Hanged, drawn, and quartered by the English, his very quarters were then quartered for distribution around the world, parceled off to Rome (his head), Lampspringe, Germany (his torso and legs), Sarnsfield Court (one forearm), Cabra (the other), and Paris (one upper arm). There is even a piece of his skull in Boston, Massachusetts.

Compared to St. Oliver's peregrinations, St. Catherine—with a rib in Brunswick, a finger in Rouen, one hand in Alexandria and her head at Mount Sinai—appears positively reclusive.

In terms of total dispersion, however, few saints can rival John the Baptist. Leaving one head in Constantinople, he sent another to Jean d'Angely, and a third to Poitier. His face went to Amiens, the back of his head to Nemours, his brains to Nogent-le- Retrou, his blood to Aachen Cathedral, a bit of one ear to St Flour-en-Auverge, his body to Sebaste, Italy, and his hair to the King of the Visigoths.

And when one abbot was questioned as to how his establishment could be displaying the saint's head, when another was on display elsewhere, his answer—while possibly apocryphal—is another reminder of the credulity of the age. "Oh, we have his head as a young man. They've got it from when he was older." Or words to that effect.

It was not only clergy who clamored for relics, however. The Emperor Charlemagne was a tireless enthusiast, distributing dismembered holy men throughout the Holy Roman Empire. Three centuries later, France's King Louis IX was such a renowned collector that when he arrived in the Holy Land on Crusade, local tradesmen literally queued up to offer him sacred souvenirs.

The reformer John Calvin once remarked that if one were to gather together every splinter of the True Cross preserved around the world, one would be left with a crucifix so heavy that three men could not lift it. King Louis had one of the largest of these slivers, together with phials filled with Christ's blood and the Virgin's milk, the Crown of Thorns, one of four known Holy Lances, a fragment from one of the Baptist's skulls, sundry segments of Mary Magdalene and more. Much more.

We read little about relics in the tales of Robin Hood, although England held a great many of the things. Aside from the treasure troves interred in Hereford and Canterbury, Durham Cathedral owned the remains of

St. Cuthbert; saints Paulinus and Ithamar were to be found in Rochester; St. William of York, very fittingly, resided at York; Saint Etheldreda in Hereward's old stomping grounds of Ely; and one of St. Oswald's arms was in Peterborough, stolen from its previous home at Bamburgh Castle by one of the abbey's monks. Within riding distance of Robin's hideout, some elements of St. Eadburh were sequestered in Southwell.

Robin, however, did not interfere with them, and from that silence we can deduce the awe in which the early chroniclers held them. While Robin merrily stole gold and treasure from the Church, he never once touched the remains of a holy man.

That would have been a crime too far.

Into the Woods We Go

Robin Hood and the Mystery of the Forest

T here is one further major player in the legend that we have not yet mentioned.

Despite the grandiosity of its current nomenclature, the Sherwood Forest National Nature Reserve, the Sherwood Forest of today is but a shadow of the vast woodland that once bore its name. Dating back to the Ice Age, it spreads today over 1,045 acres. In earlier times, it was far larger, but the growth of civilization in the form of villages and towns, and the need for wood for construction and industry have seen it diminish to a point where it would be unrecognizable even to a passing Regency buck, let alone to Robin Hood.

Even the King's Houses, a vast, seven-and-a-half acre royal palace that stood outside Clipstone village as long ago as 1164 and was a home away from home for three centuries of English monarchs, would fall first into ruin and then out of memory.

Until as recently as 2010, its remains were widely believed to be nothing more than a considerably smaller hunting lodge. Since that time, excavations and research by English Heritage, Nottinghamshire County Council, and British television's *Time Team* archaeological troupe, have all pointed toward a far more glorious past. (Amusingly, the latter's frontman, Tony Robinson, was also the writer of, and the sheriff in, *Maid Marian and her Merry Men*, two decades earlier.)

Daniel Defoe visited Sherwood Forest as he prepared his monumental *A Tour Through the Whole Island of Britain* in 1726, and he professed himself sorely disappointed by what he encountered.

"This Forest is now given up, in a manner, to Waste: even the Woods, which formerly made it famous for Thieves, are destroyed, so that *Robin Hood* would now hardly find Shelter for a Week; nor is there any Store of Deer now left, at least not worth mentioning."

And that was before the demands of the industrial revolution took to hewing down anything that even looked like a tree; and certainly before the agricultural requirements of the Great War (1914–1918) saw even more acres cleared for cultivation, to grow the foods that the conflict had rendered scarce. Neither is Sherwood alone in this cruel diminishment. Once, almost all of England was forested; today, more than 80 percent of the woodlands have been hacked back, the "green and pleasant" land of fable converted to a gray, drab, concrete wasteland.

Tourism, too, has taken its toll. Herculean is the prospect of imagining how the forest must have looked to the Merry Men when, at almost every turn, there stand gift stores, cafés, and information booths to remind you that you are now visiting Robin Hood Country, and this is not a recent phenomenon.

Almost fifty years ago, the Pulitzer Prize–winning naturalist Edwin Way Teale found his way to the Major Oak, the vast tree in which the outlaws are said to have once hidden from the sheriff.

> And what did we find? Instead of a wild and unfrequented forest
> . . . acres of varicolored automobiles jammed together in the open
> spaces. The blare of portable radios filled the air. People swarmed
> among the trees eating picnic lunches in the shade and in the
> sunshine. Ice cream stands, carnival booths, even a merry-go-round
> occupied the largest open space.

(The thousand-year-old pendunculate, or English oak, incidentally, is named not for some obscure element within Robin's tale, but for the eighteenth century antiquary Major Hayman Rooke, author of an eighteenth-century study of Sherwood's oak trees. It was also once known as the Cockpen Tree, apparently because fighting cocks were housed within its hollow trunk. In a poll conducted in 2002, the Major Oak was voted Britain's favorite tree.)

For all the uncertainties that surround Robin's existence and whereabouts, Sherwood Forest has been a remarkably constant feature throughout the centuries.

A scrap of poetry that some scholars date to the beginning of the fifteenth century includes the tantalizing line "Robyn hod in scherewod stod," while the ancient ballad "Robin Hood and the Monk" has Robin going to Nottingham, while "Littul John [went] to merry Scherwode [by] the pathes he knew alone."

Something else that is common to the legends. The forest is always sunny, a canopy of verdant green shimmering in the heat haze. Very few tales of Robin Hood are enacted beneath anything less than the most clement conditions, as though the grim aquarium that is the modern English climate was simply another gray consequence of modernity and progress. Either that, or he spent the winter months in hibernation.

Even back then, however, Sherwood was not the sole contender for Robin's home. All across the U. K., local landmarks and traditions alike bear his name and many of them even have legends attached.

Butts, Barrows, and Barns

In Herefordshire, two small hills near King's Pyon were known as Robin Hood's Butts—a butt being the small conical mound upon which an archery target was placed.

According to one legend, Robin was in the habit of standing on one hill and hitting a target on the other, some half-mile distant; according to another, Robin and Little John were responsible for creating the hills in the first place, while jumping over nearby Wormesley Hill—the butts were the clods of earth they displaced upon landing. And according to a third, the butts are the spoil from a mighty pit that Robin dug while burying his treasure.

There are more butts to be found deep into the English southwest, in the Blackdown Hills of Somerset, a group of three (there were once five) prehistoric burial mounds, or tumuli, which some locals believed were also used as targets by Robin and his men.

Others, however, claimed that Robin and Little John used to play quoits there, tossing them from one barrow to the other, and they point to the scars in the soil left by long-ago treasure hunters as the marks that the quoits made when they missed their target.

Even further afield, in isolated Cornwall, the oaken log placed at the back of the fire at Yule was traditionally known as a Hood, in tribute to the oak trees among which Robin resided; and any woodlouse that escaped from the burning wood was thus named "Robin Hood's Steed." It was believed the insect then escaped up the chimney before taking the form of a robin.

Hills in Gloucestershire and Derbyshire were named for the outlaw (although the former, now known as Robinswood Hill, is grotesquely scarred by an artificial ski slope), and a vast rock near Matlock, in the latter county, was called Robin Hood's Tor.

Remaining in Derbyshire, Robin Hood's Stride is the twenty-two-foot gap between two eighteen-foot-high rock formations known to climbers as the Weasel and Inaccessible, on Harthill Moor. It also overlooks the Grey Ladies stone circle, now a group of four six-foot stones but once a far more impressive ring of nine—including, according to the eighteenth century's Charles King, one that stood *seventeen* feet high!

The Stride's proximity to the Grey Ladies was no accident. Although another visitor, archaeologist Aubrey Burl, remarks that the stride, which is a natural formation, resembles nothing so much as "the head and pricked-up ears of a wrinkled hippopotamus," he also points out that "from the circle, the major southern moon sets between the ears, and this may be the reason for the situation of the ring."

Robin Hood's own connection to the stones, however, is long lost, although it might well be related to the sheer impossibility of anybody actually being capable of striding across the gap. Numerous similarly forged Robin-related proverbs litter the colloquial English landscape, including "Robin Hood's Penny'sworth," which means being able to buy a lot of something for very little money; "Robin Hood's Ale," which was uncommonly strong beer; and "Robin Hood's Mile," which denotes a long journey.

Up on Ludworth Moor, a pair of pillars set in a stone block are known as Robin Hood's Picking Rods, and are believed to have been erected—appropriately enough—to aid in the bending of bows while they were being strung. Down on the border with Nottinghamshire, meanwhile, Robin Hood's Cave lies within the spectacular Creswell Crags, with tradition insisting that this was one of the outlaws' favorite hideouts.

However, the network of caves that lies amidst the crags is perhaps better regarded today as an archaeological treasure trove, with one of their number, Church Hole Cave, still decorated with paintings that have been there for twelve thousand years.

Included among these are deer, birds, and what some view as highly stylized naked women, each blessed with enormous buttocks, but apparently lacking their lower limbs. They have, consequently, been dubbed "the Legless Ladies of Creswell Crags."

In Lincolnshire, an ancient boundary stone was known as Robin Hood's Cross; in Lancashire, we find Robin Hood's Well; in Ennerdale, in the Lake District, there's a natural rock formation known as Robin Hood's Chair; and there are several stone circles around the country that are, or were once, known as "Robin's Stones" or something similar, with opinion divided between whether they related to the mythic Hood or the fairy Goodfellow. (Assuming, as we shall see later, that there is a difference between the two.)

Either way, equally ancient traditions insisted that any young woman visiting the circle on certain nights of the year, or phases of the moon, would assuredly become pregnant as a consequence.

These names are old; they certainly predate the now-familiar ruse of affixing a celebrity's name to a particular locale as a means of drumming up some tourist dollars. Neither are they always attached directly to the legend.

At Flimby Colliery in Cumbria, for example, Robin gave his name to an antimony mine; and in Hoby, Leicestershire, a mound that is said to be of Roman origin is named Robin Hood's Barn, *not* because anyone believes it might have been, but because Robin didn't *have* a barn. Echoing the aforementioned Robin Hood's Stride, et al., "Going to Robin Hood's Barn" was once a popular simile for a wild goose chase, and while we don't now know how the saying and the mound are linked, we also don't share the medieval sense of humor.

The county of Nottinghamshire, of course, is riddled with reminders of Robin's preeminence. Robin Hood's Hills stand within what was once a part of the original Sherwood Forest, to form a beautiful natural amphitheatre; the Robin Hood Pit is a tumulus close to the village of Oxton; Robin Hood Meadow was a field near Perlethorpe; and Robin Hood's Well, once famed for its aphrodisiac properties, lies north of Beauvale Priory. In the village of Edwinstowe, Robin Hood Avenue and the Robin Hood Inn celebrated the tradition that it was here that Robin and Marian were wed.

The county is also peppered with mines, with the first coal mines operating around Cossall and Selston as early as the 1270s, but evidence of earlier excavations abound, both within the landscape and the myths.

Television's 1975 series *The Legend of Robin Hood* has the sheriff and Prince John operating a silver mine, manned by slave labor recruited from nearby villages. Both the 2006 *Robin Hood* and *Doctor Who*'s "Robot of Sherwood" episode also made heavy usage of similarly manned mining operations.

In keeping with its own claims, medieval and otherwise, upon Robin Hood's residence, neighboring Yorkshire, too, has a number of related landmarks.

In Chatsworth, we marvel at a chasm called Robin Hood's Leap; and five miles south of Whitby (itself renowned for its links to Bram Stoker's *Dracula*), we find the village of Robin Hood's Bay, and a legend that tells

The Robin Hood memorial in Nottingham. *Wikimedia Commons*

how Robin saved the town's fishing fleet from the attentions of some French pirates—echoes, of course, of his escapades in Scarborough (see chapter six).

Robin Hood's Fountain once lay between Doncaster and Wakefield; and on Midgely Moor, there stands his Penny Stone, a boulder distinguished by a deep, natural bowl. During years of pestilence and plague, victims of the disease would visit here, pour vinegar into the bowl and deposit what coins they could spare. In return, it was said, Robin Hood would leave them food.

We cannot read too much into these names, as anybody with a more than passing familiarity with the English countryside could tell you. The land is lousy with landmarks which tradition has titled, and most of them are named for the devil: his bridge, his punchbowl, his dike, his hill. King Arthur, too, has seats, stones, beds, and caverns the length and breadth of the county. It is easy to conjecture that Robin has no more literal a claim upon his landmarks that those two worthies have on theirs.

Besides, Yorkshire's strongest hold on the legend is delivered not by chasms, fountains or bowls. It arrives courtesy of another fragment of verse, dating from 1429.

Standing in stark opposition to Sherwood's claims on his presence, it begins,"Robyn hode en bernesdale stode," an insistence that would appear to situate him firmly in Barnsdale, near the town of Doncaster, on what was one of England's most important highways, the still much-traveled remains of the Roman Watling Street.

Close by, too, is the village, and former coal-mining community of Robin Hood, whose significance is further suggested by the early ballads that mention the "outwood"—taken by some scholars to mean the nearby Outwoods of Wakefield.

"A Lyttel Geste of Robyn Hode" also places Robin's home in the region of Barnsdale, and it may be no coincidence that other chronicles report highway robbery as a very popular pastime in that neighborhood, outlaws leaping out of the dark to hold up travelers and relieve them of their treasures.

Of course, Robin could have had bases in both places, in Barnsdale and in Sherwood. The journey now takes around an hour, but that is with the benefit of modern roads. In medieval times it was a considerably more arduous trip, but still it could have been negotiated relatively swiftly—indeed, King John himself made the trip in a day, and that was with his royal retinue in tow, all mindful of the comfort of the royal posterior. A band of outlaws, astride fast horses, would have had no such qualms.

It must be said, however, that Sherwood fits the legend in numerous different ways. As a Royal Forest, it was the property of the crown, and a number of kings (including Richard I and John) enjoyed the hunting there.

Furthermore, its wildlife fell under the protection of far more stringent (and punitive) laws than in other wooded areas, with the penalties for poaching including castration, blinding or hanging, and sometimes all three.

Another favorite penalty involved sewing the poacher into a freshly obtained deerskin, giving him a few minutes head start, and then setting the dogs on his trail—a grisly end that echoes one of the myths that attend the Greek Goddess Artemis (Diana to the Romans).

Bathing in the forest one day, she was both surprised and enraged by the sudden appearance of a passing herdsman named Actaeon. Instantly, she turned the hapless fellow into a stag, and then watched contentedly while his own dogs attacked and killed him.

Of course these laws, and the consequent punishments, were unpopular. That was the point of them. In an age when many people still lived off the land, and the Royal Forest itself encompassed any number of villages and hamlets, there can have been few greater frustrations than knowing that the forest around you was plethoric with wildlife, yet you were not permitted to touch it.

Wild boar and deer, creatures whose meat could feed a family for many a day, were all off limits, while the 1975 *Legend of Robin Hood* series reminds us that it was not only Royal land that was protected. Any noble could, so he desired, set the harshest penalties for anyone caught stealing from his land, hence Sir Guy of Gisborne's apparent habit of hanging anyone found picking berries from his bushes.

Nevertheless, the prospect of a slow starvation forced many people to eventually pit their wits against the Royal Foresters, as the forests' guards were known, and take down a buck or roe. And if they were caught, in the region of Sherwood, the sharper among them had a ready explanation to hand.

"I didn't shoot the arrow; Robin Hood did."

It might not save their lives, or whatever part of their body the sheriff (if he was feeling merciful) might deem to hack off. But it might give their captors a few sleepless nights.

In the Dark, Dark Wood

A felon offering up such a defense today—blaming a mythological (or, at least, long dead) being for committing the crime for which he is being tried—would probably receive little sympathy from anybody with the possible exception of his psychologist.

The authorities in earlier times were less sure of themselves. It is unforgivably patronizing to describe the medieval world as "superstitious"; although the dictionary definition of the word is more understanding, it is generally accepted today that a superstitious man is a somewhat foolish one, believing in beings and happenings that science and reason assure us are impossible.

But to call them, instead, "uneducated" is to be similarly ingenuous.

What, after all, is science, beyond a catchall summary for all that we are told is possible? Science is not a recent invention; although they have not always been known as such, scientists have existed throughout human civilization, dedicatedly ferreting out the "truths" behind what they perceive as reality, and building their world around the discoveries that their researches assure them are correct.

Only for the next generation to come along and show that they'd got it all completely wrong.

And what is education, if not the means by which that science is drilled into everybody's head? Regardless of where one stands on the issue, the modern debate between those who would teach Darwin's theories of evolution, and those who prefer other explanations for the development of life on earth, is nothing more than a refusal to accept as incontrovertible fact a belief that remains mere educated (if very logical) guesswork, for that is all a theory is.

So it is with superstition. Science tells us that *this* is possible, *that* is impossible, and ne'er the twain shall meet. But more people have seen ghosts than have watched a monkey evolve into a man, so why is one considered a scientific reality when the other is regarded as nonsense?

Particularly when, were one to travel back just a few centuries in time, science was firmly convinced that lead could be turned into gold, the sun revolved around the earth (which itself was as flat as a pancake), and you could cure insanity by drilling a hole in the sufferer's head to let out the evil spirits therein.

Medieval man believed in ghosts because nobody had told him he shouldn't. It is, after all, one of mankind's oldest beliefs, that the dead return to earth as wraiths and spirits, and the more good or evil the dead person was, the more likely they are to reappear.

Again, that same belief is still current today. Invariably, if an old building is haunted, it will usually be by the most famous person associated with it.

The Tower of London, for example, saw countless hundreds of executions, including many of very high rank and nobility. But it's not some forgotten Duke of Anywhere who walks the grounds in the dead of night, with his neatly severed head tucked underneath his arm. It's Anne Boleyn, the luckless queen of King Henry VIII.

In Nottingham, Standard Hill (in the shadow of the castle) is haunted not by any one of the numerous people who have lived in its houses over the centuries, but by Roger Mortimer, Earl of March, the executed lover of Queen Dowager Isabella, wife of King Edward II.

Those despairing screams that echo through the castle? No, they're not the cries of the hundreds of souls who were imprisoned or tormented there, or of their loved ones begging for clemency. They're the cries of Queen Isabella herself, mourning the death of her lover.

And when, in 2013, a worker at the Sherwood Forest Nature Reserve photographed the Major Oak following a snowfall, and a combination of shadow, snow, and the trunk's natural contours revealed a chunky humanoid shape, the English *Daily Mail* was swift to christen it "the monk in the trunk" and declare it to be Friar Tuck.

In Sherwood Forest, therefore, it was never some nameless spectral bowman who shot the king's deer just as the Foresters rode by. It was Robin Hood and his Merry Men, immortalized in song for decades, if not centuries, but still robbing the rich to feed the poor.

Familiar once to generations of English schoolchildren (who also learned and loved his epic *The Highwayman*), Alfred, Lord Noyes captured the supernatural flavor that adheres to Robin Hood in a play which he titled, simply, *Sherwood*.

> Sherwood in the twilight, is Robin Hood awake?
> Grey and ghostly shadows are gliding through the brake,
> Shadows of the dappled deer, dreaming of the morn,
> Dreaming of a shadowy man that winds a shadowy horn.
>
> Robin Hood is here again: all his merry thieves
> Hear a ghostly bugle-note shivering through the leaves,
> Calling as he used to call, faint and far away,
> In Sherwood, in Sherwood, about the break of day.

The Ghosts and Gods of Sherwood Forest

We're getting into troublesome waters here, though, with all this talk of the supernatural impinging upon the worlds of Robin Hood. Troublesome, because the stories are exciting enough as they stand, without people needing to start dragging phantoms and fairies into them.

They do it, anyway.

In 1858, a stage play was unveiled in which Robin is captured by the Gnome Demon, and contemporary reviews suggest that it was about as good as you'd expect from that description.

In 1956, the comic book *The Adventures of Robin Hood* plunged Robin into combat with Morla Le Fey, known as "the evil enchantress of England, hired by Prince John to cast a spell on Robin Hood."

And more recently, in 2012, he joined the ranks of the living dead, and did so in 3D, no less!

The movie *Ghosts of Sherwood* begins with Robin and the Merry Men battling the sheriff one more time, but this time will be the last. The sheriff's men win the day, routing the outlaws and killing them, too. Only Little John and Maid Marian survive, and they know what a world without Robin will be like. So they set about raising them from the dead.

As zombies.

Did we just call it absurd? No, although we should have. It's fun as well, though, in a semi-slapstick *Walking Dead In Tights* kind of way, but the key point is, six hundred years ago, nobody would have regarded it as anything particularly out of the ordinary.

True, zombies are a relatively recent addition to the canon of western supernatural beings, but the medieval world was already home to boggarts and goblins, elves and ogres, ancient gods and contemporary chimerae, ghosties and ghoulies and long-legged beasties and things that went "bump" in the night. One more supernatural terror would have made no difference whatsoever. And Robin, in fact, fits the bill in a surprising number of ways.

The possibility that the legend of Robin Hood is actually the survivor of some earlier folk belief has been broached by several scholars, and others besides.

As the consort of the May Queen in the medieval festivities, he would automatically have assumed the role of the Summer King, awakened from his winterlong sleep in one of the oldest religious rituals known to man.

This, in turn, aligns him with the Green Man, so popular (and popularly oft-distorted) in modern pagan literature, but also a common sight in older churches, where his image was carved into the very fabric of the building, an example of the religion's stealthy absorption of lingering pre-Christian imagery into its own iconography.

The notion that the Green Man started life in more Bacchanalian surroundings has long been suspected, however, with his possible lineage extending as far afield as the Greek God Pan, the Germanic Freyr, and the Celtic Cernunnos. Indeed, the very name of another Celtic deity, Virinios, translates into "green man" in both Welsh and Latin.

Whatever his source might have been, the Green Man is a powerful symbol of fertility and life (again, the role of the Summer King), which means it may well not have been purely for purposes of camouflage that Robin Hood is most frequently depicted dressed in green.

The Green Man is only one possible mythological identity, however.

"Robin" was also once a popular name for the devil, and might be a twist on the Teutonic god Woden (Odin in the Norse pantheon), as Christianity inverted his earlier religious significance and transformed him into the embodiment of evil. And returning to the legends surrounding Robin Hood's Butts in Herefordshire, it was once said that they were the work of the devil, after he challenged another hero, Jack O'Kent, to an earth-throwing competition.

(That said, "Robin" is also old Cornish slang for "penis"; and "Robin's Hood" was the foreskin.)

Puck and his Pals

Robin's relationship with the fairyfolk is very much a modern addition to the tales.

Already quoted in these pages, Alfred, Lord Noyes's *Sherwood* sees Robin interact with the fairies of the forest; while Henry Gilbert's *Robin Hood and his Merry Men* introduces us to Hob O'the Hill and Ket the Trow, earthly spirits whom Stephen Knight, author of *Robin Hood: A Mythic Biography*, describes as "more like Celtic survivors than the fairies from . . . *Sherwood*."

He is correct. Among the legion of romantic reinventions of the late Victorian era, fairies in particular drew the shortest straw, essentially being reinvented as neutered talking butterflies, giggling like Tinkerbelle and prone to nothing more mischievous than spiriting children away to Never Never Land and introducing them to ticking crocodiles. (*Peter Pan* was published as a play in 1904).

Prior to that, fairies (and an entire family of similarly weird relatives, from elves and gnomes, to giants and pixies) were prone to all the emotions and rages that a superstitious mind could envisage; were responsible for everything from souring milk to stampeding horses; and amused themselves by leading travelers into bogs, and stealing babies from their cradles.

But were they simply a human invention? Or were they folk memories from a time before man started measuring time? A time when the very name "Hood" could have had any number of meanings beyond those we think of today.

"Hodekin" was a very helpful Teutonic house elf—or at least, helpful if you were the master of the house. Less so if you were his unfaithful wife, though; according to one legend, whenever one particularly wanton lady of the house attempted to entertain a secret lover (which was, allegedly, fairly regularly), up would pop Hodekin to transform himself into all manner of terrifying creatures, until he had scared away her paramour.

Hodekin had an English equivalent, too, name of Robin Goodfellow, and you can probably see where this is leading.

A generally benevolent woodsprite, prone to good-humored mischief and jesting, Robin Goodfellow was not originally a single character; W. Y. Evans-Wents, in his monumental *The Fairy Faith in Celtic Countries* (1911), describes Robin Goodfellows as a race that was comparable to the pixies of Cornwall, the goblins of Wales, the brownies of Scotland, the corrigan of Brittany, and so forth.

The assumed singularity of the name, however, has seen Robin Goodfellow devolve to a single entity, and this might well be the source of the confusion that sometimes conjoins Goodfellow to Robin Hood. Several sites around the British Isles—including the stone circles we visited earlier, and Robin's Bank hill in Llyn Ebyr, in Wales—divide their legends between the two, depending upon who is relating the tale.

It is as a distinct individual that Robin Goodfellow has also become aligned with another non-human race that has likewise been personalized into a single being, the puck. Or, thanks to Shakespeare, Puck, famous now as a character in *A Midsummer Night's Dream,* but before that, a creature whose name might have been derived from the Old Norse word *puki,* meaning "unsettled," or from the Swedish *pyskie,* meaning "small fairy"—a pixie, of course.

Puck became Robin Goodfellow when he was adopted, like Hodekin, as a friendly presence around the house . . . a hobgoblin, or a goblin of the hearth (or hob, as it was once called). *Brewer's Dictionary of Phrase and Fable* (published in 1898) refers to him as a "drudging fiend, and merry domestic fairy, famous for mischievous pranks and practical jokes. At night-time he will sometimes do little services for the family over which he presides."

An even firmer description was offered by Shakespeare, as Puck makes himself known to a passing fairy.

> Either I mistake your shape and making quite,
> Or else you are that shrewd and knavish sprite
> Call'd Robin Goodfellow: are not you he
> That frights the maidens of the villagery;
> Skim milk, and sometimes labour in the quern
> And bootless make the breathless housewife churn;
> And sometime make the drink to bear no barm;
> Mislead night-wanderers, laughing at their harm?
> Those that Hobgoblin call you and sweet Puck,
> You do their work, and they shall have good luck:
> Are not you he?

Already, however, this feels like something of a blind alley.

Robin Hood had many, many, noble properties, but cleaning the hearth and washing the dishes were not among them. It is true, Jonas Armstrong's personification of Robin in the 2006 television series certainly plays on his charming, puckish qualities— a bold contrast to the often over-heroic beefcake of other characterizations—but no. If Robin Hood truly has a supernatural alter-ego, it is not Robin Goodfellow.

Maybe he is the devil after all. The sheriff certainly thought so.

The Witch of Papplewick

One of the most enthralling of all supernatural Robin Hood stories (and one in which Puck appears as a very separate character) is *The Sad Shepherd*, a pastoral penned by playwright Ben Jonson shortly before his death in 1637.

Jonson was a contemporary of William Shakespeare, whose own canon features several mentions of the great outlaw and his companions. In *The Two Gentlemen of Verona*, we hear a resounding cry of "By the bare scalp of Robin Hood's fat friar"; in *As You Like It*, a duke and his men are exiled to the Forest of Arden, there to "live like the old Robin Hood of England."

Falstaff, in *Henry IV Part One*, invokes Maid Marian during a delightful volley of invective aimed at a displeasing hostess:

> There's no more faith in thee than in a stewed
> prune; nor no more truth in thee than in a drawn
> fox; and for womanhood, Maid Marian may be the
> deputy's wife of the ward to thee. Go, you thing,go.

And in the companion *Henry IV, Part Two*, Justice Silence unleashes (for no apparent reason) a lusty chorus of "And Robin Hood, Scarlet, and John."

So Robin Hood was no more a stranger to the Shakespearean stage than he had been to that of any earlier age, and he continued so. Nevertheless, it is one of the tragedies of English literature that Jonson did not live to finish writing *The Sad Shepherd*. Less than three acts were completed, out of a projected five, and so we can only imagine how the tale might have finished, and what further twists the author had in store. Like Charles Dickens's similarly unfinished final novel, *The Mystery of Edwin Drood*, *The Sad Shepherd* builds in so many tantalizing directions that few readers, having devoured it, can resist conjecturing, "What next"?

It is a cunningly mapped out tale. It opens in the Vale of Belvoir, in Sherwood Forest, with Robin preparing to host a great feast, to which all the local shepherds and shepherdesses have been invited. Venison, the meat of the king's so keenly protected deer, is, naturally, on the menu.

Something of a cloud is draped over the proceedings, however, by the news that one of the guests, the shepherd Aeglamour, is mourning the apparent death of his wife, Earine. She was last seen several days earlier, crossing over the River Trent, and it can only be assumed that she fell in and drowned.

Certainly Aeglamour is convinced of this, and now yearns only for the waters to return her corpse . . .

> All pale and bloodlesse, I will love it still,
> For all that they can doe, and make 'hem mad,
> To see how I will hugge it in mine armes!
> And hang upon the lookes, dwell on her eyes:
> Feed round about her lips, and eate her kisses!
> Suck of her drowned flesh!

Realizing there is nothing that he can say or do that will comfort the grieving widower, Robin leaves Aeglamour to his thoughts, and returns to preparing for the feast.

Meanwhile, Marian has returned from the hunt, and mentions that she'd heard that Maudlin, the notorious Witch of Papplewick (a village in west-central Nottinghamshire) had been seen around the neighborhood, in the form of a raven—at which point Scathlock, described here as the brother of Will Scarlet, pipes up, saying he, too, had seen her boiling scraps of venison down at "the Chimley nuik." The same scraps, Robin realizes, that had earlier been thrown out, a crucial element in the "unmaking of the deer," as the ritualistic preparation of such a feast was termed—traditionally, it was the beast's pelvis that would be returned to the kill site as an offering to the crows and corbies. And, on this occasion, the witch.

Marian leaves, only to reappear a few moments later, and begin arguing with Robin. First, she demands that "Mother Maudlins, whom you call the witch" be allowed to share in the feast and then, when Robin objects, she unleashes a positively scorching stream of invective:

> you are the spie . . . that watch upon my walkes,
> To informe what Deere I kill, or give away!
> Where! when! to whom! but spie your worst, good Spie!
> I will dispose of this where least you like!
> Fall to your cheese-cakes, curdles, clawted creame,
> Your fooles, your flaunes; and of ale a streame
> To wash it from your livers: straine ewes milke
> Into your Cider sillabubs, and be drunke
> To him, whose Fleece hath brought the earliest Lambe
> This yeare; and weares the Baudrick at your bord!
> Where you may all goe whistle; and record
> This i' your dance: and foot it lustily.

She then storms off, taking the venison with her, leaving Robin and his companions utterly baffled by this sudden change in Marian's demeanor.

But, of course, it wasn't Marian. It was Maudlin assuming her form, as the witch explains while she and her daughter Douce begin preparing the venison:

> Have I not left 'em in a brave confusion?
> Amazed their expectation? got their Venison?
> Troubled their mirth, and meeting? made them doubtfull,
> And jealous of each other? all distracted?
> And, 'i the close, uncertaine of themselves?
> This can your Mother doe my daintie Douce!
> Take anie shape upon her! and delude
> The senses, best acquainted with their Owners!

Maudlin reveals, too, that it was she who was responsible for the disappearance of the shepherd's wife, Earine; that the woman is now imprisoned in a tree:

> Your brother Lorell's prize!
> For so my largesse hath lotted her,
> to be your brother's Mistresse.

The real Marian has returned to the feast by now, to be stunned by the accusations that her friends level against her. Of course she denies that she had taken the venison or thrown a single insult; naturally, she insists she was not even in the clearing at the time.

But she is thoroughly thrown for a loop by the appearance, a few moments later, of Maudlin, in her own form this time, to thank her for the gift she just brought them.

While the witch relishes her apparent victory, however, Scathlock has recovered the stolen meat. He returns with it, and Maudlin flies into a fury, unleashing a storm of curses upon the cook, first upon his attempts to prepare the meal:

> The Spit stand still, no Broches turne
> Before the fire, but let it burne
> Both sides, and haunches . . .

And then upon his own flesh:

> The Swilland Dropsie enter in
> The Lazie Cuke, and swell his skin;
> And the old Mort-mal on his shin
> Now prick, and itch, withouten blin.
> The Pæne, wee call S. Antons fire
> The Gout, or what wee can desire,
> To crampe a Cuke, in every lim,
> Before they dine, yet; seize on him.

And with that, she departs, with Robin and his men in hot pursuit—and there, sadly, Jonson's story ends. A surviving precis, or "argument," for the third act makes it clear that Maudlin's plans for poor Earrine are doomed to failure, and that the witch will never profit from her wicked behavior; and 150 years later, the playwright Francis Godolphin Waldron confirmed this when he offered up his own conclusion to the tale, so that it might be debuted at the Drury Lane Theatre in London.

In terms of delirious devilment, however, there is no surpassing Jonson's original text, and it is one of the tragedies of the mythos of Robin Hood that the *The Sad Shepherd* is neither better known, nor more widely praised.

Likewise, although a belief in witchcraft, for both good and evil, was a major component of medieval life, it is scarcely mentioned in any surviving earlier texts.

Scholarship, however, has stepped in to try and fill the void, with some of the more fanciful theories even painting Robin as a witch and the Merry Men (plus Marian) as the coven which he led.

There is little evidence, even anecdotal, to support these claims, a failing that is only exacerbated by the fact that most of what we know about witchcraft throughout this period is itself little more than hearsay and propaganda, put about by those men charged with stamping it out.

True, the anthropologist and historian Margaret Murray argued firmly for the existence of a widespread underground organization in her 1921 book *The Witch-Cult in Western Europe*. Therein, she suggests that the sheer consistency of the testimonies and confessions that the witch hunters obtained indicates some form of shared belief and experience, one that could only have developed were there a single central text (either spoken or written) that all the witches knew.

But the confessions could as easily have been doctored, or at least shaped, by the questions being asked, and any attempt to draw modern conclusions from contemporary responses can only be conjectural at best. Under torture, there can only be so many times a suspected witch is asked, "Do you serve a horned god?" before she will finally agree that yes, she does. And thanks to the mid-eighties television series *Robin of Sherwood* (see chapter 23), a lot of people now believe that Robin Hood served one as well.

Herne the Hunter

> Sometime a keeper here in Windsor Forest,
> Doth all the winter-time, at still midnight,
> Walk round about an oak, with great ragg'd horns;
> And there he blasts the tree, and takes the cattle,
> And makes milch-kine yield blood, and shakes a chain
> In a most hideous and dreadful manner.
> You have heard of such a spirit, and well you know
> The superstitious idle-headed eld
> Receiv'd, and did deliver to our age,
> This tale of Herne the Hunter for a truth.
>
> *William Shakespeare, The Merry Wives of Windsor*

We have Shakespeare to thank for Herne the Hunter. Shakespeare and Harrison Ainsworth.

According to the former, Herne was a ghostly guardian of Windsor Forest, that vast expanse of woodland that is today (partially) preserved as Windsor Great Park.

In life, claimed author (and renowned Shakespearean scholar) Samuel Ireland in 1792, Herne had been one of the forest's keepers, a few years before Shakespeare wrote his play, around 1597. "Having committed some great offence, for which he feared to lose his situation and fall into disgrace, [Herne] was induced to hang himself on this tree."

The mid-1980s TV series *Robin of Sherwood* introduced Herne to the legends of Sherwood.

Where this particular nugget came from is unclear; it is just as likely to have been a product of Ireland's imagination as it is to have been a once extant, but now vanished reference in the Windsor records. But it would be in good company if it had disappeared, sharing its fate with the tree which local lore had pinpointed as the one to which Shakespeare was referring. The original Herne's Oak was cut down in 1796 (the tree that stands on the same site was planted by King Edward VII in the early 1900s).

No matter. The legend of Herne, such as it was, continued to whisper around Windsor. Shakespeare's play was just a few years old when an unauthorized version of the play (yes, there were copyright pirates even then) was published, in which we learn that

> since Horne the hunter dyed
> That women to affright their little children
> Ses that he walkes in shape of a great stagge.

Herne himself then returned to a degree of newsworthiness in 1838, when a second tree was pinpointed as Herne's Oak. But it was four years more before the spectral hunter truly took his place at the forefront of English mythology, when he was summoned into the limelight by that most visionary of contemporary English authors, William Harrison Ainsworth.

Born in Manchester in 1805, a contemporary and friend of both Charles Dickens and Edward Bulwer-Lytton, Ainsworth arrived on the British literary scene fully formed in 1834, with the publication of *Rookwood*—the aforementioned "biography" of Dick Turpin that effectively formulated every myth and legend that has since immortalized a highwayman who was hitherto little more than a footnote in the annals of crime.

The book was a massive success, certainly overshadowing Ainsworth's second novel, the period manners of *Crichton*, but the author bounced back with another criminal hero, the housebreaker Jack Sheppard, renowned as the first man ever to break out of Newgate prison three times.

Again, Ainsworth bestrode the best seller lists, while controversy came courting in the form of the widespread condemnation of press and politicians alike.

While the media fumed over the tale's potential to unleash a plague of juvenile housebreakers—and worse—upon the land, attempts to adapt the story for the London stage were stymied when the Lord Chamberlain (whose office had to approve every play performed in the country) took the all-but unprecedented step of issuing a forty-year ban on any work which featured Sheppard's name in the title, again for fear of inspiring copycat criminals.

The book was even implicated in a sensational murder trial.

On May 5, 1840, Lord William Russell was murdered by his valet, Benjamin F. Courvoisier. In his defense, the valet claimed the idea of committing the crime had been suggested to him while reading *Jack Sheppard*.

Such claims are commonplace, some might even say encouraged, today. And a hundred years before, playwright John Gay's *Beggar's Opera* was regarded as being equally culpable in the manufacture of the criminal element.

The difference, the element which made Courvoisier's claim so shocking, was that attending a play, particularly one already notorious for the type of person it attracted, was essentially an interactive pastime. Reading, however—what could be more sedentary than that?

Few people denied that Courvoisier was emotionally unbalanced, but there was no such defense for *Jack Sheppard*, not unless a law be enacted regulating the sale of certain types of literature to the unstable. On June 21, 1840, Courvoisier was sentenced to death; a week later, an editorial in the magazine *Forster's Examiner* discussed Courvoisier's confession (it was actually his second; his first made no mention of the book).

> He ascribes his crimes to the perusal of that detestable book, *Jack Sheppard*; and it is certainly a publication calculated to familiarize the mind with cruelties and to serve as the cutthroats manual or the midnight assassin's vade-mecum, in which character we now expect to see it advertised. If ever there was a publication that deserved to be burnt by the common hangman, it is *Jack Sheppard*.

Ainsworth, of course, sprang to his novel's defense, but clearly the furor caused him to re-examine his literary ambitions. Abandoning crime, he turned instead to history and, in particular, the history of London.

Each of his next three novels, *Guy Fawkes*, *The Tower of London* and *The Old Saint Paul's* seized upon different chapters in the city's long history (respectively, the Gunpowder Plot of 1605; the tragic life and cruel execution of Lady Jane Grey in 1554; and the Great Plague and Fire of London in 1665–1666).

And then came *Windsor Castle*.

The focus of the novel lies on the events surrounding Henry VIII's courtship of Anne Boleyn, during his marriage to Catherine of Aragon; followed by his romancing Jane Seymour during Boleyn's ill-fated tenure as

Another scene from Ainsworth's *Windsor Castle*.

his queen. Of course, manifold other intrigues unfold around these regal shenanigans, but intertwined with all this is the story of Herne the Hunter.

From whence did Ainsworth's vision of Herne spring?

At least a few elements of the story were probably picked up from the same local lore that Shakespeare drew from—forests, after all, were dark and mysterious places, alive with mysterious beings and supernatural fears.

Every village, every villager, had heard some kind of story about the perils that lurked within the trees and, just like the legends of Robin Hood, the passing years would see them begin to coalesce.

For the most part, however, we must credit Ainsworth's own imagination; that, and the reading public's willingness to *believe*. For, no less than the adventures of Dick Turpin, what Ainsworth imagined, others took as fact—a tribute indeed to the author's storytelling prowess.

He was not a scholar; although he certainly researched his stories deeply, he did not pride himself on unimpeachable accuracy—if the facts did not fit his purposes, he discarded them without a second thought. Yet what he lacked in that department, he made up for it with the sheer vitality of, and his enthusiasm for, the scenes he portrayed, the characters he created and the landscapes he conjured.

Neither the windswept moors of *Wuthering Heights* nor the darkened corridors of *Jane Eyre*'s Thornfield Hall, are depicted with, or haunted by, visions more complete than Ainsworth's portrait of Windsor Park or St. Paul's Cathedral, and it might not be unduly presumptuous to compare the living death of Rochester's first wife in *Jane Eyre* with that of Alexia in *The Tower of London* six years previous.

Likewise, there are few superior depictions of a supernatural being than Ainsworth (and illustrator George Cruikshank)'s vision of Herne.

The way Ainsworth tells it, Herne was a keeper in Windsor Forest during the reign of King Richard II (1377–1399—that is, almost exactly a century after Richard I and Prince John).

An expert woodcraftsman, he frequently accompanied the king on hunting expeditions, with his two black hunting hounds at his side, and it was during one of these excursions that the king spotted the most magnificent stag he had ever seen.

Calling Herne to his side, Richard galloped in pursuit of the animal, but the stag was in no mood to run. Rather, it stopped dead, turned, and gored the king's horse with its huge antlers.

The king was thrown from his mount, and the stag lunged towards him, preparing to deliver the final death blow—at which point Herne flung himself between the two, killer and king, and took the blow himself. Then, despite his mortal wounds, he pulled out his knife and stabbed the stag in the throat.

By now the rest of the hunting party had arrived, to hear the king tell Herne that, should he recover from his wounds, he would immediately be promoted to head keeper. Herne, however, knew there would be no recovery. All he now required was a grave.

The king turned to the other keepers and hunters, promising a vast reward to anybody who could heal the dying man—which is when a mysterious figure on a jet-black steed appeared in the clearing, dismounted, and introduced himself as Philip Urswick, a local man and an accomplished healer. He claimed to have been riding with the hunt all day, although nobody had ever noticed him before, and the suspicion was that he was probably a poacher.

The king, however, was desperate. He promised that should Herne be healed, Urswick would receive both a reward and a free pardon for any crimes he might have been guilty of, at which point the stranger knelt and, with his hunting knife, cut the antlers from the dead stag's head. He then ordered that they be tied to Herne's head.

Thus bedecked, the dying man was then placed on a stretcher of twigs and branches, and carried to Urswick's hut. In a month's time, the stranger pledged, Herne would be healed.

However, the other keepers were not necessarily very enthusiastic about the prospect of Herne returning to work. His closeness to the king, and his superior skills in the forest, had uncorked a firestorm of petty jealousy and malice; to a man, they would all have been happier had Herne simply died.

So Urswick asked what they would give him if he could also guarantee that Herne would return without any of his former talents.

They had nothing to offer, so Urswick made his own suggestion—that they would, obediently and without question, carry out the first request that he made of them. They agreed.

True to Urswick's pledge to the king, Herne was back at work within a month. True to his bargain with the other keepers, he had forgotten everything he once knew about woodcraft. Reluctantly, the king released him from his service and Herne was last seen riding off into the distance,

The nineteenth-century artist George Cruikshank illustrated Harrison Ainsworth's *Windsor Castle*, the source of so many of the modern Herne legends.

wielding a chain, with the antlers still firmly affixed to his head. A few hours later, a passing pedlar found him hanged from a certain oak tree in the forest.

A party was sent out to retrieve the body, but it had vanished by the time they got there. That night, however, a mighty thunderstorm blew in, and the oak was blasted by lightning.

Life went on, but for the keepers, it was not pleasant. One after another, men were elevated to the post of head keeper, and then dismissed when it became apparent that, like Herne, they were no longer capable of performing the simplest tasks that were required of them.

Finally a delegation went to visit Urswick to ask that the curse be lifted. He told them that their only hope was to go, at midnight, to the oak from which Herne had hanged himself.

There, the hunter's ghost appeared to them and commanded that they return the following night, with horses and hounds as though for a hunt. They did as they were told, and when Herne leapt astride what had once been his own horse, they followed him into the depths of the forest.

Urswick awaited them, to call in the pledge that the men had made before Herne was healed. They were to serve and follow Herne forevermore.

For months thereafter, the cowed keepers would wait by the oak until Herne's ghost arrived, and then they hunted the forest bare. Finally the king had had enough. As the keepers prepared for their next assignation, the king joined them and, when Herne appeared, Richard demanded to know what was going on.

Herne told him the entire story, including the role of the other keepers in his downfall. He also promised to continue haunting the forest unless the king had each of the men hanged from the same tree upon which Herne had perished. The king agreed, the keepers were executed, and Herne kept his half of the deal as well—at least up to a point. He was never again seen during the reign of King Richard II. But the moment the king passed away in February 1400, murdered (some say starved to death) on the orders of the usurper king Henry IV, Herne renewed his depredations.

That was the legend as Ainsworth related it, although others abound, both composed in the aftermath of *Windsor Castle*, or preserved in the older lore of the locale itself. All, however, have a similar tragedy at their heart, a keeper committing suicide from the branches of a certain oak tree.

There is one—again penned by Ainsworth—in which Herne fell in love with a nun he imprisoned in a forest cave. Unable to win her heart, he murdered her and then, full of remorse, killed himself. Others retain the tale of him being gored by a stag, but then have him being driven insane by the pain, tying the antlers to his head himself, and then committing suicide; another has him turning into a fire-breathing stag after hanging himself; and so on.

Whatever the roots of the legend may be, and whoever the original Herne might be (there are almost as many answers to the riddle as there are for Robin Hood), there is no doubt that, beyond the writings of Shakespeare and Ainsworth, a horned hunter storming through the forests of the medieval world is an ancient and venerable tradition.

> . . . they sweep through forest and air in whole companies with a horrible din. This is the widely spread legend of the furious host, the furious hunt, which is of high antiquity, and interweaves itself, now with gods, and now with heroes. Look where you will, it betrays its connexion with heathenism.
>
> —*Jacob Grimm, Teutonic Mythology (1835)*

Woodland gods from across the pre-Christian spectrum shared at least a few of Herne's attributes, from the antlered head to the wild hunt—the Celtic god Cernunnos, the Roman Mars, the Teutonic Woden, the mysterious figure whom the Romans knew as the Thracian Rider. From any society whose mythology told of a Wild Hunt, the candidates flock in, and perhaps that is all we need to know.

We have already mentioned the wild hunt that was sighted near Peterborough, in the English midlands, in 1127. In the quoted source, it was claimed to be the spirit of Hereward the Wake. But there are others that insist it was Herne, punishing the misdeeds of the then-incumbent abbot, Henry of Poitou—a man, apparently, who "did nothing good there and left nothing good there."

The anonymous monk who composed the *Anglo Saxon Chronicle* shuddered:

> . . . many people saw and heard many hunters hunting. The hunters were black and big and loathsome, and their hounds all black and wide-eyed and loathsome, and they rode on black horses and black goats. This was seen in the very deer-park in the town of Petersborough, and in all the woods that there were between his town and Stamford, and the monks heard the horns blow that were blowing at night. Trustworthy people noticed them at night, and said that it seemed to them there might well be about twenty or thirty hornblowers. This was seen and heard from the time he came there all Lent up to Easter.

Another hunt was witnessed near York in 1154. Herne himself has sup-posedly been sighted in Windsor Great Park on the eve of both national disasters and the deaths of kings, but he can also be summonsed in other ways, such as the night in 1962, when a group of boys found an old hunting horn on the ground, and blew it.

Herne the Hunter, as seen in Shakespeare's *Merry Wives of Windsor*, an eighteenth-century painting in the style of Johann Heinrich Füssli.

Immediately they heard an answering call, and the baying of oncoming hounds. Then Herne appeared on a great black horse, his antlered head silhouetted against the moon. The boys fled.

Herne is the spirit of nature—the forests, the trees, the undergrowth, the darkness—at what early man believed to be its most untamed, the god of the blackest, most fearful shadows, brute strength, and animal cunning.

Long before writer Richard Carpenter wrote Herne into his mid-eighties televisual tales of *Robin of Sherwood*, the hunter's spirit was already abroad in the legend, in terms of atmosphere if not actual identity.

Carpenter, whose grasp of the supernatural side of British history had already produced such jewels as *Catweazle* (a Norman wizard catapulted into a late-sixties English farm), *The Ghosts of Motley Hall* (self-explanatory) and *Dick Turpin* (ditto), needed no further encouragement than that.

Interviewed for the superlative boldoutlaw.com website, Carpenter explained, "Robin Hood is one of the few perennial legends with no magic in it. There is a fragment of a ballad called 'Robin Hood and the Witch' . . . but [it] tantalizingly breaks off after a stanza."

> The Middle Ages were extremely superstitious and much remained of the old pre-christian fertility and tree worship religions. You must remember that the country was largely based on agriculture: and the crops and the turning year were extremely important to everyone.
>
> Vestiges of this still remain throughout Europe. Although the Mother Goddess was supreme . . . the male principal was considered equally important. The question is whether Herne is a shaman or if he—like shamans do—'becomes' the god at certain times after practicing certain rituals.

That question remains unanswered throughout *Robin of Sherwood*. What Carpenter could not have guessed was the alacrity with which his idea would be incorporated into other versions of the Robin Hood legend—all the more so since Herne's presence completely rewrites what we might call Robin's origin.

No more an outlawed nobleman, or whatever other concoction might be bestowed upon our hero, *Robin of Sherwood* portrays him as nothing more than Robin, growing up in the village of Loxley until the day the Normans came to destroy it.

Taken in by a local miller, Robin continues to live a "normal" life until, one day, a mysterious, shrouded, and antler-bedecked figure appears before him, introduces itself as Herne the Hunter, and commands him to take to the forest to fight against oppression as "the Hooded Man."

Throughout the series, Herne guides and aids Robin in his struggles, influencing his decisions and deploying his own brand of woodland magic to occasionally confound Robin's foes.

The result, arguably, joins the Saracen as the most significant addition to the legend since Sir Guy of Gisborne first rode to prominence. Fiction authors have certainly picked up where *Robin of Sherwood* left off, and there is now an entire library's worth of novels that feature Herne the Hunter as a more-than-major character.

Barely three decades have passed since Carpenter introduced Herne to the legend, but—like the Saracen who also debuted in this same series—it feels as though he has been there forever.

In many ways, maybe he has.

Another Historical Interlude

Later Robins from Ludd to Courtenay

History, and English history in particular, abounds with men who were, or who claimed to be, fired by the same spirit of injustice as Robin Hood.

Few, however, succeeded. The state was too strong, the insurrection was too weak, spies were as rife in ancient times as they appear to be today.

But history remembers them regardless, and where it doesn't, it ought to.

It is no surprise that the legend of Robin Hood underwent something of a populist revival during the nineteenth century, any more than we should be surprised that various other facets of a mythical, "earlier" England were likewise revived. From the fairies that were mentioned in the previous chapter, to the glorious tales of King Arthur, it was as though a society that could not stop modernizing itself was simultaneously crying out for a return to earlier values, and not only in literary and cultural terms.

The eighteenth and early nineteenth centuries were a time of great political ferment in Great Britain. The country was, arguably, at its peak; rapid advances in industrialization, the birth of modern capitalism, and a series of military successes all contributed to the nation's success.

Yes, the American colonies were lost. But victory over the French emperor Napoleon saw the country's greatest historical foe, France, reduced almost to puppet status. Germany, Italy, and Poland were carved up to suit the victors' own ends, the Dutch overseas empire had been fragmented and added to Britain's own.

Yet beneath the façade of success, the country was seething.

The population was increasing at a hitherto unimaginable rate, doubling in no more than fifty years. But outside of the nobility and the new capitalists spawned by the Industrial Revolution, the disparity between rich and poor was greater than it had ever been, and the law appeared intent upon making certain that it remained that way.

Exploited in the factories and on the land, with no right to vote or to unionize, what little money the common man did earn was snatched away again by taxes, landlords, and merchants; and whatever freedoms he might have had, too, were being eroded, all for the benefit of the wealthy.

Inevitably, the poor would fight back.

King John (a different one)

In 1720, costly foreign wars and the collapse of a massively over-valued investment vehicle called the South Sea Company saw the entire country teetering on the brink of depression.

Banks and goldsmiths followed regular investors into bankruptcy; landowners struggled to pay their employees; taxes soared, jobs were scrapped, homes were lost. And crime began to rise, as people resorted to any means possible to clothe and feed their families.

Always a problem in the past, outbreaks of poaching now rose to an industrial scale. The multitude of laws and restrictions surrounding poaching—those to which Robin Hood had likely fallen prey five hundred years earlier, and which had continued to entrap the poor ever since—were still in force, but not only had the penalties been lightened, the law itself had become more lenient.

It was no longer legal for a land owner to mete out summary justice on the spot; nor sufficient for him merely to accuse somebody of the crime. They had to be proved to be guilty, too, and a magistrate convinced of the fact.

And that was not always easy.

The poachers were cunning and, in their own way, as ruthless as the gamekeepers and land owners against whom they were ranged. Heavily armed, they were also heavily disguised, blacking their faces, donning peculiar outfits (straw hats were apparently a favorite), and having no compunction whatsoever about threatening to shoot any keeper who might try to prevent them.

Neither did their activities end simply with the killing of the deer. Apocryphal or otherwise, tales spread of other misdeeds—armed assaults on any constables who might capture one of their number; vandalizing the property and threatening the lives of any land owner who might complain of their behavior; burning barns, felling trees, mailing poison-pen letters; effectively unleashing a reign of terror across the countryside.

Or, at least, a few acres of it.

The Blacks, as these nocturnal menaces were known (as a consequence, of course, of their blacked-up faces), were effectively active in just two areas—in Windsor, where local superstition was happy to ascribe the Blacks' activities to the restless spirit of Herne the Hunter, and mock the law's attempts to arrest a ghost; and further south in Hampshire.

Both areas had much in common: vast forests, of course, but also land owners whose personal greed outweighed any other considerations they might have had. Indeed, in Farnham Park, Hampshire, one of the biggest land owners of all, Sir Jonathan Trelawny, employed a steward, Dr. Heron, who might well have considered himself the Sheriff of Nottingham reborn, so violently and vigorously did he pursue his own private aims.

In his acclaimed study of the period, *Whigs and Hunters*, historian E. P. Thompson writes,

> Heron rode ceaselessly around the woods and lands [*of Farnham Park*] . . . imposed his domineering presence at the various manorial courts, ransacked old deed and tables of fees, and succeeded on treading on the corns of . . . officers and tenants alike. He uncovered what were (in his view) atrocious goings-on; timber of the copyhold farms was wasted, farms were undervalued, officers of the court were taking unwarranted fees.

And while Heron's reign was relatively short, the men who replaced him had clearly learned from his methods. By 1718, Trelawny's lands were under an almost constant state of siege, with poaching, arson, cattle-maiming and pale-breaking (trespass) being reported on a regular basis. Nor did Trelawny's death in 1721 bring about an end to the attacks; in fact, under the new ownership of the Bishop of Norwich, Charles Trimnell, the Blacks only increased their noctivagant assaults.

In October 1721, an estimated sixteen men on horseback entered Farnham Park in the traditional garb of blacked-up faces, costumes, and (a nice touch, this) black gloves. Three deer were taken, two more were killed, and a keeper was shot and injured.

The law moved swiftly. Several suspects were rounded up, but with little evidence, and certainly with no indication of who had fired at the luckless keeper, the courts could do no more than impose the now standard punishments for the crimes—a day in the stocks, a year in prison and a fine. The bishop, of course, was outraged, but so were the convicted men's associates.

Vowing that in any competition between upholding the law and aiding the poor, the latter were always going to come out on top, these men declared themselves the citizens of what a period commentator described as a "mock kingly government," presided over by "a very robust, enterprising and substantial gentleman" . . . King John.

Was the irony intentional? Did the poachers purposefully invoke the name of Robin Hood's greatest adversary, so that they might utterly invert

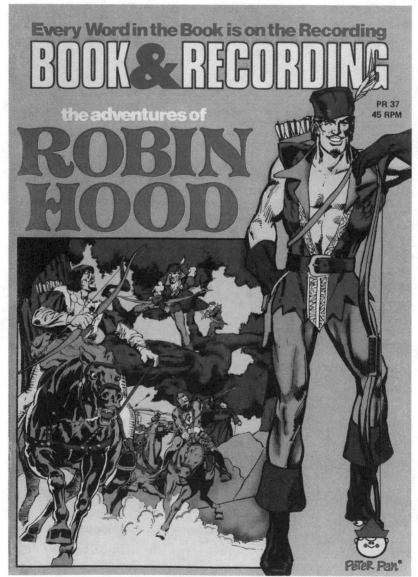

Another childhood recitation of the legend of Robin Hood.

his reputation? We do not know. But King John avowedly made certain that his name and reputation were known throughout the region.

A skilled self-publicist, he maintained a more-or-less constant commentary on the aims and intentions of his merry men and, over the course of the next year, nothing that the bishop called his own could be deemed safe. A full twenty-five miles from Farnham Park, the bishop owned further properties at Waltham Chase, and these came under attack as readily as Farnham Park itself.

This was no longer a case of hungry men stealing for their table. This was all-out war.

Daniel Defoe, in his *A Tour Through the Whole Island of Great Britain*, described the Blacks as having "of late been very unkind to the bishop, in pulling down the pale of his park, and plundering it of the deer, killing, wounding, and even disabling those they could not carry away."

Nobody was safe. A local land owner who informed on the Blacks found his fences and gates broken down, and a herd of cows driven into his standing corn field. When one of their number was convicted of poaching, and rewards were handed around the keepers who arrested him, King John and his men descended upon their homes and demanded they surrender the bounty, or they could watch their homes being burned to the ground.

Nor were the Blacks concerned only with justice for themselves.

Gentry and gentlemen alike notoriously displayed a very cavalier attitude towards repaying debts to tradesmen. King John made certain that they paid up, dispatching a few of his men to the debtor's home to deliver a letter from John himself, in which prompt payment was politely suggested. The blunderbusses that the messengers carried made sure that the message was taken seriously. And if it wasn't, then there *would* be further punishment.

When a local doctor refused to pay for some hay, King John's men ensured that he swiftly opened his purse. The doctor probably never withheld payment again.

But when a gentleman farmer refused to pay for a barn he had recently constructed, he shrugged off the ensuing threats and had the carpenter imprisoned instead. So King John wrote him a second letter, even more severe than the first, and the carpenter was promptly bailed out *and* paid.

A widowed gentlewoman who used her status to win a dispute regarding the use of a church pew had her fine gardens vandalized; the parson who had supported her found his beehives overturned.

"For a few months," E. P. Thompson writes, "the Robin Hood of legend was incarnated in 'King John.' The resentment of decades sheltered him and his band, as he rode openly administering folk justice." And, just like the real Robin Hood, his identity has never been discovered. Quite simply, in March 1723, King John gathered his followers together to announce that he would no longer be concerning himself "with publick affairs." Then he rode away, and Thompson concludes,

> The ballads of Robin Hood still went their rounds, but this flesh-and-blood Robin Hood rode back, perhaps to some small forest estate, to be forgotten . . . leaving behind him (so far as we can discover) no legend, no folk memory, not even a song.

The Black Act

It would be pleasant to report that King John's legacy led to a lessening of the abuse to which the country folk were subjected. In fact, quite the opposite was true.

Two months before King John retired from public view, it became clear that the law intended coming down as hard as it could upon the Blacks, in the form of a new parliamentary act intended to both streamline the laws that surrounded poaching, and increase the penalties for those who were caught. A day in the stocks and a year in prison clearly was no longer any kind of deterrent. Harsher justice was required, and so the Waltham Black Act became law.

It was, according to the statute book, "An Act for the more effectual punishing wicked and evil disposed Persons going armed in Disguise and doing Injuries and Violence to the Persons and Properties of His Majesty's Subject, and for the more speedy bringing the Offenders to Justice."

But this law had teeth, and it wasn't shy in using them. No less than fifty new capital crimes were introduced, including being discovered in any place "wherein deer have been or shall usually be kept . . . armed with swords, fire-arms, or other offensive weapons, and having his or their face blacked."

Other offenses were swiftly added to the law; existing ones were enlarged. According to historian Sir Leon Radzinowicz, author of *A History of English Criminal Law and its Administration from 1750*, "no other single statute passed during the eighteenth century equalled [the Black Act] in severity, and none appointed the punishment of death in so many cases."

He continued,

John Nichols Tom

Percy Honeywood, Courtenay

Knight of Malta

The Knight of Malta—or a Victorian Robin Hood?

> It is very doubtful whether any other country possessed a criminal code with anything like so many capital provisions as there were in this single statute . . .

There was scarcely a solitary criminal act that did not fall within the provisions of the Black Act. Offenses against public order, against the administration of criminal justice, against property, against the person, malicious injuries to property of varying degree—all came under this statute and all were punishable by death.

The law was originally supposed to stand for just three years, presumably until the menace of the Blacks had been expunged from society. In the event, it would not be repealed until 1822; and, meanwhile, the people continued to be bled.

New laws dictated every aspect of their life. By the early nineteenth century, the cost of living had rocketed to levels to which it would not return until the middle of the twentieth century.

A simple loaf of bread cost more than many families had to spend on food in a week. Exports were struggling to recover from wartime shortages long after the war was won, and with so many demobilized troops searching for work, employers could keep wages as low as they wished, and in the process snatch even the basic necessities of life from within reach of the common man.

The Poor Laws, which provided for workers whose wage was below the accepted poverty level, only encouraged the employers to maintain their miserable rates of pay, and so a vicious cycle kicked on. Taxes were increased to pay the higher welfare bills, more people were thus forced onto the "dole," which, in turn, led to higher taxes. Poverty begat poverty, squalor begat squalor.

Ned Ludd

Fresh advances in the manufacturing industries added fuel to the flames. Improvements in machinery were so swift, and so vast, that enormous quantities of manpower were laid off. Why employ a workforce of one hundred, when it needed only ten barely skilled machine operatives to produce the same amount of material?

Attempts by the workers to form unions were fiercely repressed. In 1799, Parliament passed the Combination Act, which effectively outlawed the formation of any organization seeking to better the lot of the working man.

Three years later, disturbances in Wiltshire by weavers anxious to halt the spread of machinery were put down with almost uncommon ferocity, and in 1811, the unquenchable spirits of Robin Hood and King John blazed once again in Nottinghamshire when the first factories were broken into and vandalized by a gang of masked men who referred to themselves as Luddites.

Like the ever-present example of Robin Hood, their leader was a spiritual rather than physical being. Ned Ludd was portrayed as a virtual giant, overflowing with supernatural ability. No factory was secure against him, no factory owner could sleep soundly at night without fearing what Ned might be doing to his property. And his influence was pernicious.

By February 1812, the disturbances had reached the great woolen manufactories of Yorkshire and Lancashire, and fresh attacks were being reported almost daily.

The Manufacturers' Committee immediately offered a massive reward (100 guineas, equivalent to almost 7,000 pounds/$10,000 today) to anybody supplying information which would lead to the arrest of the wreckers.

The military was installed in the area, but the Luddites' assaults, which had hitherto been conducted against property alone, now flared into outright warfare.

On April 11, two Luddites were shot and killed during an attack on a mill; six days later, the mill owner was shot as reprisal. Ten days on, soldiers who, during the first attack, had refused to fire upon the Luddites were publicly flogged in front of the mill, and one week after that, William Horsfall, another mill owner, was shot and killed on his way home from the market.

The assassination of the British Prime Minister Spencer Perceval on May 11 was, in some quarters, laid at the Luddites' doorstep and while these particular accusations were swiftly proved to be unfounded, the new government formed by Lord Liverpool vowed to do everything in its power to smash the uprising.

It would be almost six months, and countless more attacks, before the government could begin to claim victory. In October, a number of the Luddites' ringleaders were rounded up on the evidence of one Ben Walker and, five months later, a total of sixty-six men were tried before a special commission in York.

Seven were acquitted, fourteen more were transported to the penal colony of Australia, and three were hanged. Fourteen more followed them to the grave as the trials continued.

The power of the Luddites was smashed, but the unrest continued. For the Luddites were simply the most prominent display of disaffection in the country.

Conspiracies, Martyrs, and Massacres

The Napoleonic War had been won, but to what end? Glory on foreign fields was echoed by misery on those at home.

The government, still looking back over its shoulder at the French Revolution, and drawing none-too-distorted parallels between the mood in France at that time and that in England now, sought ever-more stringent means of "keeping the people in their place."

Mass meetings were all but outlawed, yet rioting became commonplace, a cruel cycle which culminated in August 1819 when some thirty thousand people gathered in Manchester's Peterloo Fields to hear a well-known agitator, Orator Hunt.

Panicked by the size of the crowd, the local magistrature ordered a regiment of cavalry to charge the crowd. In what is now remembered as the Peterloo Massacre, close to a hundred people were seriously injured in the ensuing chaos, half a dozen more killed.

Public opinion reflected the outrage. Even *The Times*, an occasionally outspoken, but normally placid supporter of the government, was driven to censure the decision to employ the military to break up what was essentially a peaceful meeting.

The government, however, stood firm behind the magistrates, and by the end of the year had instituted the Six Acts, which inflicted heavy penalties upon anybody involved in the "arming and drilling of the masses," and which suppressed "seditious libels"; that is, any publication (including *The Times*) which sought to criticize the government and its methods in any way whatsoever.

The so-called Cato Street Conspiracy, in 1820, added to the government's paranoia. Provoked by the Six Acts, a gang of "violent extremists" set about planning the murder of the entire cabinet at a ministerial dinner scheduled for later in the year. The plot was betrayed, however, and the conspirators arrested in a house on Cato Street in London. A few days later their leaders, the most prominent of them being a "ruffian" named Thistlewood, were similarly captured and put to death.

The people were not, however, without their champions. The suicide, in 1822, of Viscount Castlereagh, one of the most uncompromising members of government, allowed the cabinet to be reorganized along more liberal lines, while William Huskisson, the president of the Board of Trade, commenced work on the legislation which would lead, in 1824, to the repealing of the Combination Acts, thereby opening the way for the formation of free Trade Unions.

(That said, when six laborers from the Dorsetshire village of Tolpuddle attempted to exercise just that right, in 1834, the government of the day lost little time in suppressing their activities, ultimately finding them guilty on a charge of illegally administering sworn oaths, and sentencing them to seven years in transportation, or banishment to a penal colony. The six, better known today as The Tolpuddle Martyrs, were reprieved two years later, as a result of the ensuing public outcry.)

Further advances in the reform codes were made in 1828, following the elevation of the Duke of Wellington (1769–1852) to the prime ministership. But his government was doomed to fall following the repeal of the Test Act, which had, since 1673, excluded Roman Catholics from state and municipal office. In 1830, the opposition Whigs were returned to power for the first time in sixty years.

The new government met its first crisis—a summer of strikes and riots which echoed almost perfectly the unrest going on across the channel in France—head on. Much of the strife was fostered by the people's dissatisfaction with the current parliamentary system; in drawing up the Parliamentary Reform Bill in 1832, they literally averted the threat of revolution.

Other problems, however, remained, and other flashpoints flared around the unlikeliest of causes—one of which was a fresh reprinting of a book about Robin Hood.

Joseph Ritson's *Robin Hood: A Collection of all the Ancient Poems, Songs, and Ballads, Now Extant, Relative to the Celebrated English Outlaw*, was originally published in 1795. On the face of it, it was a scholarly work of historical research. However, reading deeper into Ritson's opening essay, one swiftly discovers why the government of the day felt so uneasy.

When Ritson first put quill to parchment, the French Revolution was still a newborn child, and the author was wholeheartedly in favor of its aims.

It was the work of a moment for him to interpret Robin Hood likewise, a brilliant revolutionary ferociously opposed to aristocracy and privilege, a fierce supporter of the common man,

> a man who, in a barbarous age, and under complicated tyranny, displayed a spirit of freedom and independence, which has endeared

him to the common people, whose cause he maintained, (for all opposition to tyranny is the cause of the people,) and, in spite of the malicious endeavors of pitiful monks, by whom history was consecrated to the crimes and follies of titled ruffians and sainted idiots, to suppress all record of his patriotic exertions and virtuous acts, will render his name immortal.

Replace the "pitiful monks" with "empleomaniac politicians" and Ritson could almost have been writing a contemporary biography. The events that unfolded later that same year, when a new edition of Ritson's work was placed on the streets, suggested he still could have been.

The Knight of Malta—the Last Robin Hood?

Early in 1832, a strange man arrived in the Kentish cathedral city of Canterbury. He introduced himself as Sir William Percy Honeywood Courtenay, not only a nobleman but also the rightful claimant to titles that dated back to the age of the Crusades, Knight of Malta and King of Jerusalem.

He proclaimed himself a friend of the oppressed, an enemy to the selfish aristocracy and the common man's last line of defense against the stupidity of a government that held the common man in bondage, and he appeared to live up to those promises.

His speeches aroused enormous enthusiasm and excitement, and when Courtenay expressed an interest in standing for Parliament at the December elections, few dissenting voices were heard, at least among the common flock.

Gathering his supporters on the balcony of the Rose Hotel, he would openly harangue crowds the size of which had seldom been seen in the city, distributing his own magazine, *The Lion*, to all who passed, and putting on a show so credible that he polled over nine hundred, coming within a whisker of election.

Literary immortality reached out to him, as Harrison Ainsworth wrote Courtenay into his best-selling *Rookwood*, performing as a member of a gypsy troupe. There is no telling how high his rising star might have reached.

But it all came quickly to a grinding halt. Courtenay's outspoken support for a group of local fishermen who were being investigated on charges of smuggling led to legal action against him and, in 1833, he was imprisoned on a charge of perjury. Further investigations revealed the lie behind his claims to noble birth; that he was, in fact, a runaway husband named John

Thom, the son of a Cornish innkeeper; and he was transferred to the lunatic asylum at Barming (the source of the English slang word "barmy," meaning insane).

His reign, it appeared, was over.

Meanwhile, the business of government continued on. In 1834, the authorities introduced the New Poor Laws, replacing the long-redundant Tudor acts that had hitherto tended to the requirements of the needy.

Recognizing that the former system of subsidizing the lowest wages from local taxes had served only to demoralize the laborers, and keep wages low, the new system demanded that the able-bodied poor should instead apply to the newly instituted workhouses for relief.

History—aided, to no mean extent by writers such as Charles Dickens and Charles Kingsley—has recorded this as an almost unimaginably harsh, even punitive measure, with workhouses painted as one of the most inhumane social policies ever perpetrated upon a supposedly free people.

And so they were. Married couples would be separated; families shattered; any kind of social interaction forbidden. Set to work in exchange for food and accommodation, inmates found themselves doing the most menial tasks available—grinding bone for fertilizer, breaking rocks for construction, and so forth.

From his cell in the asylum, Courtenay studied whatever reports on the effects of the New Poor Law he could lay his hands on, and when, in 1837, a group of wealthy friends succeeded in having him released into their care, the former Knight of Malta knew what he needed do.

While confined, Courtenay had undergone a religious conversion and he quickly returned to the public eye, proselytizing his new faith. Accompanied by an ever-increasing band of followers, Courtenay then returned to Canterbury, there to preach salvation to the farm workers.

He was come, he said, to free the oppressed, to succor the poor, and to abrogate the cruel New Poor Law and the "Bastilles of Poverty" that had been erected in its name.

But was he merely a savior . . . or was he *the* Savior? An extraordinary facial resemblance to the traditional image of Jesus seems to have persuaded certain of his followers that Courtenay was, in fact, the Second Coming of Christ. His love for all men, his support for the poor and needy—such things inspired a devotion in his followers which bordered upon the extraordinary.

Laborers left their fields to follow Courtenay; by the end of May 1838, he had more than a hundred rustics tramping the roads behind him, a blue-and-white flag, and half a loaf of bread impaled upon a stick, raised at

From a contemporary engraving, the Battle of Bossenden Wood, on May 31, 1838, was the last military engagement fought on English soil.

their head. This was the sight which greeted a local constable, Mears, and two other men on the morning of May 31.

The three of them had been dispatched at the request of a wealthy landowner, deprived of his workforce by Courtenay's preaching, and now demanding that those men return to the fields.

Courtenay's response was to shoot the poor constable dead.

Mears's companions fled back to Canterbury, where they alerted the military. But when a company of the 45th Regiment arrived at the scene to demand Courtenay's surrender, they, too, were fired upon and their leader, Lieutenant Bennet, was killed.

This was the signal for Courtenay's men to fall upon the troops. But sticks, cudgels and the one or two pistols in their possession were no match for a well-equipped regiment, and in the ensuing volley of shots, Courtenay himself was mortally wounded.

Eight of his followers, too, fell at the Battle of Bossenden Wood, since described as the last battle ever to be fought on English soil. Two more men later died of their wounds, and at the ensuing trial, a further twenty-three were sentenced to lengthy jail sentences. Others, still, were exiled in transportation.

Courtenay was buried in an unmarked grave in the nearby village of Hernhill, and the authorities took no chances regarding the man's possible immortality. Not only his body was kept in a barn until corruption set in before being released for burial, but the resurrection clause was then omitted from his funeral service.

But although he was dead, Courtenay did not die. His legend lived on in Hernhill and beyond, and 150 years later, the movie *A Challenge for Robin Hood* (1967) suggested that William Courtenay may even have been descended from Robin Hood himself, as the outlaw was revealed to be none other than Sir Robin de Courtenay, a knight bent upon regaining a stolen inheritance.

15

The Ballads of Bold Robin Hood

With a Hey Nonny-no, to the Greenwood We Shall Go

In 1888, no less an authority than the Harvard professor Francis James Child weighed in on the continuing debate regarding Robin Hood's reality, and came unequivocally down on the side of mythology.

Echoing the words of the antiquary Reverend John Hunter, who dismissed Robin Hood from the historical record in 1852 (Hood "lives only as a hero of song"), Child declared that Robin

> is absolutely a creation of the ballad-muse. The earliest mention we have of him is as the subject of ballads. The only two early historians who speak of him as a ballad-hero, pretend to have no information about him except what they derive from ballads, and show that they have none other by the description they give of him; this description being in entire conformity with ballads in our possession, one of which is found in a Manuscript as old as the older of these two writers.

The evidence at Child's disposal was vast.

Ask the average twenty-first century citizen to sing you a song about Robin Hood, and the likelihood is that they'll come back with just one of two ditties—either Bryan Adams's grisly "Everything I Do," so inescapably bound up with the *Prince of Thieves* movie; or, more mercifully, the theme to the 1950s television series *Adventures of Robin Hood*, a galloping little romp that rhymes "merry men" with "riding through the glen," and sums up Robin's *modus operandi* with just two well-chosen lines, "feared by the bad, loved by the good." Ah, they don't write 'em like that any more.

They don't make singers like that, either. Dick James, whose sonorous tones related the tale, eventually crossed to the other side of the microphone as one of Britain's most successful music publishers; the Beatles and Elton John are just two of the monster acts whose songwriting he handled, while his DJM label was a power in Robin's native land through the early 1970s. So, not only could he sing a good song, he knew when he heard one as well.

Ask that same question of a denizen of earlier times, however, and you might have been dizzied by the number of titles, verses, and choruses they could hurl at you. For Robin Hood was not simply numbered among England's most revered folk heroes. He was also the subject of some of its most revered folk songs, a status that lives on today thanks to the work of, again, Francis James Child.

The Child Ballads

Born in Boston in 1825, the son of a relatively poor sail maker, Francis James Child was a student at one of the city's free schools, the English High School, when he came to the attention of Epes Sargent Dixwell, principal of the Boston Latin School; impressed by the boy's intelligence and thirst for learning, Dixwell arranged for Child ("Stubby" to his friends, on account of his diminutive stature) to receive a scholarship to Harvard.

There, the boy proved as brilliant a scholar as his patron had believed him to be, excelling at literature and the classics and, in 1848, Child published *Four Old Plays*, resurrecting, indeed, four plays dating from the early English renaissance: the anonymously penned *Jack Jugler* and *Thersytes*, Heywood's *Pardoner and Frere* and Gascoigne's *Jocasta*.

All four were known to scholars, but Child's intention was to bring them to the attention of a wider audience; a goal he continued to prize when, in 1853 (now installed as Professor of Rhetoric at Harvard), he oversaw the publication of *The British Poets*—a vast work that ultimately amounted to 130 volumes concentrating on lesser- and even unknown works from throughout that nation's history.

Paramount among these were eight volumes of *English and Scottish Ballads*, the collection's scope largely informed by Child's discovery that few of Britain's ancient folk songs and ballads were available even for inspection by scholars, let alone consumption by the public. One entire volume within this series, volume five, was devoted to Robin Hood, with Child's introduction explaining,

> There is no one of the royal heroes of England that enjoys a more enviable reputation than the bold outlaw of Barnsdale and

Sherwood. His chance for a substantial immortality is at least as good as that of stout Lion Heart, wild Prince Hal, or merry Charles.

His fame began with the yeomanry full five hundred years ago, was constantly increasing for two or three centuries, has extended to all classes of society, and, with some changes of aspect, is as great as ever. Bishops, sheriffs, and game-keepers, the only enemies he ever had, have relinquished their ancient grudges, and Englishmen would be almost as loath to surrender his exploits as any part of the national glory.

His free life in the woods, his unerring eye and strong arm, his open hand and love of fair-play, his never-forgotten courtesy, his respect for women and devotion to [*the Virgin*] Mary, form a picture eminently healthful and agreeable to the imagination, and commend him to the hearty favor of all genial minds.

Francis James Child, the nineteenth-century Harvard professor who collected so many of the ancient Robin Hood ballads. *PD-US.*
Wikimedia Commons

But Child is not altogether convinced. "Securely established as Robin Hood is in popular esteem," he continues, still he reminds us that "'a tale of Robin Hood' is an old proverb for the idlest of stories."

Nevertheless, the ballads needed to be preserved; more than that, they needed to be released from the musty confines of obscure scholarship, and returned to the common folk with whom they originated. And it was that realization which laid the foundation for the remainder of Child's life's work.

By 1868, Child had arranged the publication of the folio manuscript of Thomas Percy's century-old *Reliques of Ancient English Poetry*, the largest-ever gathering of its subject matter; and formed the Ballad Society, dedicated to the preservation and publication of the multitude of similar publications of which scholars and collectors alone seemed aware.

And in 1882, he commenced work on the monumental collection that still bears his name today—properly titled *The English and Scottish Popular Ballads*, but more commonly refered to as the *Child Ballads*—and establishing it as the single-most important, if not comprehensive, gathering of folk songs ever published.

Some 305 ballads were collected not only from the UK, but also from those regions of the United States to which the English, Scots, Welsh, and Irish migrated, taking their music with them.

The ballads cover the entire spectrum of human existence, or at least as much of it as was worth setting to music. So lots of love and death, old legends and fresh fears, witches and goblins, killers and angels . . . and Robin Hood, Robin Hood, riding through the book.

Consuming almost one-tenth of the complete collection, Robin Hood is the subject of no less than thirty-three ballads, each one relaying, or replaying, one of the myriad adventures and exploits for which Robin was renowned.

Child dug back to the earliest days of the "A Lyttel Geste of Robyn Hode," and then onwards to the popular songs of more recent vintage. He collected every old volume of verse that he could find, and developed a network of fellow collectors who kept him apprised of their own discoveries.

No ballad was too obscure, or too twee, to be considered for inclusion, and while he would eventually draw a somewhat arbitrary line in the sand by excluding a number of more recent concoctions (largely on the grounds that they had no place in the genuine folk tradition), still he permitted the inclusion of a great many that he personally felt had few redeeming qualities—in fact, we have already encountered one of them earlier in this book, the "foolish ditty" that was "Robin Hood and Maid Marian."

Child's ire is raised again by another ballad, this time pitting Robin against some particularly powerful peddlers. He admits that it might well be a genuinely ancient piece. But he would nevertheless "be glad to be rid of it."

Variations on the ballad "Robin Hood and Queen Katherine" (itself retelling the earlier tale of "Robin Hood and the Bishop of Hereford" include one that Child dismisses as "a piece of regular hack-work"; and while the old professor admits to a sequel of sorts of that tale, "Robin Hood's Chase," is "a well-conceived ballad," he still cannot resist a most elitist poke at it. "[It] needs to be older."

Despite, or perhaps *because* of, Child's sometimes churlish disdain, *The English and Scottish Popular Ballads* remains the heart and soul of every collection of folk songs published since then, and the primary source, too, for the repertoires of every English-speaking folk performer of the era—such superstars as Fairport Convention and Shirley Collins, Judy Collins and Joan Baez, Jean Redpath and Steeleye Span.

"The House Carpenter" was recorded by the young Bob Dylan, "Scarborough Fair" by Simon and Garfunkel, and in 2013, Jefferson Hamer and Anaïs Mitchell scored a massive success on both sides of the Atlantic with an album comprised wholly of, and unequivocally titled *The Child Ballads*.

It is strange, then, to discover that Child's assemblage of Robin Hood ballads has scarcely been touched by modern performers, despite containing some of the most charming, exciting, and even intoxicating ballads in the entire five-volume series.

According to Grey Malkin, whose folk act the Hare and the Moon are among the Child Ballads' most imaginative interpreters, "[T]here are occasional instances of Robin put to song (such as A. L. Lloyd's "Robin Hood and the Tanner"), but these are far and few between, despite there being a suitable and varied mix of lighter Robin exploits and much darker, more murderous tales to choose from."

It has been suggested that this paucity of performance might be the result of Robin's sheer ubiquity in the modern world. British anthropologist Hester NicEilidh is one of the researchers who has tried to reverse this state of affairs.

> As I researched the Robin Hood legend through the early 2000s, I became frustrated by the tendency of scholars to treat the ballads as a literary tradition as opposed to a performance tradition. In

other words, these scholars generally approached the ballad lyrics as poetry, rather than as songs.

In response, I began to search for recorded versions of the Robin Hood ballads, but they were few and far between. For many of the ballads, particularly those said to have "no known associated tune," I could find no recorded versions.

That led me to the idea of trying to record some of my own versions around 2005/6 [*even though I was a very novice singer*] and to try to encourage other singers and musicians . . . to attempt to revitalize some of the "orphaned" Robin Hood ballads and re-integrate them into the performed folk music repertoire, to look at the Robin Hood ballads as potential performance material.

This process eventually blossomed into the Robin Hood Ballad Project, an online archive that featured fresh, and often breathtakingly beautiful, renderings of the entire surviving canon.

Sadly, as NicEilidh wryly remarks, it "did not exactly go viral," and all but three of the recordings have since disappeared from view. And the ballads remain orphaned.

Researcher Bob Askew, interviewed at the English Folk Dance and Song Society in 2015, explained that movie and television adaptations have lifted Robin Hood clear out of the folk milieu, and established him instead as a product of modern mainstream mythology—the kiss of death, of course, in a medium that prides itself on unspoiled tradition.

> Robin Hood started as a middle class yeoman fighting with a sword. He was adopted by lower class people and then fought with a staff. He was adopted by aristocrats and kings and became a nobleman down on his luck. He was incorporated into the May games, and Maid Marion was invented as a consort.

Somewhere along the line, however, Robin Hood lost his standing as a folk hero, and was transformed into a super-hero instead.

We have precious little in the way of authentic survivors from the plays of this era, at least so far as Robin Hood is concerned. The earliest complete plays that we know of are *Edward I*, published in 1593, with Robin but an incidental character behind a history of that king's invasion of Wales; and the aforementioned *George a Green*. But Anthony Munday's two plays swiftly followed and it is these that Askew is reflecting upon when he claims "Two Robin Hood plays were more popular than Shakespeare in the late 16th century."

He continues,

In the romantic era, Walter Scott made [*Robin*] an Anglo Saxon fighting Norman oppressors. In the 19th century he became a children's book hero who did not kill anybody, and who robbed the rich to give to the poor. He became a film hero once cinema was invented, and later a TV hero . . . he has been depicted with involvement with space travelers [*the Canadian animated series* Rocket Robin Hood].

The ballad stories have been used as a basis in every major adaption. So I think that Robin Hood's continuing popularity is the real reason why the ballads are not sung much nowadays. He seems to be current rather than from the mysterious past.

Yet it is the very stubbornness of the ballad stories that maintains the "modern" Robin's links to his ancient forebear, as Grey Malkin explains.

One of the aspects about the Robin Hood Ballads that I am personally intrigued by is how little has changed in their telling over the centuries, as if the authors or storytellers hit the nail on the head from the word go and tapped into something in the storytelling form that was almost perfectly constructed and timeless.

[*However*], by the folk heyday of the late 1960s and early 1970s, Robin Hood was associated with green-tighted Errol Flynn style heroics and was simply not viewed as being very cool, happening or "authentic."

In hindsight, this glaring omission could be viewed as a genuine shame, for such an illustrious and potentially counter cultural figure to be so excluded. However, arguably Robin has instead found a home in rather more visual interpretations of his forest based adventures, on both television and in cinema.

Robin Hood and the Monk

As if to prove Malkin's point, "Robin Hood and the Monk" emerges from among the very earliest of all the surviving Robin Hood ballads and already, Robin, Little John and Much Miller are battling against the forces of the Sheriff of Nottingham. The story of the archery competition, first prize—a golden arrow—is as familiar to modern blu-ray aficionados as it was to medieval peasants; and so on and so forth.

Yet there is much more in the ballads than modern interpreters choose to take, just as there is a delight to be found in the reading of them that can seldom be found elsewhere.

There is no way of knowing precisely how old the vast majority of the surviving ballads are; at best, students—and that includes the pioneering

Francis James Child—can merely record their earliest appearances in print or manuscript form, and assume that they were often already old at that point.

Nevertheless, it is clear that they encompass a remarkable span of years, with "Robin Hood and the Monk" reckoned to date back to around 1450, as the language deployed therein makes evident.

> Whan John came to Notyngham
> The ʒatis were sparred ychon;
> John callid vp the porter,
> He answerid sone anon.
> "What is þe cause," seid Litul Jon,
> "Þou sparris þe ʒates so fast?"
> "Because of Robyn Hode," seid [þe] porter,
> "In depe prison is cast.
>
> "John and Moch and Wyll Scathlok,
> Ffor sothe as I yow say,
> Þei slew oure men vpon our wallis,
> And sawten vs euery day."
>
> Litull John spyrred after þe schereff,
> And sone he hym fonde;
> He oppyned þe kyngus priue seell,
> And gaf hym in his honde.
> Whan þe scheref saw þe kyngus seell,
> He did of his hode anon:
> "Wher is þe munke þat bare þe letturs?"
> He seid to Litull John.
>
> "He is so fayn of hym," seid Litul John,
> "Ffor sothe as I yow say,
> He has made hym abot of Westmynster,
> A lorde of þat abbay."
>
> The scheref made John gode chere,
> And gaf hym wyne of the best;
> At nyʒt þei went to her bedde,
> And euery man to his rest.

According to the ballad, it is a bright Whitsunday morning when Robin decides to attend Mass in Nottingham. As usual, he is counseled to take a dozen men with him for protection but—again, as usual—he insists he will be accompanied only by Little John. And, yet again as usual, they fall into a fight on their way to the church and part.

Robin arrives at St. Mary's Church in Nottingham and is immediately recognized by a monk, who just as promptly informs the sheriff that his nemesis is on the premises.

A veritable army of soldiers descend upon the church and, while Robin fights valiantly (and breaks his sword over the sheriff's head), the sheer weight of numbers eventually overcomes him. He is captured and dragged back to Nottingham to be hanged.

Back at the camp, news of the calamity reaches Robin's men, who fly into fits of despair. Only Little John seems unconcerned. Their earlier disagreement presumably forgotten, he reminds them that the Virgin Mary would never allow harm to befall Robin Hood, and he lays out a plan.

The following day, as a monk travels through the forest to deliver news of Robin's capture to the king, Little John and Much Miller ambush him. The monk is killed, and they convey the news to the king themselves.

He rewards them with a sizable sum of money, appoints them yeomen of the crown, and sends them back to Nottingham with a letter bearing his seal, demanding that the prisoner be brought to him unharmed.

The pair returns to Nottingham to find the sheriff still celebrating his triumph. Together they drink, then once the sheriff is sleeping, John goes to the jail, kills the guard and rescues Robin. Then they return to the forest, and the sheriff is made a fool of once again.

"Too much," wrote Child, "could not be said in praise of this ballad, but nothing need be said.

> It is very perfection in its kind; and yet we have others equally good, and beyond doubt should have had more, if they had been written down early, as this was, and had not been left to the chances of tradition. Even writing would not have saved all, but writing has saved this (in large part), and in excellent form.

Child is correct. As has already been mentioned, the first undisputed historical reference to Robin Hood as a legend (or, at least, as something more than a man) appears in "Visio Willelmi de Petro Ploughman" (today more commonly referred to as "Piers Plowman"), a vast narrative poem written around 1377 by William Langland.

An account of Piers's quest for religious enlightenment, the poem is effective both as allegory and satire, with the king depicted as a cat and the people as mice, cruelly beholden to a series of hopelessly contradictory laws that demanded some form of resolution. One popular interpretation of "Piers Plowman" is that it was among the texts and theories that inspired Wat Tyler's Peasants Revolt of 1381.

So far as Robin Hood is concerned, its significance lies in what other scholars might consider a mere lyrical aside, a reference to fact that the common man was far more familiar with the words and meaning of the popular songs of the day, than with the Latin services that he heard each week in church.

> I kan noght parfitly my Paternoster as þe preest it syngeþ,
> But I kan rymes of Robyn Hood and Randolf Erl of Chestre,
> Ac neiþer of Oure Lord ne of Oure Lady þe leeste þat euere was maked.
> [I don't know perfectly my Our Father as the priest sings it;
> I know rhymes of Robin Hood and Randolf Earl of Chester,
> But neither of Our Lord nor of Our Lady the least that ever was written.]

Thus is it confirmed that at least some of the adventures of Robin Hood had been set to music, and had traveled through the land, well before the end of the fourteenth century.

This information brings us no closer to agreeing who Robin Hood actually was, or when he lived, but it certainly gives us a timeframe with which to work; and one to which subsequent balladeers would adhere.

How ironic it is, then, that the identities of these balladeers is no less shrouded in mystery than that of the man about whom they were writing.

Throughout the centuries that preceded the invention (and, more crucially, general availability) of the printing press, there were no music publishers in the medieval world; no central repositories in which a song-writer might lodge his latest creation.

Quite simply, a song would be sung by one person; heard and learned and adapted by others; and spread literally by word of mouth. And in every retelling, it would change. Open Child's balladry to almost any page, and one can readily marvel at how many different versions there are of almost every ballad in the book.

Sometimes, the variations are merely colloquial—a version collected from a singer in the north of the land would employ very different language to one from the south. But often, the content, too, changes, and sometimes to such a degree that the only concrete links between two versions of a ballad might lie in the names of its characters, and the loosest outline of the story.

This process has not always been documented. Child published as many variations as he was able to find, but no matter how many versions of, say, "Long Lankin" (a particularly gory tale of slaughter and retribution) he might have unearthed, there were undoubtedly many more that circulated in centuries gone by. And so it is with the Robin Hood ballads, even though the majority of those that Child collected contrarily seldom appear in more than one form, usually that which had been recorded in earlier times by scholars who sought only to preserve what they personally considered to be the "best" version of each song.

The famous diarist Samuel Pepys was a keen ballad collector, and published a number of Robin Hood's ballads in his quaintly titled *Garlands* of 1663 and 1670.

Two editions of Thomas Evans's *Old Ballads* (1777 and 1784) and antiquarian Joseph Ritson's highly acclaimed (and oft-mentioned) *Robin Hood: A*

Richard Todd in a classic pose from *The Story of Robin Hood and His Merrie Men* (1952).   *Photofest*

Collection of All the Ancient Poems, Songs, and Ballads, Now Extant . . . served up further offerings. So did the great libraries of the age, carefully preserved collections of manuscripts and writings that may not even have existed as more than a handful of copies.

Child, therefore, did not merely reprint the ballads. He reported on them too, discussing their provenance, and commenting, too, on the work of previous collectors.

For example, what appears to be another very early balladic retelling of the Robin Hood story is "Robyn and Gandelyn," written around 1450 and preserved among the aforementioned Sloane Manuscripts.

Child, however, is adamant that the ballad has nothing whatsoever to do with our hero. First, he discusses and quotes an earlier scholar who suggested that this Robyn was indeed Hood. And then he sniffs haughtily, "Thought is free."

A Lytell Geste of Robyn Hode

In Child's opinion, the oldest complete, extant Robin Hood ballad is also the longest and, in terms of later retellings, the most influential of them all.

"A Lytell Geste of Robyn Hood" was published in London by the enviably named Wynken de Worde sometime around 1500, although there is little doubt that it was largely compiled from songs and verses that had already been circulating for decades before that—in fact, Child names four of which he was aware: "Robin Hood and the Monk," "Robin Hood, Little John and the Sheriff," "Robin Hood and the King" and "Robin Hood's Death."

Perhaps these were the songs with which Piers Plowman was so familiar, and whose appeal to the "common man" was further remarked upon by another period author, Bower, during the 1440s.

> Robertus Hode et Litill-Johanne, cum eorum complicibus, de quibus stolidum vulgus hianter in comœdiis et in tragœdiis prurienter festum faciunt, et præ ceteris romanciis mimos et bardanos cantitare delectantur.
>
> [*"Robin Hood and Little John, of whom the foolish vulgar in comedies and tragedies make lewd entertainment, and are delighted to hear the jesters and minstrels sing them above all other ballads."*]

Half a century after that, John Major, the author of the *Historia Maioris Britanniæ* (*the History of Greater Britain*) noted,

Robertus Hudus Anglus et Paruus Ioannes, latrones famatissimi in nemoribus latuerunt, solum opulentorum virornm bona diripientes. Nullum nisi eos inuadentem, vel resistentem pro suarum rerum tuitione, occiderunt Centum sagittarios ad pugnam aptissimos Robertus latrociniis aluit, quos 400 viri fortissimi inuadere non audebant. Rebus huius Roberti gestis tola Britannia incantibus utitur. Fœminam nullam opprimi permisit, nee pauperum bona surripuit, verum eos ex abbatum bonis ablatis opipare pauit.

[*"The Englishmen Robert Hudus and Little John were robbers who hid in the woods, from whence they attacked the wealthy . . . taking goods from the wealthy Abbots, with which they fed the poor . . . " The passage goes on to explain that they were so powerful that not even a force of four hundred dared attack them, and soon all of Britain had heard of the things they had achieved.*]

The songs were spreading and the "Geste," suggests Child, was simply an attempt to compile them all into one place—the medieval equivalent of the modern compilation album.

But what of those that were overlooked by the "Geste"? Some of them have come down to us as mere scraps, but our hero certainly appears within the so-called Porkington Manuscripts, a collection of works dated to the late fifteenth century:

Ther were tynkerris in tarlottus, the met was fulle goode,
The sowe sat one him benche, and harppyd Robyn Hoode.

And he can be found within "a Song on Woman" from the Manuscript Lambeth, which also dates from the fifteenth century:

He that made this songe full good
Came of the northe and of the sothern blode,
And somewhat kyne to Robyn Hode.

Child continues, "These passages show the popularity of Robin Hood ballads for a century or more before the time when the 'Geste' was printed, a popularity which was fully established at the beginning of this period, and unquestionably extended back to a much earlier day."

Part of the Geste's appeal has to be its length, which again is testament to its compiler's own researches into the existing literature. At close to fourteen thousand words, it is not only the most thorough of all the early tales of Robin Hood, it is also one of the longest ballads of its time.

That said, it was not necessarily performed as a song. Rather, it would probably have been relayed as a spoken-word story, with musical accompaniment, the themes shifting with every new scene, or *fytte*.

There are eight of these *fyttes*. In the first, Robin Hood is preparing to hold a feast, but insists that there has to be a guest of honor—a quest which Little John fulfills when he chances upon a down-on-his luck knight, Sir Richard-at-the-Lee.

Apparently, Sir Richard's son had killed somebody during a joust and was imprisoned until bail was arranged. The knight borrowed the money, £400, from St. Mary's Abbey in York, but now the debt has come due, and the knight does not have the money to meet it.

The abbot is therefore preparing to take the knight's lands and property in lieu of the cash, so Robin loans Sir Richard the money, and orders Little John to accompany him to York, where he settles the debt.

He then returns home (via a swift detour to aid a yeoman in a wrestling match!), and presents Robin with an expensive bow and arrow as a token of his gratitude.

Months pass—whiled away by Little John in the service of the Sheriff of Nottingham, whom he had impressed in a recent archery tournament.

Thomas Bewick depicts Little John in action.

Tiring of this life, however, John and the sheriff's cook finally depart the castle, taking with them a large portion of the sheriff's personal treasure.

Robin, meanwhile, is beginning to miss the money he loaned the knight, and so he makes his own way to St. Mary's and not only steals back the original £400, but removes another £400 on top, telling his victim that he is acting on the orders of the Virgin Mary.

Then, when Sir Richard does finally arrive to repay the loan, Robin instead gives him even more money.

By now the sheriff has discovered the loss of his treasure, and he has identified the culprit as well. Already well aware of Little John's prowess with the bow, but newly enraged by his connection with the outlaw Robin Hood, the sheriff arranges a new archery contest, the first prize for the winner being a golden arrow.

Robin enters and, naturally, wins, but the contest was a trap. He and his men are ambushed and, though they make their escape, Little John is injured. Robin takes him to Sir Richard's castle to recover, but the sheriff is on the trail. With additional men supplied by the king, the sheriff captures Sir Richard—only for Robin to both rescue the knight and kill the sheriff.

Now the king gets involved, disguising himself as an abbot and venturing into the forest, where he meets and befriends both Robin and the knight. A friendly archery contest is arranged, which the king easily wins.

He then reveals his true identity, and takes Robin into his service, where he remains for the next fifteen months, before returning to Barnsdale, getting the old gang back together, and resuming the life of an outlaw for the next twenty-two years.

That this element of the tale echoes that of the porter, Robin Hood, whom we met in chapter one should come as no surprise. Even the most fanciful ballad often took something from reality, be it a name, an event or a life. Other incidents in the "Geste," meanwhile, have themselves become staples of the modern story.

Robin Hood and the Golden Arrow

The archery contest, with its prize of the fabulous golden arrow, is a key element in almost every major retelling of the Robin Hood legend, from the most faithful to the most fanciful.

Imagining he can flush Robin out of hiding, the sheriff arranges a competition that he knows the outlaw will be unable to resist—and, of course, he is correct.

Although he is well aware that the whole thing is a trap, Robin simply cannot hold back from entering the competition and, just as the sheriff planned, he wins. But via subterfuge, cunning, and sheer nerve, he also gets away with the arrow, an escapade that is still regarded among his most impressive. In fact, another of the ballads included in Child's collection,

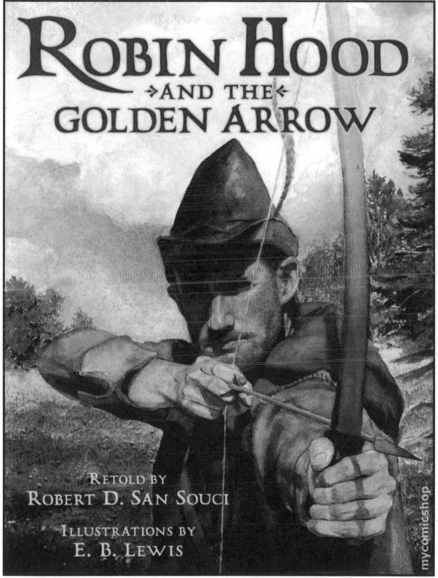

A popular retelling of one of the best-known legends of them all.

"Robin Hood and the Golden Arrow," is effectively a twenty-three stanza rewrite of the original tale, probably written around three hundred years later.

There is, however, a further installment to the tale, which devours the remainder of the original ballad.

Back in the forest, Robin is reeling beneath the (admittedly, understandable) urge to make certain that the sheriff knows full well who won the prize. Various ideas are batted back and forth, but finally Little John suggests writing a letter, affixing it to an arrow, and then firing it into the center of Nottingham:

> The project it was full performed;
> The sheriff that letter had;
> Which when he read, he scratched his head,
> And raved like one that's mad.

The earlier story, that of the competition, remains one of staples of the Robin Hood legend. It appears in the 1950s series *Adventures of Robin Hood*, it's well told in the 1980s' *Robin of Sherwood*; it even showed up, in 2014, in an episode of the long-running science-fiction television series *Doctor Who* (the excellently titled *Robot of Sherwood*) with the Sheriff of Nottingham in league with an alien invader whose spacecraft is both powered by gold, and vulnerable to it as well.

Taking the golden arrow for which he and Robin had so recently been competing, the Doctor fires it into the heart of the alien spacecraft, knowing that just this few extra pounds of the metal will overload the ship's circuits and cause it to explode in the atmosphere.

The sheriff is killed; the peasants he had enslaved are rescued; and Robin is reunited with Maid Marian (whom the sheriff had also imprisoned). Only one question remains. Throughout the episode, the Doctor was adamant that Robin Hood was a legend. Only now, he's not so certain.

Join the club.

16

A Robin Hood Broadside

Later Laments and Sensational Sonnets

C hild never wavered in his belief that Robin Hood was "absolutely a creation of the ballad-muse." But he was very picky about the ballads to which he would ascribe Robin's invention.

Child's personal fancies were for the earliest ballads, an opinion analogous today to the music fan whose tastes are steeped in classic rock, and who regards more modern sounds as little more than crass commercialism.

"The earliest of these ballads," he wrote, "are among the best of all ballads, and perhaps none in English please so many and please so long. . . . On the other hand . . . a considerable part of the Robin Hood poetry looks like char-work done for the petty press, and should be judged as such."

Thought is free.

Child was not, however, alone in his distaste for what he considered to be these latter-day concoctions. A century earlier, Joseph Ritson seized upon one particular ballad, "The King's Disguise, and Friendship with Robin Hood," as having been "written by some miserable retainer to the press, merely to eke out [a] book; being, in fact, a most contemptible performance."

Another commentator, American academic Bertrand Harris Bronson, poured his scorn out on "Robin Hood and the Prince of Aragon" and its "forty-six rather deplorable stanzas," with his fury further compounded by the revelation that this admittedly slight offering not only survived in England, it was one of the ballads that made the crossing to North America as well, in the repertoire of the earliest settlers (it would eventually be retitled, "Robin Hood and the Prince of *Oregon*").

One can understand such points of view, of course. There is a beauty to the earlier ballads that is quite lacking from many of their later counterparts; a sense that the first writers wrote for the love of the song, and the joy of their audience, while those that came later were motivated more by the lure of filthy lucre.

Here is Child discussing "Robin Hood and the Tinker," a verse that almost certainly dates from the eighteenth century: "[T]he fewest words will best befit this contemptible imitation of imitations," although he concedes that it is mere coincidence that allows elements of the offending verse to echo an earlier, superior, ballad. "It does not appear to have been known to the writers of broadsides."

And you can still feel him shudder as he wrote those final few words.

Broadsides—How Low Can You Go?

The word "broadside" was adopted from a naval term, in which a fighting ship would simultaneously discharge all the cannons on one side of the vessel at an enemy.

Published broadsides were less lethal, obviously, but they made a similar job of peppering all within range with their opinions, viewpoints or storytelling.

Roughly designed, privately printed, and sold on street corners for a penny or less, broadsides were, more or less, the only economical alternative to the high-priced newspapers of the day—and, like the newspapers, the most popular issues were those that dealt with the most sensational murders. The so-called Murder in the Red Barn, for example.

In 1828, William Corder, a prosperous farmer in the neighbourhood of Bury St. Edmunds, in England's East Anglia, met, and impregnated, Maria Marten, the beautiful daughter of a local farm laborer.

He convinced the ignorant girl of the need for utter secrecy by informing her that she could be arrested for carrying a bastard child. But he also swore to marry her, and they arranged to meet at a local landmark, the Red Barn, where a horse and cart would be waiting to take them to Ipswich, where they would be wed.

Maria consented, bade her parents farewell, and departed to begin her new life.

Two days later, Corder returned alone, claiming Maria was still in Ipswich, trying to sort out certain difficulties which had arisen over the marriage license. Later, he announced that she had moved on to London and that he would soon be traveling down to meet her.

And, at the end of September, Maria's parents received a letter from Corder, announcing the two were married and living happily on the Isle of Man.

One night, however, Maria's mother dreamt that her daughter was dead, and that her body lay in the Red Barn. Six months later, she finally convinced the authorities to conduct a search of the barn, and sure enough, Maria's body was discovered, buried beneath the floor.

Corder—who had, in the meantime, married another woman—was arrested in London and brought back to trial at Bury St. Edmunds. He pled guilty, saying Maria had in fact shot herself with a pistol she had stolen from his home. His only crime, he said, was attempting to conceal the body.

Another retelling of the Robin Hood stories.

Unfortunately for Corder, the jury preferred to believe Maria's brother, who testified he had seen Corder leaving the Red Barn on the fateful day, carrying a pickaxe. Corder was found guilty, and hanged at Bury on August 11, 1828.

His trial was an immediate sensation, and provoked a rash of ballads commemorating the event, one of which, Jemmy Catnach's "Confession And Execution Of William Corder, The Murderer Of Maria Marten," sold a reported 1,166,000 copies, and remains a staple in many folk repertoires to this day:

> With her heart so light she thought no harm
> To meet her love did go
> He murdered her all in the barn
> And he laid her body low.

Another of Catnach's ballads sold an estimated 2,500,000 copies at a penny a time. The ballad's writer, incidentally, received just one shilling for his work, although his renown was sufficient for none less than the author William Makepeace Thackeray, during his years as a brutally satirical journalist, to title a "dissertation upon ballads" *Horae Catnachinoe.*

"A good murder is a great godsend [to newspapermen]," he remarked on another occasion. He might easily have added, "And to songsmiths."

But of course, one could not rely on a good murder coming along every day, or even often enough to provide any writer with the semblance of a decent living. Nor a juicy scandal, nor a political embarrassment. No less than today, the average reader of the eighteenth and nineteenth centuries craved excitement, and it was the media's job to satisfy that craving, if not with singalongs torn from the headlines, then with fresh revelations about already-established favorites.

That same process, as we have already seen, still plays out today, and though the medium has changed, the heroes remain the same. From Dick Turpin to Casey Jones, from Jesse James to Sweeney Todd, the legendary figures that stalked the ballads and broadsides of a century-and-more ago are still alive and well—and many a historian will tell you straight, there is no more truth in a modern documentary on the life of "the real Robin Hood" than there is in the pages of, for example, "A True Tale of Robin Hood," written in 1632 by one Martin Parker, and published in London by Francis Grove.

The ballad's full title, by the way, would be a sight to behold on a modern album cover: "A True Tale of Robbin Hood, or, a Brief Touch of the Life and Death of That Renowned Outlaw, Robert, Earl of Huntington, Vulgarly

Called Robbin Hood Who Lived and Dyed in AD. 1198, Being the 9Th Year of the Reign of King Richard the First, Commonly Called Richard Coeur De Lyon. Carefully Collected Out of the Truest Writers of Our English Chronicles and Published for the Satisfaction of Those Who Desire Truth From Falsehood by Martin Parker."

Child, however, is not impressed.

> Martin Parker professes . . . to follow chronicles, not "fained tales." Perhaps he regards broadside-ballads with historical names in them as chronicles: at any rate, though he reports some things which are found in Grafton, and in Major as cited by Grafton, much the larger part of his True Tale is now to be found only in ballads. When he does not agree with ballads which have come down to us, he may have used earlier copies, or he may have invented. . . . Perhaps Parker calls his compilation a True Tale because a tale of Robin Hood was a proverb for an incredible story: "Tales of Robin Hood are good for fools."

Much of Parker's "true tale" has been traced to earlier balladic writings—"A Lyttel Geste," of course; "Robin Hood and the Bishop," "Robin Hood and Queen Katherine" and "The Noble Fisherman."

But his originality (or otherwise) should not be an issue, any more than it is with the "Geste" itself. The truth of the matter is, "A True Tale of Robin Hood" is an exciting tale, 120 stanzas long, and encompassing so much of the standard legend that it is better viewed as a precursor to any number of twentieth century retellings, than as an object for scholarly scorn.

Protest Songs, Seventeenth Century Style

Robin Hood, after all, was never intended for study. He may or may not have been based upon a living person; he may or may not have performed even a fraction of the deeds for which he is credited. But it doesn't matter.

To his audience . . . we'd call them fans today . . . he represented something they could believe in, the knowledge that no matter how unjust their world might be, how wicked their overlords, how cruel their masters, how poor their families, it did not have to be that way.

Someone, somewhere, was fighting for change, and it should certainly come as no surprise to discover that many of the most powerful ballads dated from periods of dramatic, and sometimes traumatic, social change.

Like King Arthur and Don Quixote, similarly "legendary" (meaning, we really don't know whether or not they existed) heroes who battled against the odds, Robin Hood represents the true spirit of mankind, a hero who stands not for the state, for politics or business, but for what we would now call the man on the street—the person who just wants to get on with the day-to-day business of living, but is buffeted nevertheless by the decisions and demands of the wider world.

It's a spirit that still lives on; through the 1960s, in the so-called protest music of Bob Dylan, Joan Baez et al., *and* the anti-war songs that provided

From the days before movies spun off soundtrack albums, the sheet music for the theme to the 1922 Douglas Fairbanks "photo play."

the soundtrack for the Vietnam conflict; in every rock and pop song that confronted "the man" head on and demanded he listen to what the rest of us have to say.

You see it invoked in modern-day political campaigns, too, when a candidate takes to the podium or the airwaves to explain how they stand against corporate lobbyists and special interest groups—although one does sometimes wonder how many more years they'll be able to get away with recycling the same old soundbites, before somebody points out that they've not done a very good job of their mission so far. At least Robin Hood usually won his battles, and we still remember him today.

Politicians, on the other hand . . . there's a terrific tale told in the first series of the 2006 *Robin Hood*, where the sheriff captures Much the Miller, but rather than execute him and thus create a martyr, he takes the opposite tack altogether, and ennobles the funny little man.

As the Earl of Bonchurch, the sheriff believes, Much will soon become accustomed to the finer things in life—wealth and status, political power, all the usual benefits and, in so doing, he will see the sense of preserving the status quo. In other words, he will become as corrupt as everybody else who attends the sheriff's Council of Nobles.

In the TV series, the sheriff's plan fails. The spirit of altruism that Robin has inculcated into his Merry Men is too deeply entrenched to be warped by a handful of baubles. In reality, that same quality cannot so easily be taken for granted.

At the same time, it must be admitted that there is a vast amount of repetition to be found among the ballads, and not only within the slight (and easily parodied) rhyming devices that amuse so many latter day commentators. "Hey nonny no" and "derry down dey" were simply the period equivalent of today's "yeah yeah yeah" and "baby, baby, whooo."

Many of the ballads that Child collected were effectively further variations on an earlier verse, perhaps purposefully adapted, but just as likely to have developed over time into a new scenario.

For example, the ballads "Robin Hood and the Potter," "Robin Hood and the Butcher," "Robin Hood and the Shepherd" and "Robin Hood and the Beggar" all involve the outlaw first waylaying a passerby, and being soundly thrashed as a consequence.

Rather than invite his conqueror to join the Merry Men, however, Robin instead offers to purchase the merchant's goods (or, in the beggar's case, his clothing), and then travels to Nottingham to sell them.

There, he first insinuates himself with the sheriff's wife by offering her a sample of his goods at reduced prices, and then tricks the sheriff into following him into the forest—in the "Potter" poem, the lawman is lured by the promise of being introduced to Robin Hood; in the "Butcher" ballad, the sheriff intends on selling the merchant some livestock.

On every occasion, however, he is walking into a trap; is relieved of his money, and sent home in humiliation; and on every occasion, his wife makes it very clear that he brought his misfortunes down upon his own head. In fact, it's rather a shame that we know nothing more of Mrs. Sheriff than what we learn from these ballads. She sounds like a remarkable woman.

Another popular theme sees Robin either fighting, or charming, his way out of trouble.

In the ballad "Robin Hood's Delight," for example, Robin, Little John and Scarlet are ambushed by three foresters. The battle rages for six hours, at which point Robin and his men are at a serious disadvantage.

Robin begs a moment's rest, and goes to blow his hunting horn. But the keepers aren't going to fall for that old trick. Either he fights on, or he yields to them, at which point Robin compliments their strength and prowess, and suggests they finish their contest in a Nottingham ale house, exchanging their weapons for alcohol, and drinking until they cannot hold another drop. Which they do.

In the hands of other broadside authors, however, Robin became embroiled in a series of brand new adventures—and that, surely, is one of the functions of an evolving tradition. There is a lovely seventeenth century ballad called "Robin Hood's Golden Prize," for instance, in which Robin disguises himself as a friar and begs for charity from two passing monks.

A magnificent recitation of the ballad, recorded in 1956 by Kathleen Danson Read, imbibes the story with all the action that a medieval audience must have experienced. They turn him down, explaining that they have just been robbed, and rendered penniless. Robin, of course, does not believe them, but he feigns sympathy regardless, pulling them from their horses and suggesting, "then we will pray for [money]."

He forces the pair to their knees and, for the next hour, they pray, until Robin decides that it is time to discover whether or not their supplications have been answered.

Ignoring the monks' protests, he digs deep into their pockets and, miraculously, discovers a small fortune in gold. He allows the monks to each keep 10 percent of this unexpected bounty, and then makes off with the rest.

It's a great story, and a terrific addition to the canon. It is also more or less identical to a German folk tale of perhaps a century earlier, only there it is three out-of-work soldiers who have cornered a monk from a nearby Benedictine monastery.

But no harm, no foul. In an age before litigation supplanted artistry and interpretation as the single-most crucial arbiter of song or story, language and literature alike developed out of such blatant borrowings—a point that is hammered home harder every time another impoverished second-rate songwriter accuses a wealthy hit maker of "stealing" the spirit of his ditty. If the original piece was so magnificent, after all, then why wasn't *it* already a smash?

Of course, as the immortal Jemmy Catnach discovered, there was precious little money to be made from composing broadsides. They were cheap and cheerful, designed solely to appeal to as many people as possible. They were the pop songs of the day, and they were intended to be as ephemeral, too.

But, as Grey Malkin counsels, we overlook them at our peril. Because, no less than Child's beloved early songs, even the most mealy-mouthed of later creations

> are heroic, they are humorous, they are tense and they are sometimes bawdy (and in the case of "Progress to Nottingham," grisly and bloody). There are not many characters that survive the centuries so intact and untouched; [*King*] Arthur, perhaps, but few others.
>
> Robin Hood is a living archetype; few cannot immediately picture Robin Hood upon mention of his name. The Robin of the Child Ballads deserves special attention, he deserves a few psych or folk rock interpretations. And he is out there still, in the woods, shapeshifting through the ages, always relevant and always needed.

17

From Ballads to Books

The Legend Continues . . .

Although there is certainly no shortage of books telling stories of Robin Hood, just two truly tell what we might call *the* story—*Ivanhoe*, by the Scots author Sir Walter Scott; and *The Merry Adventures of Robin Hood of Great Renown in Nottinghamshire* by the American writer and illustrator Howard Pyle.

Published sixty-four years apart, in 1819 and 1883 respectively, the two books are significant not only for their content, however. They also bridge the years during which the pursuit of reading truly exploded across all levels of the general public. Indeed, Scott was very much among the earliest pioneers of reading, as opposed to studying.

No, he did not "invent" the novel—extended fictional narratives have been around since the earliest days of man, and even if one confines the genre only to books that started life as printed tales, Cervantes's *Don Quixote* got in there over two centuries earlier, with Daniel Defoe, Jonathan Swift, and Mrs. Radcliffe (to name but three) all adding their two-cent's worth in the years since then.

But the early nineteenth century was a time of great social change, beyond the political turmoil that also marked the era. More people could read than ever before; and books were becoming cheaper and more available, if not in bound form then at least as regular serials, published a chapter or so at a time as comparatively inexpensive magazine-style serials. And Scott was one of the names, if not the principal one, who ensured people kept coming back for more.

Born in 1771 in Edinburgh, Scott was initially best known (and highly regarded) as a poet. In 1814, however, he published *Waverley*, an adventure set during the Jacobite Uprising of 1745—a rebellion, just seventy years earlier, whose events and repercussions were still within living memory.

Scott's own father was a lad of sixteen when Bonnie Prince Charlie first raised his standard, and Scott grew up with tales (embellished, of course, by the passing years) of the uprising blazing in his belly.

Add to that a long-standing fascination with both Scots history and folklore, and the wonder is that *Waverley*—and the succession of novels that followed it—was not birthed sooner.

Scott wrote at a prodigious rate, twenty full-length, deeply researched, and densely packed novels over the next fifteen years, including many that remain much beloved classics today—*The Heart of Midlothian*, *The Bride of Lammermore*, *Kenilworth*, and *The Pirate* among them.

But it is *Ivanhoe* for which Scott is, perhaps, best known—not only because of its story, but because of its setting, too. Medieval England was a fresh arena for the author, whose previous writings had concentrated on the history of his homeland; and it was fresh for many of his readers, too.

The era was one that people knew only passingly, from the little snippets of everyday life passed down through ballads and folk tales; Scott brought those snippets to life, painting a portrait that positively ached with the notions of romance and chivalry—attributes that few people would hitherto have ever associated with the age.

Thanks to *Ivanhoe*, they became indivisible. Everything we *think* we know about the Middle Ages, if not invented by Scott, was at least popularized by him, from the pageantry of a jousting tournament to the brave knight riding to the aid of a damsel in distress.

Likewise, in choosing to place his tale in the immediate aftermath of Richard the Lionheart's return to England in 1194, Scott was able to place both the history and the mythology, of that king's reign into a perspective that, again, still influences the thinking of many people.

The heart of the story revolves around the aspirations and adventures of Wilfred of Ivanhoe, a young man who finds himself disinherited by his father for the sin of supporting King Richard (who, after all, was still regarded as a Norman), as opposed to following Lord Aethelstane, a Saxon nobleman whose own claim to the English throne was vouchsafed by a direct line of descent from the ill-fated King Harold—the short-lived monarch who ended his days at the Battle of Hastings.

In to this is projected a certain Robin of Locksley, *not* as a leading character, per se, but certainly a recurrent one, whose acts of heroism echo those of the traditional Robin Hood, at the same time as layering fresh nuance onto the legend.

It was Scott, for example, who first depicted Robin winning an archery contest by splitting his opponent's arrow with one of his own; and it is thanks to *Ivanhoe* that so many subsequent histories refer to Robin Hood as Robin of Locksley—although it should be noted that he is merely a yeoman in these tales, and Locksley is simply the village that he hails from. There was no talk of lost inheritances here.

Play-along with the *Robin Hood: Prince of Thieves (1991)*.

A Romantic Heritage

Scott was not Robin Hood's sole supporter at this time, however. The poets
J. R. Reynolds, Leigh Hunt, and John Keats all invoked his memory in verses
published shortly before *Ivanhoe* appeared, with the latter adapting one of
the legend's own past maneuverings by wondering how Robin and Marian
would get on, were they to be reawakened in the modern world:

> And if Robin should be cast
> Sudden from his turfed grave,
> And if Marian should have
> Once again her forest days,
> She would weep, and he would craze:
> He would swear, for all his oaks,
> Fall'n beneath the dockyard strokes,
> Have rotted on the briny seas;
> She would weep that her wild bees
> Sang not to her—strange! that honey
> Can't be got without hard money!

Perhaps the most important (if not influential) work from this period,
however, was Thomas Love Peacock's *Maid Marian*, a novella published in
1822 and unique in that it brings together for the first time *in prose* many of
the manifold details that are scattered through the ballads and early plays,
and forges them into a cohesive narrative.

Others had, of course, accumulated this material in the past.
Bettesworth and Hitch's now-ninety-year-old *The Whole Life, and Merry
Exploits of Bold Robin Hood, Earl of Huntington (etc., etc.)* had long since been
forgotten. But just thirty years earlier, in 1795, Joseph Ritson's two-volume
compendium proved a work of such depth that scholars still scramble to
add anything to its pages, more than two centuries on.

That, however, is who Ritson's work was aimed at—scholars and historians. Peacock was searching for a wider audience.

Peacock's Robin is Robert Fitz-Ooth, Earl of Locksley, and Huntingdon—
the identity created by the scholar William Stukeley back in 1742; Marian is
Matilda Fitzwalter, daughter of the baron of the fictional Arlingford, and we
join the couple as they stand at the altar of the similarly invented Rubygill
Abbey, about to be wed.

Suddenly a troop of soldiers march in and, halting the abbot mid-
ceremony, declare the wedding at an end, in the name of King Henry I.
Fitz-Ooth is denounced as a traitor and flees with the soldiers in heavy
pursuit, but not before completing the marriage ceremony in his own words:

"Sweet Matilda," said the earl, "did you give your love to the Earl of Huntingdon, whose lands touch the Ouse and the Trent, or to Robert Fitz-Ooth, the son of his mother?"

"Neither to the earl nor his earldom," answered Matilda firmly, "but to Robert Fitz-Ooth and his love."

"That I well knew," said the earl; "and though the ceremony be incomplete, we are not the less married in the eye of my only saint, our Lady, who will yet bring us together. Lord Fitzwater, to your care, for the present, I commit your daughter. —Nay, sweet Matilda, part we must for a while; but we will soon meet under brighter skies, and be this the seal of our faith."

Peacock writes with incredible grace and humor; a few lines on, as the earl's loyal archers struggle desperately to hold back the tide of soldiers, we read of one arrow only narrowly missing the abbot

who, in mortal fear of being suddenly translated from a ghostly friar into a friarly ghost, began to roll out of the chapel as fast as his bulk and his holy robes would permit, roaring "Sacrilege!"

With his terrified monks hot on his heels, the abbot runs for his life, only to trip over his own voluminous outfit, and precipitate an almighty pile-up;

[*as he*] fell suddenly prostrate in the door-way that connected the chapel with the abbey, and was instantaneously buried under a pyramid of ghostly carcasses, that fell over him and each other, and lay a rolling chaos of animated rotundities, sprawling and bawling in unseemly disarray, and sending forth the names of all the saints in and out of heaven, amidst the clashing of swords, the ringing of bucklers, the clattering of helmets, the twanging of bow-strings, the whizzing of arrows, the screams of women, the shouts of the warriors, and the vociferations of the peasantry, who had been assembled to the intended nuptials, and who, seeing a fair set-to, contrived to pick a quarrel among themselves on the occasion, and proceeded, with staff and cudgel, to crack each other's skulls for the good of the king and the earl.

And we're still only a few pages in!

Fitz-Ooth, meanwhile, has fled to the forest with those of his men who remained loyal, living the life of an outlaw—which, it soon transpires, he had been toying with for some years beforehand. It was his long-standing habit of poaching the royal deer that set the king against him in the first place (an echo of those ballads that muse vaguely over sundry forestry offenses), and the baron is determined that his daughter should renounce the felon.

Matilda, however, is made of sterner stuff, as she proves when she appears in the great hall one morning, clad in green and carrying a bow.

> "I am going a-hunting," said Matilda.
> "A-hunting!" said the baron. "What, I warrant you, to meet with the earl, and slip your neck into the same noose?"
> "No," said Matilda: "I am not going out of our own woods to-day."
> "How do I know that?" said the baron. "What surety have I of that?"
> "Here is the friar," said Matilda. "He will be surety."
> "Not he," said the baron: "he will undertake nothing but where the devil is a party concerned."
> "Yes, I will," said the friar: "I will undertake any thing for the lady Matilda."
> "No matter for that," said the baron: "she shall not go hunting to-day."
> "Why, father," said Matilda, "if you coop me up here in this odious castle, I shall pine and die like a lonely swan on a pool."

And so she departs, and ultimately she is reunited with Fitz-Ooth in the forest, where they happily adopt fresh identities. Matilda, henceforth, will be known as Maid Marian; Fitz-Ooth as Robin Hood.

Maid Marian is a magnificent romp, in equal parts stirring, heroic, and comical, guiding us through all the familiar tales of Robin and his adventures with a deft eye not only for action, but also for the sometime-silliness of the early ballads and tales. Reading Peacock, one is never certain quite how seriously he is taking his source material; whether or not he is gently parodying both its form and its content.

Certainly the self-penned ballads that he introduces to the text ache with suppressed mischievousness, while the dialogue is seldom less than scintillating—such as this passage, the Baron and a Friar making merry with word play.

> "Ho! ho! friar!" said the baron—"singing friar, laughing friar, roaring friar, fighting friar, hacking friar, thwacking friar; cracking, cracking, cracking friar; joke-cracking, bottle-cracking, skull-cracking friar!"
> "And ho! ho!" said the friar,—"bold baron, old baron, sturdy baron, wordy baron, long baron, strong baron, mighty baron, flighty baron, mazed baron, crazed baron, hacked baron, thwacked baron; cracked, cracked, cracked baron; bone-cracked, sconce-cracked, brain-cracked baron!"

"What do you mean," said the baron, "bully friar, by calling me hacked and thwacked?"

"Were you not in the wars?" said the friar, "where he who escapes untracked does more credit to his heels than his arms. I pay tribute to your valour in calling you hacked and thwacked."

"I never was thwacked in my life," said the baron.

Or later, when the baron leaves the room after arguing with his daughter. Utterly bucking the traditions of contemporary literature, he "walked away without a song."

Robin Hood, the Opera

Did Somebody Mention Songs?

Today, when a novel is a hit, it is oftentimes swiftly immortalized on film or television. In earlier times, it would transition to the stage or the opera house.

Thomas Love Peacock's *Maid Marian* would be dramatized, in December 1822, as *Maid Marian, or The Huntress of Arlingford*; while the success of Sir Walter Scott's *Ivanhoe* saw no less than half a dozen rival productions open within months of the novel's publication—for the most part unauthorized, but nonetheless popular.

Concepts such as copyright and intellectual property were considerably less well formed then than now, and while many authors did grumble at seeing their work so crudely appropriated by strangers, there was also a sense of well-being to be had, knowing that if the book was purchased by just a fraction of the people who turned out to see the stage show, no amount of expensive advertising could ever have reached such an audience.

Robin Hood himself had long ago transitioned from the amateur productions of village fêtes and May games by then; was already firmly established on the legitimate English stage by then.

In August 1717, revelers at the annual St. Bartholomew's Fair in London rejoiced in what was surely a delightfully bawdy production called *Robin Hood and Little John*; six years later, at Southwark Fair, impresario George Lee staged *The Adventures of Robin Hood, Earl of Huntingdon, and his Mate Little John*. Doubtless other productions, long forgotten today, echoed these successes at less well-reported fairs and festivals.

British theatre was changing, however. Music had long been a part of the stage show, but true music*als* were unknown beyond the world of opera—which itself was an arena far beyond the interests of the common man.

In 1728, therefore, playwright John Gay resolved to counter the country's stifling immersion beneath the weight of incomprehensible European offerings by creating a wholly English opera. It was called *The Beggar's Opera* and it reinvented theatre.

The Beggar's Opera seized upon an English archetype—a hard-drinking, hard-living highwayman—and portrayed him in archetypal English terms, with catchy tunes and memorable lyrics, alive with slang and political commentary. And while the government of the day condemned both the play and its potential effects on the populace, the notion of the English Opera swiftly took root.

In August 1730, less than two years after Gay's *Beggar's Opera* opened in London, *Robin Hood: An Opera* was performed at St. Bartholomew's Fair at a booth operated by messrs. Lee and Harper.

Anonymously penned, this plaintively titled three-act/nineteen-song production is remembered today only by the barest details, noted in the accompanying playbill:

> Shewing how he was banish'd by the Instigation of the Earl of Pembroke, for the Love of the Fair Matilda; His bold Adventures with his Man Little John; and the Band of Outlaws; on which Information the King went with his Army to Pembroke, and Robin Hood's happy Return to Court; With the Comical Adventures of Little John and he Pindar's Wife.

However, William Eben Schultz, PhD, author of *Gay's Beggar's Opera: Its Contents, History and Influence* (1923) enthusiastically proclaims it one of the earliest ballad operas that "show to what extent Gay founded a new school of drama," and its appearance within the *laissez-faire* context of the fair suggests that its appeal was firmly rooted in both common language and coarse song.

Robin arrived on a more conventional stage in December 1750, when Moses Mendez's two-act *Robin Hood: A New Musical Entertainment* debuted at the Drury Lane Theatre. Unfortunately, despite proudly laying claim to an all-new selection of songs composed by the Society of the Temple of Apollo (actually, the magnificent pseudonym for future music historian Charles Burnay!), it did not linger—a later review reflected, "[I]t had little more than musical merit to recommend it [and] met with no great success."

Neither does the plot seem particularly inspired, being largely concerned with Robin's attempts to unite the lovesick Leander with his true love, Clarinda (another echo of the shepherdess Clorinda?), despite her father's determined push for her to wed a pretentious fop named Glitter.

This Robin achieves by disguising himself as the aristocratic Sir Humphrey Wealthy, and convincing Clarinda's father (the equally appropriately named Graspall) that Leander would make a far more suitable son-in-law. Clarinda's engagement to Glitter is broken off, and to compound the latter's misery, Robin robs him as well.

> But you, Squire Ape, must leave your Horses here
> Your Rings, youyr Money and your other Geer
> Trudge home on Foot and when you leave the Wood
> Tell all you see, you met with Robin Hood.

Robin Hood's next appearance on stage could be said to have been the product of public demand.

The 1770s saw a major revival in the pursuit of archery, with clubs springing up all over the country and more than one commentator remarking on the number of would-be Robin Hoods to be found practicing the sport. Soon, even the Prince of Wales was proclaiming his enthusiasm.

The publication, in 1777, of Thomas Evans's collection, *Old Ballads: Historical and Narrative, with Some of Modern Date*, furthered the fervor as readers were reintroduced to such delights as "Robin Hood and the Curtal Friar" and "Robin Hood and Little John."

In the summer of 1783, the Royal Circus and Equestrian Philharmonic Academy staged a mounted *Robin Hood*, and the following April, songsmith William Shield and author Leonard McNally's *Robin Hood, or Sherwood Forest* offered the people even more of what they wanted when it stepped out at Covent Garden Opera House.

With its Irish-born author renowned at the time for past novels *Retaliation* and *Tristram Shandy*, McNally's play fascinates via its incorporation of not only the expected balladic material, but also several pieces that are not traditionally associated with Robin Hood.

McNally wrote:

> The three principle ideas which combine the subject are not original, but borrowed from the ballads of Robin Hood, "the Nut Brown Maid" and "the Hermit of the Dale" . . . taken from an old ballad called "The Herdsman."

Thus we find reference to "Robin Hood's Birth, Breeding, Valor and Marriage" in the welcome return of the love interest Clorinda (although here she is a noblewoman, the niece of Baron FitzHerbert, as opposed to a shepherdess), "The Bishop of Hereford" and sundry others. But by far the most pronounced influence on the production was poet Oliver Goldsmith's "The Hermit"—

> Turn, gentle hermit of the dale,
> And guide my lonely way,
> To where yon taper cheers the vale,
> With hospitable ray.

—with its lead characters, Edwin and Angelina, imposed upon by Robin Hood (played by a Mr. Bannister), Little John (Mr. Quick), Allen a Dale (Mr. Davies), and Clorinda (Mrs. Martyr).

Further romance is present in the love triangle enacted between Little John, Will Scarlet, and Stella, the sister of Allen a Dale, but again, the play met with disapproving critics. According to the *The London Magazine*,

> The author of this opera has done nothing but write the dialogue, which is every where scanty, and compile the ballads which are selected from Milton, Goldsmith, Shirley, Bate, Jonson's collection, Irish ballads &c &c. There is not that structure of fable in it which we usually call plot; the story is simple, and the termination much as the audience are led to expect.

The review conceded that "there are many strokes of pointed satire, particularly in the Justice scene," in which Little John questions why

> we [*who are*] honest are put out of the law, but who are the greater thieves, we who feed on royal venison or those who prey upon his majesty's liege subjects [*under cover of law or authority*]?

But still there was scope for additional complaint.

> The characters and manners of the times in which Robin Hood is said to have lived [*are*] totally disregarded. Robin is a sentimental MacHeath [*the highwayman hero of* Beggar's Opera] and Stella, whom the author meant as a rural, pastoral innocent, is a most unnatural combination of ignorance and artfulness, simplicity and cunning . . .

But the critics be damned. *Robin Hood, or Sherwood Forest* was a success not only in London, but it appears to have played in other cities too, a sure sign that the public paid no more attention back then to what they read than they do today. The play was still undergoing periodic revivals as late as 1820.

In the meantime, Robin continued to appear on stage in a wealth of other guises. Alongside William Cloudesley and Adam Bell, he is a secondary character in Thomas Holcroft's *The Noble Peasant* (1784), and he made his debut in pantomime at Christmas 1795 in William Pearce's *Merry Sherwood, or Harlequin Forester*—Harlequin being a staple character in all such productions at that time.

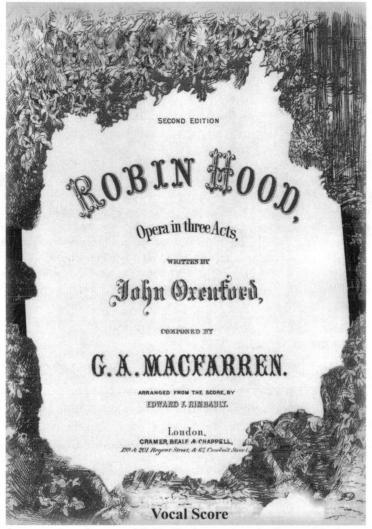

A now-neglected opera of *Robin Hood* was written by George Macfarren and John Oxenford; it was first performed in 1860.

Into the next century, Robin continued to flourish. Her Majesty's Theatre in London produced the three-act *Robin Hood* in October 1860, its plot revolving around the archery contest; and 1891 saw Americans Reginald De Koven and Harry B. Smith enjoy considerable success with their operetta *Maid Marian* (better known today by its American title, *Robin Hood: A Comic Opera*, to which title the British production converted sometime before De Koven unveiled a second opera called *Maid Marian* in 1901).

The success of Francis James Child's newly published ballad collections, meanwhile, opened up fresh avenues for other musical offerings, among them the writings of Sir Henry Rowley Bishop.

Shakespeare and Sir Walter Scott both had major works adapted for the opera by Bishop, but a sure sign of the composer's popularity can be gleaned from this description of a visit to a "smoking concert," staged at "a vast hotel east of Temple Bar," which appeared in *The Musical Standard* magazine in 1879.

> The clatter of hundreds of voices is silent; the waiters flitting here and there transfixed, by order, in their places, and the crowd of men and lads is held spellbound. A charming madrigal of old-world sweetness follows; and then one of Sir Henry Bishop's incomparable glees. Is there anything in the world more refreshing, sweeter or gayer than these rippling ballads? He must indeed be dead to the influence of sweet sounds who is not carried out of himself and his business cares into the romantic atmosphere of the fascinating days when bold Robin Hood, that forester good, drew bow in the merry greenwood.

An Opera for the Eyes

The popularity of the so-called "English Opera" was not slow in communicating itself to other media. With both adult and child literacy on the rise, and reading already under attack, from some circles, for drawing people away from such traditional hobbies as the theatre and the pub, publishers hustled to meet the demand.

The works, and subsequent renown, of Ainsworth, Dickens, Bulwer-Lytton, Thackeray, and so many more had their roots in this demand, but so did a morass of less noteworthy authors. Like modern television companies forever recruiting fresh meat for their reality shows, many mid-nineteenth century publishers were suddenly akin to sausage factories, simply churning out new books and publications, and not really caring a hoot for the quality either.

So long as a story was engrossing, exciting, arousing and entertaining, aspiring authors had more or less a free hand when it came to devising their next masterpiece, and the world of modern fiction was wholly shaped by their efforts.

The murder mystery, the detective novel, fantasy, sci-fi, romance, erotica, enthralling adventures, all were birthed (or, at least, came to fruition) in the seething cauldron of the mid-to-late Victorian literary boom—with many of them, furthermore, tracing their roots back to a genre whose name, even today, can arouse a fission of anticipation—the Penny Dreadful.

Cheaply printed, cheaply priced, the first Penny Dreadfuls began appearing in the late 1830s, direct descendants of the serialized novels of Dickens, Ainsworth et al.

Published on a monthly, or even weekly basis, with stories continuing from issue to issue, they were seldom oriented towards children—the works of author G. W. M. Reynolds, in particular, delighted in a savagery that even the adult world often found difficult to comprehend.

Robin Hood was among the earliest stars of this new publishing sensation. Pierce Egan the Younger's *Robin Hood and Little John: or, The Merry Men*

Pierce Egan, author of some of the most rip-roaring penny dreadfuls.

of Sherwood Forest debuted in 1838, and to the cautious adult perusing its pages as a possible gift for a youngster, it set out its stall very cautiously.

> The materials for a Life of Robin Hood are but scanty; for, although his fame is universal, the existing details of his life are but few, and so surrounded by the mists and obscurity of age, that but little certain can be gathered.
> Many traditions have been handed down respecting him, bearing some stamp of authority if it be only in the fact that the feats narrated are within the bounds of credibility, while they illustrate

Another gloriously gaudy "penny dreadful."

the customs and manners of the period; yet, on the other hand, there are many which are quite beyond the pale of human belief, and must be discarded accordingly. Among his Biographers, some have contended for the nobility of his birth; others have repudiated it: the latter have labored hard to support the proofs they have advanced, but they have little foundation in fact, and, in truth, tend more to mystify than to enlighten the enquirer on this subject.

It all sounded very scholarly indeed; in fact, there is even a most learned joke on the opening page, a pair of travelers passing through Sherwood, one of whom is named Ritson.

It takes positively ages, or at least pages, before the first maiden is deflowered, the first knave is disemboweled, the first heart pierced by arrows, the first grisly ghost goes abroad.

But once they are unleashed, *The Merry Men of Sherwood* is revealed among the most swashbuckling sagas Robin Hood has ever pranced through, a model not only for every action movie made in his name since, but also a few that Hollywood is still reluctant to attempt.

Only slowly did the dreadfuls shake off their adult readership—or, perhaps, the adults shook off the need to read them—and, by the mid-1860s, these graphic tales of sensationalism and gore were being targeted almost exclusively at the working-class young, the logical extension of a trend first acknowledged by a House of Commons inquiry into juvenile delinquency, in 1852.

Killers and criminals drawn from both literature and history (and, of course, that peculiar half-world where the two come together) gallop prominently across almost every page, and Robin Hood remained among their commanders-in-chief.

Maid Marian, the Forest Queen, ran to thirty-one monthly installments, *Little John and Will Scarlet; or, The Outlaws of Sherwood Forest* extended to forty, while Pierce Egan's pioneering serial continued so successfully that not only was it to reappear as an oft-reprinted novel, it even spawned a French edition which, according to legend, owed its translation to none other than Alexandre Dumas. (His chosen title, *Robin Hood, Prince des Voleurs*, by the way, lives on via the silver screen—it translates as *Robin Hood, Prince of Thieves*.)

The adult consensus on the dreadfuls was that they were indeed dreadful; that they glorified crime, tempting their readers into lives of cheap thrill-seeking which could only lead them into the utmost degradation and despair.

Modern authors, too, glory in finding fault with the dreadfuls, singling out not only the gratuitous violence that was common to them, but to the casual sexism and racism that was the backdrop to almost every tale—Robin Hood's adventures, for example, are full of the latter, every time a purebred Saxon (as indeed were Robin and his men) is inclined to insult a passing Norman.

Of course, this is a latter-day concern—at the height of the British Empire, the superiority of one race over another wasn't simply taken for granted, it was not even worth considering. Far more concerning was the debilitating effect that the dreadfuls were having on that superior race.

In 1878, foreshadowing the controversies that neutered the world of American comics during the 1950s, the statesman Lord Shaftesbury claimed to have noted the dreadful to be creeping "not only in the houses of the poor, neglected, and untaught, but into the largest mansions, penetrating into religious families and astounding careful parents by its frightful issues."

A decade later, the impossibly prudish Edward Salmon's study of modern reading trends, *Juvenile Literature As It Is*, warned that the very existence of this pernicious rubbish would inevitably lead to the "moral and material ruin of the working class," a point that seemed to be proven in 1891, when a young East London boy was found guilty not only of murdering his mother, but also leaving her body to rot in an upstairs bedroom, while he, his sibling and a lodger continued to live beneath the same roof.

Among the evidence gathered from the house by the police was a stack of penny dreadfuls. No further proof of their corrupting effect on young minds could be demanded.

The young minds didn't care. Under the guidance of publisher Edwin Brett, juvenile England was educated into the lives, adventures, and philosophies of such characters as Varney the Vampire, Black Rollo the Pirate, May Turpin—Queen of the Road and Jack-o'-the-Cudgel.

Impressionable youth was invited to witness The Dance of Death and The Boyhood Days of Guy Fawkes, The Headsman's Doom, and worse. And then there were The Wild Boys, who lived in London's sewers, and came out at night to encounter bodysnatching doctors, bare-breasted women, and thieves and murderers of every description. Originally published in 1866, an attempt to revive their adventures in 1877 actually led to a police action, and the series' suppression!

The most popular of all dreadfuls were, without doubt, the adventures of Black Bess, the perhaps suitably named Edward Viles's blood-and-thunder-

soaked recounting of the Turpin legend, drawn out over 254 weekly installments, and running from the spring of 1863–1868. Frequent reissues kept
it selling until well into the 1890s, by which time sales were estimated at
over two million.

Naturally, Viles denied his work had any bad influence over its readers,
going so far as to write, in the preface to the bound edition which appeared
in 1868, "[I]f anyone is weak-minded enough to be carried away by the idea
that a highwayman's career as depicted in these pages can be equalled in
reality at the present day, he must be an imbecile indeed."

But wasn't that precisely the point that the dreadfuls' opponents were
trying to make? That reading this degenerate filth could transform the
smartest man in the world into a raving, drooling fool?

And that includes admirers of the true, traditional Robin Hood.

Howard Piles it On

If there was any corollary to the depredations of the dreadfuls' authors;
any one writer who stood firm against the rising tide of sewage flooding
out of the penny press publishing houses, it was the American author and
illustrator Howard Pyle.

His *The Merry Adventures of Robin Hood of Great Renown in Nottinghamshire*
was published in 1883, a humbling, wholesome homily to all that is pure,
pristine, and upstanding about Robin Hood.

Once again, his inspiration is drawn from the ballads, but so beautifully
interwoven (both by the text and Pyle's charming illustrations) that each
one appears fresh—as indeed several of them might as well be. Mindful of
his juvenile audience, Pyle purposefully eschews the sometimes gratuitous
death count that Robin's usual actions were capable of causing (the fifteen
foresters he slaughtered as a youth, for example, are now reduced to just
one), and concentrates instead on the sheer heroism of the legend.

It is a world not too far removed from Scott's *Ivanhoe*, but one that will
also feel familiar to fans of the 2006 *Robin Hood* television series. There, too,
Robin is utterly averse to killing, although Pyle's work perhaps takes that
altruism a little too far.

Only one further killing is recorded at Robin's hand, and that falls when
Pyle turns his attention to the ballad "Robin Hood and Guy of Gisborne"—
in which the two men have no alternative but to battle to the death. Robin
wins the day, but even as he wipes the gore from his sword, we overhear
him musing:

This is the first man I have slain since I shot the King's forester in the hot days of my youth. I ofttimes think bitterly, even yet, of that first life I took, but of this I am as glad as though I had slain a wild boar that laid waste a fair country. Since the Sheriff of Nottingham hath sent such a one as this against me, I will put on the fellow's garb and go forth to see whether I may not find his worship, and perchance pay him back some of the debt I owe him upon this score.

Nevertheless, the appeal of Pyle's book, both to contemporary readers and the generations that have enjoyed it since, is clear. The life and adventures of Robin Hood are painted in bright, broad strokes, his actions

Fairbanks, as Robin, on the cover of a 1923 issue of *Photoplay* magazine.
Wikimedia Commons

unimpeachably heroic, his foes unmistakably black, and his world, the same chivalric utopia that *Ivanhoe* encouraged.

It is a landscape of stark simplicity, good and bad, right and wrong. We know, without an ounce of political awareness, that Robin stands for all that is true and honest in this world, and the sheriff represents all that isn't.

There is no allegory, no satire, no sense that, buried in the mists of time, some medieval grudge is still being played out. The stories, simply, are stirring fables, and even Pyle's choice of language—all but creaking beneath a surfeit of "thees" and "thous," "verilys" and "forsooths"—works within the context of the tales. A chapter or two into the book, and you don't even notice it any longer. But how jarring it is to then pick up a book in modern English.

Even in its most hackneyed form (which this, most assuredly, is), there is a shimmering beauty to what we can only call the pseudo-medieval tongue; one that captures all of the now-perceived romance and glory of the age— and this is true whatever the subject, whether it be Robin wooing Marian with the sweetest words at his disposal, or Little John shooting the sheriff in the ass . . .

> Little John twanged his bowstring with a shout, and when the Sheriff dashed in through the gates of Nottingham Town at full speed, a gray goose shaft stuck out behind him like a moulting sparrow with one feather in its tail. For a month afterward the poor Sheriff could sit upon nought but the softest cushions that could be gotten for him.

You see? Sheer poetry.

From Sherwood to Shenandoah

Robin Hood in America

allads and folk tales were Britain's first-ever export to the New World. They traveled in the memories and repertoires of the Pilgrims, and in the luggage of all the settlers and colonists who followed them.

When the British crown filled Virginia with transportees, songs were the only items that the prisoners brought with them. When the villagers of Roanoke gathered around the fire, the old ballads were what comforted them, reminders of the land they had left behind and, in a way, oases of familiarity as they struggled to understand the mysteries of their new home.

Across the eastern seaboard, where the British took root, so did their heritage; and when, in the late nineteenth century, Francis James Child began gathering up the folk songs of the British Isles, and paving the way for every subsequent explorer and collector, the vibrant new United States proved as fruitful a hunting ground as the musty old libraries of the mother country. Fully one-third of the ballads included in his monumental work were found to be familiar in the USA.

The British were not alone in bringing their heritage to their new home-land, of course. Alan Lomax, in his landmark *Folk Songs of North America*, wrote,

> Each group of settlers in the New World tried to establish a musical community like the one they had left in Europe. They dotted the map with little Swedens, little Lithuanias, little Italies and so on, while the music of Spain, Portugal, France, Great Britain, and West Africa spread over domains in the western hemisphere. Everywhere in the New World we find songs that were popular in the days when the colonists set sail . . .

The Original Cowboy

Robin Hood was, in some ways, a peculiar survivor. As Lomax continues, "[M]ost of the ballads which gained wide popularity in America have to do with sexual conflict viewed through feminine eyes"—he cites such glorious murder ballads as "Barbara Allen," "Lord Lovel," "The Elfin Knight," and "The Cruel Mother," and if we inspect the repertoires of the traditional singers who precipitated the early 1960s folk revival in the coffee houses of New York, Boston, and elsewhere, we readily find support for his claims.

No less than back in the British Isles, however, Robin Hood scarcely impacted on these repertoires. But he was present, regardless, and always had been, a hero not in the civilized homesteads of the eastern cities, but out in the wilds, among the men who scrapped for land and a living alike, among some of the continent's most inhospitable landscapes.

The superbly named Hermes Nye, a giant of the American folk scene throughout the 1950s, described himself as a professional Texan—one whose "sneaking fondness for the English things from Percy and Child" was especially excited "when I can find Texas versions"; and Robin Hood met that stipulation.

It is not hard to see why Robin Hood should appeal to these men, in those surroundings. Divorce the wild west and the gold camps from their Hollywood equivalents, and we discover a society that was clinging to even that loose designation by its fingertips.

In a community perched on what must have felt like the very edge of civilization, the law of the land was tenuous at best; "survival of the fittest" (or the craftiest, or the richest) was the only rule that mattered, and the alacrity with which those communities elevated the biggest and toughest men to legendary status—to whit, every cowboy hero you have ever heard of—is solid evidence of their need for role models, both in reality and in song.

Robin Hood might have inhabited a very different time and landscape, but his story was universal, regardless—once again, the little man taking on the world and winning.

His heyday may not have been long; those aforementioned local heroes and happenings would soon have displaced old Robin, once their own legends were set to music—Jessie James, the Texas Rangers, the Dying Cowboy, Charlie Quantrell.

But professional Texan Nye recorded versions of both "The Death of Robin Hood" and "Robin Hood's Golden Prize" in 1957; while the meeting of Robin Hood and Arthur a Bland, "Robin Hood and the Tanner," was still circulating in the former prison colony of Virginia as late as the 1920s, when it was incorporated into a volume of *Traditional Ballads of Virginia* by Arthur K. Davis, albeit with a little tweak to render it more relevant to its new surroundings:

> When Phoebus had melted the shackles of ice
> And likewise the mountains of snow
> Bold Robin Hood, that archer so good
> Went frolicking abroad with his bow

There are no mountains in Sherwood Forest.

Idylls of the Hood

Long before that, however, Robin Hood had transitioned out of the balladry of the settlers, and into more comfortable surroundings.

The teeming metropolises of New York, Boston, Philadelphia, and Charleston all hosted popular productions of Leonard McNally and William Shield's London hit *Robin Hood, or Sherwood Forest* before the end of the eighteenth century; and in July 1872, the musical burlesque *Robin Hood Or, The Maid That Was Arch, and the Youth That Was Archer* opened at the Academy of Music in New York, and (following its transfer to the Walker Theatre) remained on Broadway until the following May.

There were no further major productions of *Robin Hood* offered to the American public for close to two decades after that, but he rarely faded from view. Both Howard Pyle's *Merry Adventures* and Francis James Child's *The English and Scottish Popular Ballads* made their debuts during this interregnum—American authors who fascinated scholars and laymen alike with their treatment of the hero, and perhaps confirmed for the benefit of future historians that "merry olde England" was little more than a cypher for any society that felt the thrill of independence and freedom.

Indeed, it might be said that Robin Hood was now more popular in the United States than he was at home, a suggestion given further weight by the contrasting fortunes of the aforementioned Reginald De Koven and Harry B. Smith's musical, *Robin Hood: A Comic Opera*; and, shortly after, Alfred, Lord Tennyson's *The Foresters*.

Two Tales of Two Cities

A failure when it transferred to London in 1891, *Robin Hood* was contrarily a major hit from the moment it opened at the Chicago Opera House in June

1890. Indeed, not only did it repeat its success in New York the following year, the opera then enjoyed regular Broadway revivals throughout the first half of the last century, and was most recently performed in 2004, in the eminently capable hands of the Ohio Light Opera.

The production's plot was simple, effectively telling how Robin and his men set out to foil the sheriff's plan of marrying his nephew, Sir Guy of Gisborne, to Maid Marian—who is, of course, Robin's sweetheart. In the ensuing mayhem, Robin is captured and sentenced to death, but receives a last-minute reprieve from the returning King Richard, and all live happily ever after.

Of course, any musical is as much a vehicle for its songs as its plot, and *Robin Hood: A Comic Opera* had a real winner nestling within. "O Promise Me" had been written by De Koven, to lyrics by English poet Clement Scott, back in 1887; imported into *Robin Hood* to accompany Robin and Marian's eventual marriage, it then became a firm favorite among the country's newly-weds deep into the next century.

The success of *Robin Hood* in 1890–1891 was swiftly followed, in 1892, by another new production, in the form of Arthur Sullivan and Alfred, Lord Tennyson's *The Foresters*. And again, its London fortunes were in sharp contrast to its American prospects.

The opera had troubled beginnings. Tennyson and Sullivan wrote it in 1881, intending it as the successor to the poet's earlier *The Cup*. However, Henry Irving, proprietor of London's Lyceum Theatre, rejected it out of hand. Both his, and his theatre's, reputations were built upon some of the most sensational productions of the age; the venue's business manager, a young man named Bram Stoker, later based the appearance of his literary vampire Dracula on Irving's penchant for dramatically flowing black capes, while the Lyceum's 1888 production of *The Strange Case of Dr. Jekyll and Mr. Hyde* was so convincingly brutal that the lead actor, Richard Mansfield, was among the very first suspects in the hunt for Jack the Ripper!

The pastoral pleasures of *The Foresters*, its blithe blending of Robin Hood with the fairy denizens of Shakespeare's *A Midsummer Night's Dream*, simply could not compete with that.

In 1887, Tennyson tried again, this time offering the opera to the American actress Mary Anderson as a follow-up to her proposed production of, again, *The Cup*. She, too, turned it down, but her brother Joseph was less dismissive, particularly after noting the success of *Robin Hood—The Comic Opera*.

He recommended *The Foresters* to the impresario Augustin Daly, and by late 1891, arrangements were in place for the musical to debut on the New York stage in March 1892. It was instantly successful and the following spring, bedecked in all manner of flowery American plaudits, the show finally made it to the Lyceum Theatre in London—where all of Irving's original misgivings were borne out.

Tennyson's contributions to the legend of Robin Hood, *The Foresters*, was a major hit in 1890s New York.   *Wikimedia Commons*

Undeterred both by the so-recent death of Tennyson himself, or the monumental respect in which both of its authors were held, *The Foresters* was unanimously condemned for its tedium and simplistic storyline. The *London Times*, for example, pointed out the opera's "feebleness of dramatic conception" and "the author's inattention to the shaping of character," with the reviewer haughtily sniffing,

ARTHUR SULLIVAN
Mendelssohn Scholar, 1856

Arthur Sullivan, Tennyson's collaborator on *The Foresters*.   *Wikimedia Commons*

> The verdict to be passed upon *The Foresters*, which was last night brought to the test of a stage representation at Daly's Theatre, is that it is rather a pastoral poem than a play—a poem prettily set and nicely delivered—but lacking in the qualities distinctively belonging to the work of the born dramatist—namely, movement, clearness of characterization, and grip. As the literary merits of this, the last work of the late Lord Tennyson are already sufficiently known, there is no need to treat *The Foresters* from the poetic point of view.

The success, that same year, of another Arthur Sullivan–composed opera, a new production of *Ivanhoe* (libretto by Julian Sturgis) added further salt to the wounds. More than a century later, *Ivanhoe* remained a legend in London operatic circles, as *Opera News* magazine recalled in 2010:

> *Ivanhoe* was produced as the opening work in 1891 at Richard D'Oyly Carte's brand-new Royal English Opera House, now the Palace Theatre in London's Cambridge Circus. It enjoyed an impressive, unparalleled run of 155 consecutive performances (with a double cast), which no other grand opera to this day has equaled in its first outing. It had a sumptuous mounting, with hundreds of supers [*extras*] and lavish costumes and scenery by the decorative talents from the Savoy Theatre.

The Foresters, too, lived on in the memory, but so did its damning reputation. In his 1959 biography of Sir Arthur Sullivan, author Gervase Hughes was still wondering "how did the author of *The Idylls of the King* come to put his name to such puerile rubbish?"

American reviews of the opera, on the other hand, were as enthusiastic as its audiences.

A Broadway smash, *The Foresters* then enjoyed a successful seven-city tour, and is still regarded in the USA as Tennyson's greatest theatrical success—and the wellspring, perhaps, for the century-plus of subsequent Robin Hoods whose song-and-dancing is as vivid in 2015's *The Heart of Robin Hood* as it must have been in the very first Mayday amusements, more than half-a-millennium ago.

The American contribution to the overall legend, however, was still in its infancy. For a new power was gathering force on the fringes of the entertainment industry, and with its emergence, Robin Hood would ride forth into every home in the land.

Hood Goes to Hollywood (Silently, at First)

There is no greater indication of how just firmly Robin Hood has taken hold of the American imagination than his ubiquity on the silver screen.

The film industry in the United States was barely a decade old before Robin first rode into flickering black and white, since when over two dozen more interpretations have galloped out of the studios—a total greater than the related output of every other country in the world, which itself embraces productions from as far afield as Japan, Mexico, Italy, Brazil, and Germany, as well as the United Kingdom.

Understandably, this tally includes some truly dreadful efforts, as well as some bona fide classics, but the role has nevertheless entranced some of the best-known names in film history, from Douglas Fairbanks and Errol Flynn to Olivia de Havilland and Audrey Hepburn, from Walt Disney and Mel Brooks to Kevin Costner and Frank Sinatra.

Likewise, the stories and their settings have soared through time, from the twelfth century landscapes that we regard as "traditional," to the Chicago of the 1930s; and they have somersaulted in style as well, from drama to comedy, animation to musicals. Through them all, however, Robin Hood remains the same. The greatest hero ever known.

It was in 1908 that Robin Hood made his onscreen debut—first with a short English-made film, director Percy Stowe's *Robin Hood and his Merry Men*; and then, just months later, in the US-made *Robin Hood*.

Neither movie is in existence today—like the ballads of centuries before, the rate of attrition among early films was horrendous, with many more known to have been made than are still available to be watched, and more that we have no record of at all.

Thus we know little more about Stowe's movie than the fact that it was made by the director's own Claredon company and distributed by the period goliath Gaumont; that the screenplay was by Langford Reed, and that the plot revolved around Robin (and the freshly wooed Marian) forming an outlaw band in order to rescue a colleague from the gallows.

Even less has been preserved about its Stateside companion, however, beyond the fact it was made by the Kalem film company, and the suspicion that both movies were probably inspired to life by the recent success of a stage production of Alfred, Lord Noyes's *Sherwood*.

They were, however, only the first salvo.

Movie makers on both sides of the Atlantic were constantly seeking ever-more exciting heroes to satisfy the newborn industry's fast-burgeoning audience, and Robin and his ilk were seldom far from their thoughts.

The first three-reel movie ever made in the UK, in 1911, concerned the medieval Scots hero Rob Roy; and Sir Walter Scott's *Ivanhoe*, with its own connections to Robin, wasn't far behind it.

An American production, it starred King Baggot as the titular Ivanhoe, Walter Thomas as Robin Hood and Leah Baird as Rebecca, and was largely shot amid the gorgeous atmospheres of Chepstow Castle in Wales. (A British version of *Ivanhoe* also appeared around the same time; to avoid being confused with the US film, it was retitled *Rebecca the Jewess*.)

Robin's popularity in other media, of course, ensured the spotlight never strayed far from Sherwood Forest. Playwright John Drinkwater published *Robin Hood and the Pedlar* in 1912, the same year as Henry Gilbert's much-loved *Robin Hood and the Men of the Greenwood* appeared on bookshelves.

Ostensibly another retelling of the legend aimed at the children's market, it was hallmarked, somewhat controversially, by a firm grip on liberal politics.

The very first line of the preface . . . "Once upon a time, the great mass of English people were unfree" . . . is true, of course it is. But it also served as a reminder that Robin Hood's work might never be done, by pointing out that there were still English people unfreed today. It was the age, after all, of the Suffragettes, fighting and occasionally dying simply to convince the government to give the vote to women.

A precocious child reader, turning from the pages of Gilbert to the front page of the newspaper would have understood the need for a modern Robin.

Gilbert's Robin is recognizably that of the ballads. But his language is modern, the excitement unrelenting, and Robin emerges as a hero for the modern age, in action . . .

> Never was there a cruel deed done by some lord on his vassal but Robin exacted some recompense from the haughty knight; and when a poor man's land was invaded by a stronger, it was Robin's hidden archers who made the place too hot for any but the rightful owner to dwell upon it.

. . . and in appearance.

> His head of dark brown curls was covered by a velvet cap, at the side of which was stuck a short feather, pulled from the wing of a plover. His face, bronzed to a ruddy tan by wind and weather, was open and frank, his eyes shone like a wild bird's, and was as fearless and

noble. Great of limb, was he, and seemingly of a strength beyond his age, which was about twenty-five years. In one hand he carried a long-bow . . .

Even today, that description is instantly recognizable, and it would soon be seized upon by the movies.

Robin Hood—Outlawed hit the theatres in 1912. Starring A. Brian Plant as Robin and Ivy Martinek as Marian, this Charles Raymond–directed three-reeler introduced a new baddy to the legend, one Sir Hubert de Boissy (Jack Houghton), as he replaces Guy of Gisborne as Robin's rival for Marian's hand.

However, Gisborne was back that same year in the American-made *Robin Hood*, a movie version of Reginald De Koven's first theatrical treatment, produced by the Éclair Company in Fort Lee, New Jersey, and released on August 22, 1912. It stars Robert Frazer as Robin, Barbara Tennent as Marian, and Alec B. Francis as the Sheriff. (Fortunately, this movie still survives; a restored print was shown at the Museum of Modern Art in 2006.)

In 1913, one of the stories from Howard Pyle's *Merry Adventures* came to life in the plainly titled *Robin Hood* (released in the UK under the title *In the Days of Robin Hood*), which was partially made in the experimental two-color process known as Kinemacolor. The film was one of many classic stories produced by the Natural Colour Kinematograph Co. in England.

The innovation was certainly a major plus for the film—according to *Variety*, it was impossible not to be entranced by "the royal purple robes of office, to say naught of the trend of the yeoman and their women folk toward vivacious color effects and the picturesque and dashing bottle green costumes of the vagrant band."

In fact, forget the film, marvel at its production. "By reason of its cromatic qualities, the color filmed version of the story must supersede any rival black-and-white film covering the same subject." By which one assumes the reviewer ("Corb") intends Robin Hood in general, as opposed to in person. For it is not a Robin Hood movie per se.

Shot almost entirely on location in what remained of Sherwood Forest, *Robin Hood* is more concerned with Will Scarlet and his misadventures at the hands of the evil Baron Fitz Alvine, the scheming father of the lovely Lady Christabel (hitherto known as Allen a Dale's lady in Pierce Egan's novel).

It is the baron, outraged at Will's pursuit of his daughter, who has the young man outlawed, forcing him to take to the forest, where he meets with Robin (played by Harry Agar Lyons) and the rest of the Merry Men.

However, he is recaptured and sentenced to hang, thus precipitating the movie's climax, a heroic, and successful, rescue attempt.

California stood in for Nottingham in another 1913 production, *Robin Hood and Maid Marian*. This time the story drew upon the familiar tales of King Richard's secret visit to Nottingham, and the contest for the golden arrow. William Russell was Robin Hood, Gerda Holmes was Maid Marian, and John Dillon was the Sheriff of Nottingham.

The Swash is Buckled

Fairbanks and Flynn—the Merriest of Men

R obin Hood took something of a cinematic backseat over the next few years—as indeed did many facets of everyday life in Europe and the United States, as the Great War played out between 1914–1918, and the world then tried to settle back into some form of normalcy.

The Hollywood machine did not stop, of course, and a whole new generation of movie stars had arisen, with Douglas Fairbanks ranked among the mightiest of them all. Indeed, the title of his latest vehicle left nobody in any doubt as to the star's pulling power. Released in 1922, *Douglas Fairbanks in Robin Hood* (as the film was officially titled) was, quite simply, an unalloyed spectacular.

If any actor was born to play Robin Hood, it was Douglas Fairbanks. Pushing forty by the time cameras rolled, but possessed of a suave and youthful charm that exquisitely matched his tough guy demeanor, Fairbanks was born in Denver in 1883 and worked in theatre before joining Triangle Pictures in 1915, making his official debut in a screen adaptation of the 1913 Broadway play *The New Henrietta. The Lamb*, directed by W. Christy Cabanne, was co-written by pioneering director D. W. Griffith.

An affair with Mary Pickford established Fairbanks firmly as one-half of Hollywood's first true superstar couple, and he would soon be joining her among America's most highly paid actors (only Charlie Chaplin rivaled the pair's popularity and box-office draw).

In 1916 Fairbanks launched his own production company; in 1917 he published a self-help book; and in 1919, together with Pickford, Chaplin, and Griffith, formed the United Artists Corporation.

Tragedy struck in 1920, just months after Fairbanks and Pickford finally married—that October, his sister-in-law, actress Olive Thomas (married to Pickford's brother, Jack) died in Paris under what are still regarded

Douglas Fairbanks and his wife, Mary Pickford, the king and queen of
1920s Hollywood.   *Library of Congress, Prints & Photographs Division,*
ggbain.30610

as mysterious circumstances—she drank a glass of mercury bichloride, a
topical drug prescribed to her husband to ease the symptoms of syphilis.

The ensuing scandal shook the entire Pickford dynasty, but Fairbanks
remained unscathed, thanks at least in part to his latest cinematic brain-
wave—a series of movies that played to both his good looks and his physical
build. In 1920, Fairbanks invented the action hero.

He chose his parts well, and his costumes and settings even better. Even today it is hard not to thrill to the first in the sequence, *The Mark of Zorro*, or to its successor, *The Three Musketeers*.

Robin Hood was not Fairbanks's first choice for his next film—he was initially pondering *Romeo and Juliet*. Owen Wister's western *The Virginian* and Alexander Dumas's *Chico the Jester* were likewise possible follow-ups, only for all three to be rejected on what must seem very obvious grounds; they were not sufficiently action-packed for Fairbanks's reputation.

A remake of *Ivanhoe* was next on the list of possibilities, but Fairbanks shrugged that aside, and he initially gave his brother Robert's suggestion of Robin Hood short shrift as well.

But with his director friend Allan Dwan also enthusiastic about the outlaw, Fairbanks took the time to read the legends and, the deeper into the tales he got, the more he could see its appeal. On New Year's Day 1922, gathering together both friends and employees, the actor declared that his next movie would be *Robin Hood*, and would become the most lavish movie ever made. It would also become the most expensive (the budget approached a million bucks). But still, *Robin Hood* stands proud among the greatest of all cinematic retellings of the old story.

A large part of the overall expenditure was devoted to the set, constructed at the Pickford-Fairbanks Studio in Hollywood. Nothing less than an entire twelfth century Nottinghamshire village, and a vast castle to match, were called for, Designed by Wilfred Buckland and Frank Lloyd Wright, and constructed by a crew of five hundred men, the ninety-foot edifice was said to be the biggest structure built for a silent film—including the Babylon set for Griffith's 1916 epic *Intolerance*.

A working portcullis and drawbridge were installed, ingeniously powered by a gasoline engine. Lighting was largely confined to natural sunlight, directed by vast metallic reflectors. A full-sized moat was constructed, and lifelike armor, made from canvas and hemp added authenticity to the setting.

The ensuing sprawl—the castle alone towered ninety foot into the air—was so overwhelming that when he finally saw the completed thing, Fairbanks came perilously close to simply walking off the set and canceling the entire thing. There was no way, he felt certain, that any actor could not be swallowed up by the sheer immensity of the set.

Dwan, however, was not about to let go. For days he worked on Fairbanks, and finally convinced the actor with his own spot of dazzling stuntwork, leaping onto a fifty-foot drape that hung from the castle ceiling, and seeming to slide effortlessly down it, to the ground.

It looked great, it looked dramatic, it looked precisely like the kind of stunt that Fairbanks's reputation demanded. And it continued to do so, even after Dwan pulled back the curtain to reveal the great metal slide that was positioned behind it.

If the set was amazing, the casting was superlative. Fairbanks, of course, played the title role, with Enid Bennett as Lady Marian Fitzwalter, and Paul

Robin (Douglas Fairbanks) and Marian (Enid Bennett) share a private moment in the 1922 silent movie.   *Photofest*

Dickey as Sir Guy of Gisborne—who we meet at the very outset of the film, coming second best to the Earl of Huntingdon at a jousting contest. An army of extras and plentiful Merry Men completed a cast that sometimes resembled the population of a small city.

Based on a screenplay by Fairbanks himself, writing under the pseudonym of Elton Thomas, the movie initially sticks with at least a degree of tradition, with the earl appointed King Richard's (Wallace Beery) second-in-command as he prepares to depart for the Holy Land.

He has not been there long, however, when he receives a message from Marian, telling him of all that has been wrought in England during the king's absence—the greed of Prince John, the sheriff's reign of terror, and the crushing of the people.

The earl takes his news to the king and asks that he be allowed to return home to try and right the wrongs. Richard, however, refuses to believe a word he says, preferring to assume that the earl has lost his nerve. (A similar confrontation arises in the 1970s *Legend of Robin Hood* TV series, although this time, it takes place on the eve of the king's departure.)

Huntingdon continues with his plans regardless, but he does not get far. Prince John had already dispatched Gisborne to the Holy Land on a mission of his own—to ensure that neither king nor earl return to England in one piece.

Learning of the earl's intention of fleeing, Gisborne has him imprisoned as a deserter; now the earl needs to escape, too, before he can make his way home and, rejoicing in his new status as an outlaw, takes up the mantle of Robin Hood.

The action is all but non-stop; Fairbanks does everything short of swing from trees and leap from rigging, a swashbuckler of the very finest, and most knightly mettle. Raids and rescues, dramatic fights and feats of derring-do, scaling castle walls and flying from buttresses. It may be a silent film, intended to be accompanied by a live orchestra in the large cinema palaces, and an organ in the s theatres, but one can imagine the noisy excitement of audiences, whooping and cheering their way through the spectacle.

The movie is not without its idiosyncrasies, however.

Victorious in the opening joust, the earl is visibly discomfitted, and not a little fidgety, when he is obliged by the watching king to kneel before Marian to receive the ceremonial crown. "Exempt me, sire," he pleads. "I am afeared of women."

But worse is to follow. King Richard, of course, has never heard such nonsense in his life and, having first laughed uproariously through the earl's cringing performance, he unleashes a veritable bevy of beauties onto the reluctant nobleman—who by this point better resembles one of the ungallant gallants who people *Monty Python and the Holy Grail* than the hero of the free world.

Surrounding Huntingdon, the women—young and beautiful every one—proceed to paw and pursue him with such vigor that he has but one means of escape, leaping into the moat, only to surface on the other side and find himself confronted by . . . "another woman!"

The king has not finished with him yet, though. At the feast that evening, Richard gathers together the most nubile young ladies in the hall and pledges "a castle and lands to the maid who wins him." He then has the earl tied up, and leaves the ladies to do their worst.

It's an astonishing sequence, but its consequences are vital. Apparently cured of his fear of females, Huntingdon immediately falls in love with Marian . . . just as he is about to leave the country.

It's a long movie—we are thirty minutes in already; and another hour must pass before Huntingdon returns to England to become Robin Hood. Which leaves just forty minutes in which the movie's title character can strut his stuff, often by means of flashback.

But just because the movie was over, that did not mean Fairbanks would abandon the part. When *Robin Hood* had its premiere in New York in October, Fairbanks was there with his bow-and-arrow; and when a reporter suggested he demonstrate his skill with it, Fairbanks did not let him down. From the roof of the Ritz Hotel, he pointed out a gargoyle sitting at least a hundred yards away, took aim, and hit it on the first attempt.

A second arrow was not so true, however. Fairbanks let fly and the shaft soared off into the distance. It was later discovered in a local emergency room, being removed form the backside of a passing Polish immigrant.

Douglas Fairbanks in Robin Hood ended the year ranked among the most successful movies ever made, and certainly Fairbanks's own box-office best. It also uncorked a string of further Robin Hood movies, all hoping to emulate the success of the star's, occasionally with an unexpected twist.

One such twist was provided by the humorist Will Rogers, in a 1924 short he made for producer Hal Roach. In *Big Moments from Little Pictures*, Rogers includes a brilliant sendup of Fairbanks as Robin Hood. Shown cavorting in the countryside with his Merry Men, Rogers-as-Robin effortlessly leaps backward onto the branch of a tree (with the help of reverse-motion pho-tography) and then finds himself unable to climb back down. The Merry Men soliticiously provide him with a stepladder and assist him as he gingerly makes his way back to terra firma. No one, it is said, laughed louder or longer at this parody than Fairbanks himself.

Director Clarence Bricker's *Robin Hood Jr.* was the first of several movies to document the activities of the outlaw as a lad, while *Lady Robin Hood* served up precisely what it said on the tin, by delivering Evelyn Brent in the title role, with the barely known Boris Karloff as the Sheriff of Nottingham. Equally intriguingly, the action was set in then-present day California, under the reign of a wicked governor!

Of course, there was still room for traditional tales. In the UK, *Robin Hood's Men* was one installment within a series of two-reel movies titled *Fights Through the Ages*; and 1932 saw John J. Thompson and Aileen Marson star as Robin and Marian in another short, straightforward adventure, *The Merry Men of Sherwood*.

In the US, MGM had tentative plans for a Robin Hood musical starring Jeanette MacDonald and Nelson Eddy; and there was a western called *Robin Hood of El Dorado.* There was even a Japanese offering in 1924, directed by Banshô Kanamori and starring Shinpei Takagi in *Robinfuddo no yume* (*Robin Hood's Dream*).

And in print, the children's author Richmal Crompton was inspired to introduce Robin Hood to the world inhabited by young "Just William" Brown, the archetypal eleven-year-old whose devotion to mischief and menacing ultimately spread across thirty-eight books published over forty-eight years, 1922–1970.

William and his gang of like-minded delinquents, so aptly known as the Outlaws, had already romped raucously through five collections of stories when *William the Conqueror* was published in 1926, and in every single one, William always started out with the best of intentions, only for them to fall into inevitable disarray and disgrace every time.

And so it is in *William and the Philanthropist*, when a rainy afternoon spent reading a book about Robin Hood inspires William to lead his men in emulation of the noble medieval hero.

> "Let's get guns an' shoot all the rich people," said Ginger ferociously.
>
> "Yes," said William scornfully, "an' then get put in prison. No, we've either gotter find some—some unfathomable woods where we can attack the travelers an' no-one's ever able to find us, or else do it all in secret . . . like robbers do. D'you think robbers walk up to people with guns an' shoot them straight off, cause if you do, let me tell you they don't. There wun't be any sense in it, would there, Ginger?"
>
> "I dunno," said Ginger . . .

They decide, in the end, to adopt stealth. Each one of them will steal something of value from a rich person, and give it to a poor person.

And so they do. With inevitable, chaos-strewn consequences.

Enter the Errol

The misplaced heroics of William Brown notwithstanding, it would be 1938 before Robin Hood was finally able to step out from beneath Fairbanks's shadow, in the guise of perhaps the only man who *could* out buckle Dougie's swash—Errol Flynn.

Like Fairbanks, Flynn came to the role already a full-formed action hero. Twenty-six years Fairbanks's junior, the Australian-born actor made his homeland debut in a 1933 production of *Mutiny on the Bounty*, before moving to England to work in repertory theatre.

He quickly broke into the local movie industry, starring in the crime thriller *Murder at Monte Carlo* for Warner Bros.; then, still under contract to that company, he relocated to Hollywood in 1935.

He immediately made his mark. Stepping effortlessly into the now aging (early fifties!) Fairbanks swashbuckling shoes, Flynn was the runaway star of the pirate epic *Captain Blood*, and quickly followed through with the Crimean war story *The Charge of the Light Brigade* and Mark Twain's English historical *The Prince and the Pauper*.

The Adventures of Robin Hood was next.

Again, it was destined to become an expensive offering. Shot in Technicolor, at $2 million it was the costliest film Warner Bros. had yet made. But the critics flocked (and still flock) to proclaim it the best Robin Hood of all time, and it certainly captured all the action and excitement that made the original ballads and stories so remarkable, with lashings of period charm and romance to round out the action.

And again, its leading man was a revelation. James Cagney had originally been earmarked for the title role, which itself could have emerged a fascinating piece of casting.

Plans for that movie had been laid back in 1935, coincidentally around the same time as the Canadian newspaper the *Toronto Telegram* launched the comic strip *Robin Hood and Company*. But whereas the newsprint Robin would live to fight for five years' worth of adventures (and was then reborn in comic book form until 1946), his celluloid twin seemed destined to failure. Cagney walked out on the project following a dispute with the studio, and with the script still only half-written; and though we ponder curiously whether Robin might ever have called his opponents a dirty rat (not that Cagney ever uttered that phrase), perhaps his legacy had a lucky escape.

Cagney, after all, was Cagney, no matter which part he was playing—indeed, his main interest in the role was as a respite from the criminal characters and general lowlifes that he was traditionally lumbered with. But there was also good reason why he was so frequently offered those roles. Because few people could imagine him playing any others.

Douglas Fairbanks Jr, too, was sounded out for the role, but turned it down apparently without a second thought—presumably for very obvious reasons. It was hard enough to carve out his own unique reputation while bearing the same name as his immortal father. How much more difficult would it be if he started remaking the old man's movies?

Flynn, on the other hand, *became* Robin Hood, while Olivia de Havilland was a shoo-in for Marian, if only because she and Errol had already made two movies together, and were fast shaping up as one of Hollywood's favorite screen couples.

Basil Rathbone, better remembered today for his string of Sherlock Holmes movies, played Sir Guy of Gisborne and proved that the great

Robin (Errol Flynn) and Sir Guy (Basil Rathbone) face off in the classic 1938 movie.   *Photofest*

detective's icy demeanor, cunning intelligence and sharp tongue were as cutting in the hands of a baddie as a goodie (he, too, had played opposite Flynn before, in *Captain Blood*); Claude Rains made a magnificent Prince John; and there was even a look back at the Fairbanks movie, when Alan Hale Sr. was invited to reprise his Little John.

Two directors oversaw the movie; William Keighley, concentrating on the outdoor shooting, Michael Curtiz working with the in-studio sequences, while the movie's locations included a couple of spots that the Fairbanks movie had utilized sixteen years earlier.

Costuming and sets were as lavish as they ought to have been, and when the Academy Awards came in, it was these that best distinguished *The Adventures of Robin Hood*. Nominated for best picture, it lost out to Capra's *You Can't Take It With You*. But Best Art Direction, Best Film Editing, and Best Original Score would all be lining Robin's mantelpiece before the evening was out.

And yes. If you think you recognize Marian's horse, you probably do. It's Trigger, singing cowboy Roy Rogers's immortal mount.

No less than its greatest predecessor, *The Adventures of Robin Hood* was played . . . not for laughs, but for family fun. It's a romp, littered with sparkling dialogue ("You speak treason," says Marian; "Fluently," replies Robin), but its action scenes are fabulous, Flynn pulling out every stunt in his repertoire to ensure the audience is never less than spellbound. Even the soppy bits are brilliant.

The movie does take some liberties, of course; echoing *Ivanhoe* and the legends of Hereward the Wake, it is concerned not only with robbing from the rich, giving to the poor and riding through the glen, but also with recreating the conflict between subjugated Saxons and conquered Normans—a warlike scenario that predicted, and was perhaps even intended to warn of, that which would soon be playing out for real across Europe.

Although World War Two was still a nightmare yet to happen, and politicians on both sides of the imminent conflict continued to speak reassuringly of peace, the storm clouds were gathering across the continent.

Almost precisely two years after *The Adventures of Errol Flynn* played out its star-studded premiere, Hitler's Germany rolled into Belgium, France, Luxembourg, and the Netherlands, having already occupied Poland, Norway, and Denmark.

In each of those lands, resistance groups would form and fight back, as ferociously as the Saxons ever battled the Normans—although one might pause to consider a most singular irony. In Robin's time, the Saxons were the good guys; in 1940, their descendants were the belligerent Germans. (Saxony, the earlier people's original homeland, is a region of Germany.)

Fighting their fight with distinctive black arrows (thus acknowledging a debt to another literary classic, Robert Louis Stevenson's *The Black Arrow*), Flynn's outlaws are again ranged against a beastly Sheriff of Nottingham, and there could have been no sharper thorn in his backside. As another of his henchmen, Sir Geoffrey, complains to Gisborne, "[O]ur men can't even lay a hot iron to the eyes of a tax dodger without getting a black arrow in the throat! It's an outrage."

A number of movies from this immediate pre-war period do, in their own way, reflect upon the growing unease across the Atlantic; and many real-life guerilla groups and freedom fighters have adopted their own signature weapon, or method of killing, so that their handiwork will always be instantly identifiable.

But rarely is either portrayed with such aplomb as it is rendered here.

It is this same dash and verve that ensures the movie's continued freshness. So much of the legend is almost monotonously familiar today—one could, without even glancing at the script, outline the highlights of any upcoming Robin Hood movie or TV show.

It was little different in 1938. Armed with just a passing familiarity with any of the past movies or plays, novels or ballads, audiences of the day *knew* they would see Sir Guy courting Marian; Robin and Little John battling it out on the bridge; the archery tournament (and the climactic arrow splitting); Friar Tuck carrying Robin across a stream on his back.

But Flynn and company ensured that all were played out with such verve that each one felt brand new.

The movie is set during the period when King Richard was in captivity, with Prince John and the High Sheriff of Nottingham scheming to persuade Leopold V to keep him that way.

Sir Robin of Locksley leads the resistance, accompanied by a growing band of followers—Much first, then Will Scarlet, and so on. Rousingly, they bind themselves to a solemn oath, to fight until England is free, and to do so with all the gallantry they can muster.

> Do you, the freemen of the forest, take oath to despoil the rich only, to feed the hungry, clothe the naked, and shelter the old and the sick, and to protect all women, Norman or Saxon, rich or poor?

Against their noble plans, Sir Guy of Gisborne seems to have taken an utterly contrary oath—to fight until the entire country is draped beneath a pall as black as his own heart. His love of Marian, of course, is his undoing; she plays him along with all the guile and wiles at her disposal, while delivering a constant stream of information to Sherwood Forest.

In the midst of all this, Richard finally returns to discover for himself precisely what his perfidious little brother has been up to.

He and his men are disguised as pilgrims, but of course they are recognized by one of John's allies, the Bishop of the Black Canons, who hastens to tell his master. A knight, Dickon Malbete, is dispatched to kill the king before anybody else catches sight of him, but Marian overhears the plotting and attempts to get a message to Robin. At which point, she is unmasked as a spy by Gisborne.

He has her arrested, unaware that she had already confided the plot to her nurse, Bess, who is in turn involved with Much. So it is Beth who sends the message, and it is Much who finds and kills the assassin.

But now we are moving into the movie's final sequence—Robin, reunited with his king, leading his men into the castle; a great battle scene as they fight for control of the building, and a climactic clash between Robin and Gisborne, one of the greatest sword fights ever seen on film.

Gisborne is killed, his colleagues are exiled, and Robin is made Baron of Locksley and Earl of Sherwood. He and Marian wed, and Richard resumes his interrupted rule.

It was Claude Rains who is credited with conceiving the movie's climax—or, at least, in ensuring that the film would end with "a slam-bang hell of a battle, or something equally spectacular—and expensive."

Early drafts of the script planned for the film to begin with Robin and Sir Guy jousting, an echo, of course, of the Fairbanks film. Rains, in a much-circulated memo, objected furiously:

> The jousting tournament can never be anything but a prologue which, if done with the magnificence [envisaged], will have the disastrous effect of putting the climax of he picture at the beginning—and I'll be goddamned if that is a good construction dramatically. . . . The Fairbanks picture, in order to live up to its tournament fade-in, had to ring in the whole goddamned Crusades; and a light taste of the real Robin Hood story was dragged in a tag at the end to justify the use of the name.

Rains's condemnation is harsh, but it's also somewhat accurate. *The Adventures of Robin Hood* restored Robin to center page.

How could he ever have strayed away from it?

Hammer and Sword

The Endless Cinema Show

It is, perhaps, surprising that there should have been no Robin Hood films made throughout the duration of World War II. The movie industry by no means ground to a halt while hostilities were underway, and escapism remained just as popular as ever—if not more so, as Basil Rathbone proved with the continuing success of his Sherlock Holmes escapades, and Flynn with such heart-pounding delights as *Santa Fe Trail*, *They Died With Their Boots On*, *Desperate Journey*, and *Objective, Burma!*

Nevertheless, Sherwood lay largely silent through the war years, with the sound of arrows, staves, and swords only returning once peace had befallen the rest of the world.

In 1946, Columbia Pictures' production of *The Bandit of Sherwood Forest* saw Cornel Wilde take on the mantle of liberator and hero. As the movie opens, twenty years have passed since Robin Hood first haunted the forest, and the man in tights (Russell Hicks) is growing old. It is his son, Robert Hood, who must now fight the good fight, in an England ravaged by the aged Lord Regent, William of Pembroke.

History is not especially well served by the choice of villain, although the background is relatively sound.

King John *was* dead—according to legend, he was finally taken down by the "surfeit of lampreys" he consumed at a feast; and Pembroke *had been* elected regent, to safeguard the realm until John's rightful successor, nine-year-old Henry III, was old enough to rule in his own right.

It is also true that the barons who had been so unruly throughout the last years of John's reign remained fractious, all the more so after the pope annulled the Magna Carta in 1216, and it is into this fray that two generations of Hood now wade, with reality distorted to portray Pembroke as a scheming fiend who not only personally withdrew Magna Carta, but who also imprisoned young King Henry.

In other words, here comes the new enemy, same as the old enemy.

For all its historical faults, it's an entertaining movie. Bereft of the need to recycle the old story, it revels in the chance to tell some new ones, with *Variety*'s review explaining that

> it's a costume western, in effect, offering the fictional escapades of . . . a hard-riding, hard-loving hombre who uses his trusty bow and arrow to right injustice and tyranny back in the days of feudal England. . . . With his longbow, sword and trusty horse, Wilde proves himself more than a match for the villains, saves the young king's life . . . and wins true love and a knighthood.
>
> There is a concentration of chases and "they went that-a-way" flavor about the doings . . . *[but]* all that indicates a feature [that] will find the most favor among juvenile patrons.

And so it did, and with such success that not only would another son of Robin Hood star in *Rogues of Sherwood Forest* (1950), with John Derek taking the lead role; but the outlaw gained a daughter, Deering, and she, too, would soon be taking center stage, in the contrarily titled *Son of Robin Hood* (1958)—the misleading title intended, of course, to preserve the movie's greatest shock until the story is ready to give it away. June Laverick plays the title role with delightful gusto.

There was even a new comic-book adventure, within the so-fondly remembered *Classics Illustrated* series, but another conflict was looming, one which would soon be offering Hollywood the fight of its life.

Television was coming, slowly at first and tentatively. But its overlords were as ambitious as any silver screen mogul, and soon their attentions turned to Robin Hood, too. After almost a half-century of having Robin Hood to itself, and all but extinguishing both literary and theatrical competition, the movies would soon be having to share.

But not yet. The first attempt to transfer Robin's stories to the small screen, *The Tales of Robin Hood* in 1951, with Robert Clarke in the title role, met with such a lack of enthusiasm that it never got past the pilot phase—which itself was released to the theatres to meet scarcely any more enthusiasm.

So the movie houses just got on with it.

Miss Robin Hood

In 1948, Jon Hall and Patricia Morison starred in *Prince of Thieves*, effectively retelling the story of Allen a Dale's love for the Lady Christabel—and offering connoisseurs another glimpse of Alan Hale Sr.'s portrayal of Little John, more than a quarter of a century after his first.

Four years later, a female Robin returned in *Miss Robin Hood*, a British effort that not only successfully replanted the concept of Robin in the present day, it did so via the imaginative medium of a newspaper comic strip.

"Miss Robin Hood," the strip in question, concerns the adventures of its titular heroine and a gang of teenaged girls who spend their time robbing banks and then distributing the proceeds to the poor—which, in early fifties England, was a sizable chunk of the population.

The country was still struggling to rebuild from the war, rationing was still in force, the cities were still littered with decade-old bomb sites, and many of those who lost their homes due to enemy action were still housed in varying degrees of temporary accommodation.

Miss Robin Hood's attempts to right a few of the most basic wrongs would undoubtedly have attracted a lot of supporters.

Unfortunately, the newspaper's publishers were not among them, and so "Miss Robin Hood" was canceled and its writer, Henry Wrigley (Richard Hearne) was out of a job. At which point he was head-hunted by one of the strip's most ardent fans, the aging director of an orphanage in the London suburb of Hampstead, Miss Honey (played by the redoubtable Margaret Rutherford).

It's not a conventional job offer, though. She wants Miss Robin Hood to ride again, with Wrigley himself in the title role, and the orphanage as the recipient of his ill-gotten gains.

English films of this era are frequently bunched together beneath the overall banner of "Ealing" films, out of deference to the country's leading period filmmaker, located at Ealing Green in west London. Despite a cast that featured many of that studio's favorite characters (Rutherford, Sid James, Kenneth Connor, Reg Varney, Doris Hare, James Robertson Justice), *Miss Robin Hood* was *not* an Ealing production and, as such, has tended to fall through the historical cracks somewhat; all concerned made so many movies that are more fondly remembered, after all.

Reviews were not spectacular, either—the *New York Times* described *Miss Robin Hood* as "just a bit too labored—too fatuous—to be continuous fun." But Rutherford's Miss Honey, "a good-natured looney" as the *Times* review continued, is one of her finest cinematic creations, and a script by Patrick Campbell and Val Valentine is loaded with precisely the kind of laughs that its cast (a who's who of British comedy, after all) were adept at drawing out.

In fact, it's a terrific film, and if it steps away from the traditions of Robin Hood himself, that's not necessarily a bad thing. As is made clear elsewhere in this book, every era demands a Robin Hood of its own (even the future—check out the 1960s animated series *Rocket Robin Hood*).

Some are just fortunate enough to find one. Or more.

Enter Disney

For whatever reason, 1952 saw a slew of Robin Hood–related movies, with Robert Taylor and Elizabeth Taylor's remake of *Ivanhoe* being joined by the

Robert Clarke, as Robin, in *The Tales of Robin Hood and His Merrie Men* (1952), filmed in England, was the second full-length live-action Disney adventure story, the first being *Treasure Island* (1950).   *Photofest*

Disney studios' first stab at the tale, the very sensibly named *The Story of Robin Hood and his Merrie Men.*

Often overlooked in favor of (or, more accurately, overshadowed by) the same studio's animated classic of two decades later, *The Story of . . .* was very much cast from the same mold as the Fairbanks and Flynn movies, a well-produced, extravagantly budgeted and expertly cast romp through the clichés of Merrie Englande, but so magnificently rendered that you barely notice that you've seen it all before—the archery contest, the capture of the sheriff, the rescue of Will Stutely, the meetings with Little John and Friar Tuck, the robbed rich and fed poor.

Richard Todd is another in the growing sequence of dramatically dashing Robins, Joan Rice a delightfully spirited Marian, and there is no attempt to sugarcoat the reality of the original stories—when one of the sheriff's most feared henchmen, Red Gill, shoots Robin's father in the back (the penalty for refusing to swear loyalty to the loathsome creature), Robin unhesitatingly kills him in return.

Later, the sheriff is crushed to death by his own castle drawbridge, truly one of the most imaginative ends ever to befall the character, and all a very far cry from the treatment the legend would receive from the same studio in 1973.

Walt Disney's *Robin Hood* was not the first time the story had been rendered either in animation or, for that matter, an animal nation. Back in 1939, Warner Bros, portrayed Robin as a squirrel in the cartoon short *Robin Hood Makes Good.* He was that well-known duck Daffy in, of course, *Robin Hood Daffy,* and he even shares a stage with Bugs Bunny ("you long-eared knave!") in 1949's *Rabbit Hood,* set in a Nottingham so violently opposed to poaching that one of the signs reads "not even eggs." Hood, incidentally, is portrayed by Errol Flynn, cunningly clipped from the 1938 movie . . . but don't tell Bugs that.

"Naah, don't be silly. It couldn't be him."

No it couldn't, because in Disney's world, Robin is a fox (except when he disguises himself as a stork to enter the archery competition), and Marian a vixen. Little John is a bear, Friar Tuck is a badger, Allen a Dale is a rooster, the sheriff is a wolf, Prince John is a lion, and so forth through the forest. We meet a snake named Sir Hiss, a couple of vultures called Trigger and Nutsy, and the captain of the guard is a crocodile. And it's a tribute to the studio's genius that not only do we accept these substitutions, we can also see why those creatures were selected.

Although the studio's animators had visited English legend in the past, with 1963's superlative Arthurian epic *The Sword in the Stone,* Disney had not initially intended to make a Robin Hood movie.

Rather, delving deep elsewhere within the realm of medieval folklore, Reynard the Fox was the studio's first choice, the tale of a cunning and cruel trickster who spends his time scheming new ways of taking advantage of the other animals in the forest. A wealth of folk tales have grown up around him, the earliest hailing from the Franco-German region of Alsace-Lorraine, and dating back to the eleventh century, but quickly spreading across western Europe.

By the end of the twelfth century, Reynard's legend was being compared (by the period French author Pierre de St. Cloud) to those of Homer's Paris and Helen, the Arthurian hero Tristan, and Chrétian de Troyes's Yvain, the Knight of the Lion, and while it seems clear today that Reynard's tales were

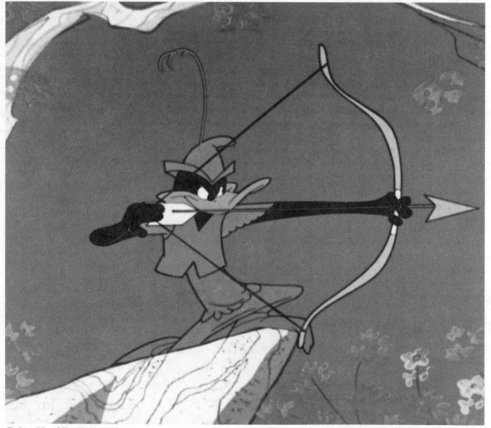

Robin Hood Daffy (1958), starring Daffy Duck, one of the less predictable onscreen Robins to have perpetuated the legend in the twentieth century.   *Photofest*

largely intended as satires upon the events and people of the age, nevertheless his popularity was boundless.

But was he suitable material for a Disney movie? Apparently not. The
fox was retained, but his identity and motives underwent a 180-degree
turn. No longer a trickster (unless it was the sheriff or the prince who were
being tricked), no longer cunning or cruel (ditto), the vulpine Robin was
debonair, charming, loyal, and loving.

And he gets the girl . . . or the vixen . . . at the end.

The Hammer and the Bow

What hindsight regards as one of the most unexpected entrants into the
world of Robin Hood took its bow in 1954, when Britain's now-legendary
Hammer Studios released its first Robin Hood movie.

Robin could be a sly old fox when he needed to, but only Disney gave him the physique
to match.   *Photofest*

Though it is more than forty years since the studio could last be relied upon to pump out new movies, nevertheless Hammer remains synonymous with a very specific kind of production. It specialized in horror, exquisite bloodbaths of B-movie sensation, in equal parts gory, tacky, sexy, silly, chilling, and childish. Dracula, Frankenstein, the wolfman and the mummy were recurrent motifs, celluloid corridors stalked by witches, weirdos, and gloriously demented scientists.

Yet Hammer also maintained a stable of less gruesome fare; in fact, to the average filmgoer of the 1940s and early 1950s, Hammer Films was one of those shoestring movie studios whose name really didn't mean much. It would be 1955 before the studio turned its attention to horror. Prior to that, it just made movies.–

Not very memorable ones, either. The studio's name might register somewhere in the credits of a medium-maudlin B-picture, *Sporting Love* or *The Bank Messenger Mystery, Who Killed Van Loon?* or *We Do Believe In Ghosts*, but Hammer's hottest properties at that time were the ones they borrowed from the radio, special agent *Dick Barton* and policeman *PC 49*.

Radio dramas were exceedingly popular in those years before television was switched on across the UK, and putting faces and pictures to adventures that had hitherto existed only in audio was definitely a step in the right financial direction.

So, it turned out, was making a big-screen version of a show that *had* been screened on TV, but which reached only a fraction of its potential audience because . . . well, because only a fraction of its potential audience had a TV.

The Quatermass Experiment, written by sci-fi author Nigel Kneale, was one of the television hits of 1953. Six episodes were broadcast, but they were filmed live and were never to be seen again—at the time, the BBC had no reliable method of recording its own output.

Media coverage of the broadcast, however, was widespread and open-armed; Quatermass, a grumpy scientist fixated on establishing Britain as the leaders of the race into space, was widely proclaimed a new hero for the age, a resourceful near-genius who epitomized the country's own growing romance with technology. And he was not going to let any scary old alien invader ruin his plans.

If ever a TV show demanded an instant movie remake, it was *The Quatermass Experiment*. Or Xperiment, as Hammer retitled it once the British Board of Film Censors had decreed it could only be screened to over-eighteens, and saddled it with an X certificate.

But Professor Quatermass was not the only small-screen icon Hammer had its eye on. Also airing in 1953, in March (a few months before *Quatermass* invented "must-see TV"), the BBC aired its take on Robin Hood, a series of six thirty-minute episodes starring Patrick Troughton (a future *Doctor Who*) as Robin, David Kossoff (later renowned as a religious broadcaster) as the sheriff and Kenneth Mackintosh as Little John.

Targeted at the children's market, *Robin Hood* has likewise long since vanished from this world; television, in those earliest days, was regarded as ephemeral, instant gratification. Like a concert or a theatrical performance in the days before cellphones became an instant movie camera, you either watched a show "live" or you didn't see it at all.

So the cast of Robin Hood would gather as if for a stage production, speak their words and act their parts, and the television audience watched them as they did so. And when the last note of the theme music faded away, that was it. It would never return. Just one episode of this first Robin Hood series is known to survive, crudely recorded for reference using the only available makeshift equipment, although it is not, sadly, the one that most people have heard of.

In a 1973 interview, Troughton recalled,

> In one scene we had back projection . . . it was a picture of the forest, you see. And on this occasion we'd got a film crew to do the back projection and I don't think they quite realized that we were live on television. Anyway we started the scene . . . and we turned around and the forest had come in sideways, and all the trees were that way round instead of that way round. And then there was more crashing and banging and the screen went blank, and then all the trees came up right and we had to go on playing.

It was a popular show, though, and the following year saw Hammer release *The Men of Sherwood Forest*. It was never intended as a direct adaptation of the television series—a different writer, Allan MacKinnon; a different cast (Don Taylor was Robin Hood); and a different target audience also stood to separate the movie from its small-screen cousin. But certainly the inspiration was there, as it would be again in 1961, when a second Hammer Hood film rose in the wake of a second TV series.

Regardless of its origins, and its distance from what would become the studio's *raison d'etre*, 1954's *The Men of Sherwood* was a significant movie for Hammer—their first-ever color film, and the first suggestion that British actors could buckle their swashes as dashingly as their American counterparts. Or not . . . Don Taylor, playing Robin Hood, was born in

Pennsylvania, and had long since cut his Hollywood choppers on the likes of *Song of the Thin Man*, *The Naked City*, *Father of the Bride*, and *The Flying Leathernecks*. He wasn't the biggest star name in movies, but he played the part like the greatest star of all.

Robin is already an outlaw, and already bedeviling the sheriff as the movie opens, but the ante is swiftly increased. A messenger has been robbed and killed as he passed through Sherwood Forest, and his assailants were masked outlaws. Of course Robin Hood gets the blame, but equally naturally, Robin knows the truth. The messenger was carrying news about King Richard, news that the sheriff did not want to become public. Now the search is on for the real murderers.

It's a simple plot, but it worked well; sufficiently, in fact, for Hammer to return to the same theme a few years later.

Hammer's second visit to the land of Robin Hood, *The Sword of Sherwood, Forest*, arrived in 1960, and this time it *was* a direct successor to a television series—the genre-busting Anglo-American *The Adventures of Robin Hood*, whose Richard Greene had held sway over screens on both sides of the Atlantic since 1955 (see chapter 23).

Greene alone of the established cast appeared in this new movie, although that is not to say it was lacking in the casting department—not with Peter Cushing, already firmly established among the masters of Hammer's now-blossoming horror line, appearing as the Sheriff of Nottingham.

Cushing was born on May 26, 1913, in the small town of Kenley, Surrey; was raised in Dulwich, south London, and then Purley, back in the county of Surrey, where home was a striking Art Deco house built by his Quantity Surveyor father on St. James Road.

Originally pointed towards a career in his father's line, Cushing won a scholarship to the Guildhall School of Music and Drama, worked in local rep for a few years and then, audaciously, took himself off to Hollywood to become a star. He landed a role in *The Man In The Iron Mask* in 1939, and also appeared alongside Laurel and Hardy as a student in *A Chump at Oxford*. But it was with that other great man of the British stage, Laurence Olivier, that Cushing made his mark, appearing as Osric in 1948's *Hamlet*.

It would have been easy for Cushing to fall into a kind of anonymity around now, just one more actor whose face was oftentimes more familiar than his name, thanks to the amount of work he was undertaking. Nevertheless, Cushing established himself.

In 1952, a BBC production of *Pride and Prejudice* cast him as Fitzwilliam Darcy; in 1954, he appeared as Winston Smith in an utterly spellbinding adaptation of Orwell's *1984*, scripted by *Quatermass* creator Nigel Kneale and so unanimously applauded that the BBC was forced to gather the entire cast and crew together and perform it all again within a week of the original broadcast.

In 1957, Cushing entered into what is probably his best-known association, joining the Hammer stable and, over the next fifteen years, establishing himself alongside Christopher Lee as the face of the studio's horror output. He is Van Helsing in the Dracula movies, he is the Baron in the Frankenstein films, and he appears to have loved every moment of it. "Who wants to see me as Hamlet?" he once asked. "Very few. But millions want to see me as Frankenstein, so that's the one I do."

Even this early into his career, typecasting could, and indeed should, have devoured him. But Cushing never fell prey to lazy audience expectations, primarily because he was so versatile. And his sheriff was one of the all-time greats, oozing soft-spoken charm and manners even as he plotted the direst fate for his foe.

The Sword of Sherwood revolves around a plot to assassinate Hubert Walter, the (real-life) Archbishop of Canterbury and Lord Chancellor, and a powerful supporter of the absent King Richard. He was also one of the men who negotiated the peace treaty that brought an end to the Third Crusade and, later, was responsible for raising the ransom payment that released the king for captivity. The plot itself is fictional, but one can certainly understand why Prince John and the sheriff might have conjured one—although, in this case, the sheriff's enmity is purely provincial. The Archbishop simply made the mistake of speaking out against one of his land-grabbing schemes.

Robin himself is portrayed with somewhat more ambiguity than usual— he is, for instance, a willing participant in the assassination plot until he realizes precisely who the target is; while Marian (played by Sarah Branch) has no feelings whatsoever for the man she believes to be a mere common criminal until she, too, realizes that he fights for a noble cause.

So it's another slender story, dignified by some excellent performances (Oliver Reed is Lord Melton, and brings all his bullying charm to the role) and, in common with so many of the studio's efforts, some great sets and lashings of atmosphere.

Contemporary audiences were certainly impressed, and that despite some early fears. Among the television show's fans, Hammer (and director Terence Fisher)'s reputation as specialists in horror left many convinced that their hero would wind up battling Dracula; while Hammer's aficionados hoped for nothing less.

But *The Sword of Sherwood*'s diet of earthly action and nefarious drama satisfied the first while winning over the latter; and though the movie is seldom mentioned in modern Hammer histories, it deserves to be seen more often.

Hammer returned to Sherwood for 1967's *A Challenge for Robin Hood*; and again there was a familiar face in the crowd as John Arnatt, who played

"Whistle My Love" was one of the big hits from the 1952 Disney movie.

the sheriff's deputy in the Richard Greene TV series, was promoted to the higher rank.

As with its predecessor, the movie boasts a slight story . . . in fact, it's even slighter, this time . . . but that does not detract from the sheer fun of the film. The early focus is on an inheritance squabble; Sir John de Courtenay is on his death bed, reading out his will—his lands are to be divided between his two warring sons, Henry and Roger, and to his nephew Robin (Barrie Ingham). Roger, who expected to be given everything, flies into what the old chroniclers might have called a heredipetous fury, murdering his sibling and then framing Robin for the crime.

The boy has no alternative but to flee, hightailing it into the forest, accompanied only by his friend Friar Tuck. There they fall in with a band of outlaws, themselves all dispossessed landowners. Their campaign for justice begins.

Meanwhile, Roger has a new ally, the sheriff; and a new guest. Marian is the sister of one of Robin's band, and now she is a prisoner in the castle. So is Will Scarlet, another of the outlaws, and the sheriff decides to hang him, sensibly guessing (and here we collide with the ballads) that Robin will soon come to his rescue.

And so he does, but the sheriff's plan to capture him fails; both Will and Marian are freed, only for the latter to again fall into the sheriff's clutches. Her rescue, a terrific fight scene, and suitably nasty ends for Roger and the sheriff all await during the movie's climax, and it's no surprise to find many modern viewers describing *A Challenge for Robin Hood* as the best of all Hammer's walks through Sherwood Forest.

Although it is run very close by Hammer's final Robin Hood opus.

As the 1970s dawned, Hammer was trying to break into the television market, with their highest hopes pinned on *Wolfshead—The Legend of Robin Hood*. With David Warbeck as Robin and Ciaran Madden as Marian, the story did much to divorce itself from the now-established legend. It is set, for example, in Barnsdale Forest, as opposed to Sherwood, and takes for its starting point the earliest of the ballads and legends—those concocted before Nottingham and its wicked sheriff became part and parcel of the tale.

Rather, Robin is still a commoner, albeit a noble-spirited one, while Sir Roger of Doncaster and the Abbot of St. Mary's are drawn from "A Lyttel Geste of Robyn Hode" to serve as the villains of the piece. And it's very tempting to speculate how the series might have developed, had it survived past a pilot episode.

Would it, for instance, have taken the twist into historical mystery that was so intrinsic to the 1980s *Robin of Sherwood*—whose creator, Richard Carpenter, was good friends with *Wolfshead* writer David Butler? The opening narration certainly suggests that possibility:

> England in 1190 was an unhappy land. Its people divided into two distinct classes: the Saxons, a slave race, and the Normans, masters who ruled without justice.
>
> More than a century before, the Saxons had been a free and happy people. But in 1066, they were beaten at Hastings by Duke William of Normandy—William the Conqueror. And to preserve their rule, the Normans built their castles and introduced brutal, repressive laws.
>
> The harshest were the Forest Laws. A man could be tortured and hanged for hunting for food to feed his starving family. Or made a wolfshead —an outlaw whose head was worth no more than a wolf's.

We will never know. Hammer spent a couple of years trying to interest various television networks in the series, all to no avail; finally, in 1973, the hour-long *Wolfshead* was released, with little fanfare and even fewer admirers, onto the UK cinema circuit, usually as the support film on a double bill.

Hammer itself was approaching the end of its life. The horror market had moved on, leaving their efforts looking quaint and corny—now, *The Exorcist* was the benchmark, and the studio had neither the budget nor the inclination to compete with that. Instead, Hammer turned the bulk of its attention back to where its golden age began, adapting popular television shows for the movies and, a scant few months later, the studio closed.

Robin Gets Raunchy

The Original Men In Tights

Robin Hood was a truly international hero by now. Early in the sixties, Italian studios produced the supremely thrilling *Robin Hood e i pirati* (*Robin Hood and the Pirates*) and *Il Trionfo di Robin Hood* (*The Triumph of Robin Hood*) while the Netherlands thrilled to *Robin Hood en zijn schelmen* (*Robin Hood and his Knaves*); a decade later, fresh efforts would emerge from Spain, Mexico, Brazil and even the USSR—where, incidentally, Robin Hood became Robin Good.

In 1964, he even washed up in 1930s' Chicago for a last gasp Rat Pack gangster flick, *Robin and his 7 Hoods*.

Frank Sinatra appears as Robbo, Dean Martin as Little John, Sammy Davis Jr. as Will, Bing Crosby as Allen A. Dale, and Barbara Rush as Marian Stevens, all ranged against Peter Falk's masterful Guy Gisborne, a rival gang leader.

It's a more violent, cynical Robin than we are used to, although that is only in keeping with the movie's setting. Yes, he does donate $50,000 to an orphanage, and is rewarded with newspaper headlines that speak of him taking from the rich and giving to the poor. He promptly sets up a string of charitable foundations to continue the giving, but this side of the business is not undertaken out of the goodness of Robbo's heart; he has simply realized how useful it is to have the tides of public sentiment firmly on his side.

Marian, too, is an artful broad—when Robin is framed for a murder, she steps in to run the gang herself, and when Robin finally returns, it is to discover that every one of his foundations is now a front for a massive counterfeiting organization.

It is a far better movie than it sounds; and it packed a powerful soundtrack as well; Sinatra's "My Kind of Town (Chicago is)," composed by Jimmy Van Heusen with lyrics by Sammy Cahn, was first heard here, and few films have a greater claim on immortality than that.

Or a lesser claim than *The Ribald Tales of Robin Hood* (aka *The Erotic Adventures of Robin Hood*), a joint American/West German production featuring lots of nudity, dirty jokes, and innuendo.

The relaxing of America's censorship laws at the end of the 1960s saw an explosion of what we now call sexploitation movies—primarily characterized by thin plots, large breasts, bad jokes and the promise that you will witness more sex than you actually do.

Frank Sinatra—and company—promoting the 1964 movie *Robin and the 7 Hoods*.

Photofest

The best of Russ Meyer's most legendary flicks fall into this category, but the true master of the genre was producer David F. Friedman, whose canon is awash in big-budget, and lavishly non-costumed comedy epics, many of which shared *The Ribald Tales'* taste for historical literature.

The Erotic Adventures of Zorro, The Adult Version of Dr. Jekyll and Mr. Hyde, The Notorious Daughter of Fanny Hill, The Amorous Adventures Of Don Quixote & Sancho Panza, and *The Secret Sex Lives of Romeo and Juliet*—all these and more eased their way off the production line, and not one of them did more to justify its title than throw on some suitable outfits (before quickly throwing them off again) and drop a few relevant names.

But they were (and remain) absurdly entertaining, with Robin's adventures incorporating, and then amending, a handful of familiar tales. The outlaw's capture of the sheriff, for example, is familiar to us all, but none of the ballads have him being stripped naked by the Merry Men. Likewise, the sheriff's jail is known to be a terrible place. But has it ever before doubled as an S&M torture chamber?

There was more unbridled sniggering to be found in 1971's *Up the Chastity Belt*, veteran British comedian Frankie Howerd's similarly (and hilariously) arch inspection of medieval life.

The heart of the movie is concerned with the peasant Lurkalot (played by Howerd), as he strives to make a living selling the titular devices . . . and the long line of men who would prefer he kept them to himself. Robin (Hugh Paddick) is a fairly minor character in the overall plot, although he is a crucial one—he and his men rescue King Richard (Howerd again) from being burned at the stake, and they retire to the forest to feast and frolic.

> Richard: Robin, I cannot thank you enough for your timely rescue.
> Robin: It's a pleasure, ducky. We haven't had such a giggle since we rolled the Sheriff of Nottingham in a cow pasture, have we lads?

Groan-inducing puns and the most monumentally convoluted double meanings had long been a staple of Howerd's act . . . of British comedy in general, in fact (it's such a shame that the *Carry On* team of comedians never turned their attention Sherwood-wards), and when you remember that this was an era, too, in which political correctness was not even a glimmer in a liberal's eye, it is clear that nothing is sacred. And that includes Robin and his Merry Men's hitherto inviolable heterosexuality.

> Robin: Well, ducky, what do you think of our camp?
> Richard: Yes, I think that's the word for it.

And a little later . . .

Frank Sinatra brought the story of Robin Hood to Prohibition-era Chicago.   *Photofest*

Robin: We're not looking our best at the moment, we lost most of our sequins. All that swinging through the trees, you know.
Richard: You swing?
Robin: Every night.

Sherwood Shock Treatment

By the mid-1970s, it felt as though every conceivable aspect of Robin Hood's life had been explored from every conceivable aspect. The ballads had been mined and mined again, the plays were played out, the stories were chasing their tales.

There was, however, one tradition that the movie makers had shied away from.

We all knew by heart how Robin Hood had lived.

But how did he die?

Robin and Marian (1976) is not wholly concerned with these end times, but mortality hangs over it like a shroud, regardless. Indeed, the movie's original title, *The Death of Robin Hood*, shapes the story from start to finish, and was only abandoned when Columbia Pictures opted for what they considered a more marketable, and less depressing, name.

Both Robin (Sean Connery) and Marian (Audrey Hepburn) are clearly approaching the autumns of their lives, although neither was exactly decrepit at the time of the movie—Connery was forty-five; Hepburn, returning to the screen following an eight-year absence, just a year his senior.

The Crusades are over, and the Richard's French wars, too. Indeed, the king is dead now, and John finally sits on the throne in his own right. But when Robin and Little John return to their homeland after years spent fighting alongside Richard, they are not feted, or even regarded as heroes. They are just two more weary war vets, in a land that is already overflowing with them.

And what were they fighting for, anyway? Certainly not freedom—all the evils that John attempted to perpetrate during his last snatch at power are now his to command by right. Exhausted though they are, Robin and Little John realize they have no alternative. They must fight on.

It's gentle, but there is a definite sense here that an era was ending, in the real world as well as that unfolding on the screen. The war in Vietnam was finally over; the last of the troops had come home; and they, too, found themselves confronting an uncertain future, overwhelmed by the experiences they had shared overseas, in a land that apparently didn't care one iota.

It's a scenario that only slowly gathered pace in Hollywood, before reaching its apogee with Sylvester Stallone's initial Rambo movie, *First Blood* (1982), and it's easy to speculate that the spirit of *Robin and Marian* at least vaguely informed the later film—the titular warrior even deploys a bow and arrow!

Connery's Robin is considerably less volatile than Rambo, of course, although the political commentary remains to the fore. As the Vietnam war wore on, media coverage had grown increasingly hostile, not only towards the politicians and generals who continued to wage it, but also to the men on the ground—memories of the My Lai massacre were still fresh, and the notion of American soldiers blithely slaughtering harmless villagers had taken firm, and damaging, root in the popular consciousness.

Robin and Marian confronts the falsehood face on; as the movie opens, Robin and Little John are refusing a direct order from Richard to storm a castle that is believed to home a priceless treasure. The king cares nothing for the fact that the castle is being defended by just one old man (and a one-eyed one, at that), or that it is filled with women and children. All he wants is the treasure, and when the pair try to reason with him, he orders their execution, before dispatching less conscientious soldiers into the castle, with instructions to massacre everybody within.

Robin and Little John are reprieved by the king's untimely death on the battlefield—killed, appropriately enough, by the one-eyed man. But their return home offers them no respite from tyranny.

While Robin fought, his pre-war paramour Marian prayed. Taking holy vows, she entered an abbey and has risen now to the rank of abbess. But shortly after Robin visits her, King John's latest squabble with the Church sees the sheriff order her arrest.

Of course Robin and his men rescue her, and when one of her captors, Sir Ranulf, sets off in pursuit of the gang, his men perish in a hail of arrows. Thoroughly routed, Sir Ranulf returns to Nottingham and asks for a fresh fighting force, no fewer than two hundred men.

Richard Lester, directing the 1976 movie *Robin and Marian*.   *Photofest*

The sheriff agrees, but on the very brink of a massive armed showdown, he and Robin agree to settle their differences instead with a duel—one that the sheriff comes very close to winning. Only as he gloats over his injured foe, sprawled on the ground before him, does the sheriff realize that he should have just finished off the outlaw while he had the chance. Fighting through pain and weakness, Robin raises himself just enough to strike his adversary a fatal blow.

Now the battle between the Merry Men and Ranulf's soldiers commences, but Robin is too badly injured to play a part in it. Instead, Little John and Marian carry him back to the abbey, where Marian keeps her healing herbs and potions.

While Little John stands guard outside, she prepares a draft; drinks from it herself and then hands it to Robin. He, too, drinks—and then realizes it was poison.

The last scenes of the movie follow tradition, Little John weeping over his longtime friend, as Robin uses the very last of his strength to shoot an arrow through the window, out across the abbey grounds, to come to earth on the spot that will be his and Marian's grave.

But Marian's final words are probably the most affecting ever spoken in the annals of Robin Hood:

> I love you. More than all you know. I love you more than children. More than fields I've planted with my hands. I love you more than morning prayers or peace or food to eat. I love you more than sunlight, more than flesh or joy, or one more day. I love you . . . more than God.

Big Bows, Big Budgets, Big Hair

Once again, it is probably safe to say that the story of Robin Hood had been taken about as far as it could be. But Richard Carpenter's *Robin of Sherwood* so masterfully rewrote the legend for television that entirely new pastures opened up.

Overnight, the three season series created a canvas that continues to inspire fresh daubings today, more than thirty years after the Hooded Man first donned his characteristic headgear—a new, mystically inclined Robin who passes still through the worlds of fantasy novels, comic books and, latterly, audio dramas. (See chapter 23)

On the big screen, however, it was as though the eighties had never happened. Nor the seventies, nor even the sixties. Fifteen years had elapsed since *Robin and Marian*, yet when the curtain raised on *Prince of Thieves*, Kevin Costner's epic 1991 contribution to the theme, even Errol Flynn might have raised an eyebrow and described it as "a little old-fashioned."

Prince of Thieves is not a great Robin Hood movie. There is no denying that it's enjoyable, an action-packed roller-coaster ride that leaves you more or less breathless throughout. But just as the critics got their jollies from finding flaw with everything from direction to script to the fact that medieval Englishmen tended not to speak with broad American accents, so Robin scholars quickly learned to hide their heads in their hands at the very mention of the movie's name.

Half a century earlier, sharp-eyed viewers of Errol Flynn's movie took great satisfaction from pointing out the decidedly twentieth century motor car that is briefly visible in twelfth century Nottingham. If *only* that were *Prince of Thieves*'s sole problem.

Such observations are churlish, however. *Prince of Thieves* was not intended to appeal to critics; was not intended to satisfy scholars. It was intended to be a box-office behemoth, a movie smash hit that would fill the multiplex night after night, and would spin off into other media too.

Toy stores groaned beneath the weight of a range of four-inch-high Robin Hood action figures, all modeled on characters from the movie, although comparisons with past entrants into the realms of replica Robins were not especially flattering.

Among the manifold gifts that have fallen from our breakfast cereal boxes, Robin and his Merry Men were a highlight of the 1960s giveaways.

They certainly could not compete with the half-dozen plastic figures that tumbled out of certain 1960s-era Corn Flakes packages, and which included Robin, Little John, Friar Tuck, Allen a Dale, the Sheriff of Nottingham, and a very prominently busted Marian . . . in fact, Costner and company's replicas looked more like an unfortunately aged, and ill-advisedly reformed boy band than a gang of fearless outlaws.

The music scene was more forgiving. From the movie's soundtrack, Canadian rocker Bryan Adams's "(Everything I Do) I Do It For You" topped the US chart for seven weeks, the Canadian for nine and the British for an unparalleled sixteen.

More than fifteen million copies were sold worldwide, with a lot of them probably going to the same people who established *Prince of Thieves* as the second-highest grossing film of 1991 (behind *Terminator 2: Judgment Day*), with $390 million in the bank.

As Francis James Child once huffed, "Thought is free."

But again, it's not all bad. Alan Rickman joins Peter Cushing in the ranks of the greatest sheriffs Nottingham has ever had, a glowering presence who can convey more menace breathing than most people can with outright menacing—later in his career, Rickman would bring a similar dimension to his portrayal of Snape in the Harry Potter movies, and there he was one of the good guys. Sort of. In *Prince of Thieves* he is the prince of evil, and he plays the part with such grace and style that it's difficult not to be rooting for him no matter how vile his latest outrage.

He even kills Gisborne, for goodness sake!

The fight scenes are fabulous, the death scenes inventive—who can resist a little cheer as Friar Tuck weights the greedy Bishop of Hereford with all the treasure he can find, and then throws him out of a window? And though history will howl in despair as the sheriff recruits a band of Celtic warriors to aid him in his pursuit of Robin, mindless of the fact that he was about five hundred years too late to find them, there is no faulting the ferocity with which these anachronisms fight. Nor can the cinematography be scorned, especially the shot that followed Robin's arrow to its target. From that point of view, *Prince of Thieves* merited every one of the commercial accolades it accrued.

More Men in Further Tights?

Prince of Thieves was not Robin's only big screen adventure that year, although the other one, John Irvin's *Robin Hood*, wound up going almost directly to video to avoid Costner crushing it at the box office. With Patrick Bergin playing an oft-times manic Robin, and Uma Thurman a magnificent Marian, *Robin Hood* was a refreshing return to basics after the brobdingnagian excesses and liberties of its rival, and in any other year it might well have done well.

As it was, it even largely avoided the attentions of Mel Brooks, as he turned to Sherwood for his next movie, *Robin Hood: Men in Tights*.

This was familiar territory for Brooks. Back in 1975, he created the US TV series *When Things Were Rotten*, a somewhat hit-and-miss comedy based on the Robin Hood legend, and starring Dick Gautier as Robin Hood.

The series itself was destined to survive for just thirteen episodes, and is seldom regarded as a high-water mark in Brooks's career. But it clearly meant something to Brooks, who lost no time in delivering an utterly over-the-top riposte to the gargantuan success of *Prince of Thieves*, and an affectionate poke, too, at a lot of other cinematic lionizations of Robin Hood (there are some great jabs in the direction of Errol Flynn, for instance).

Not to be taken seriously in the slightest, *Men in Tights* is nevertheless an important movie, if only because it reminds us of the one crucial point that *Prince of Thieves* made, but which a lot of people were too bound up in "authenticity" to realize.

That is, Robin Hood is *not* a fossil; is *not* a sequence of canonical tales that, though they maybe interpreted, can never be violated. He is *not* a single story.

For the first eight centuries of its existence, the tradition of Robin Hood was constantly growing, perpetually shifting, forever developing.

Of course it has its Ur-text, "A Lytell Geste of Robyn Hode." But that was never anything more than a foundation. Fresh Merry Men, the addition of Marian, the incorporation of Gisborne, the positioning in Sherwood, and so on and so forth; none of these ingredients would ever have been added to the stew had the medieval mind shared the modern scholar's obsession with "sticking to the story."

If it had, Robin would never have fought pirates, would never have ridden on Friar Tuck's back, would never have confronted the witch of Papplewick, would never have split the arrow at the archery contest.

Why shouldn't Asneeze be arrested for jaywalking? Why shouldn't there have been a band of warlike Celts living quietly in Scotland? Why shouldn't Marian wear an immovable chastity belt (there are multiple echoes of the Frankie Howerd movie scattered through *Men in Tights*)?

Had any of these developments come down to us on fragile, fifteenth century parchment, lovingly crafted by tonsured monks writing with feathers, we would have no problem whatsoever with incorporating them into our studies. Perhaps, in several centuries' time, future scholars will treat them as though they had been.

But until then . . .

Until Then?

A slew of lesser Hood adventures decorated the rest of the 1990s and flowed into the 2000s, too—all watchable in one way or another (see appendix), without really offering much in the way of fresh invention to the saga.

It was left to Ridley Scott, and 2010's *Robin Hood*, to change that scenario, although in his case (as if to contradict everything you have just read), he perhaps changed too much. Little of it for the better.

The movie suffered a fairly troubled beginning. Originally visualized as a study in relationships, a love triangle that captured a surprisingly likable sheriff, a surprisingly *un*likable Robin and, playing them off against each other, a cunning and manipulative Marian, *Nottingham* (as it was to be called) already had Russell Crowe on board as a leading man when director Ridley Scott arrived in April 2007, and tossed almost everything else to the wind.

The original script, by Ethan Reiff and Cyrus Voris, was reworked by Brian Helgeland, and then again by Paul Webb. Out went the twisted romance angle. Out went Christian Bale, the movie's original Robin Hood (Crowe was intended to play the sheriff). And out went Sienna Miller, as Marian, because—according to the British *Guardian* newspaper—"Crowe has simply become too fat to play the lead role. [His] failure to lose the weight he gained for Scott's 2008 thriller *Body of Lies* has reportedly forced [Miller's] departure . . . as the svelte actor's presence might have magnified Crowe's corpulence."

Scott's own working schedule necessitated one delay in filming; the 2008 Screen Actors Guild strike caused another; and the changing seasons demanded another—again according to the *Guardian*, "[P]roducers were forced to delay shooting following concern that the leaves in the location doubling for Sherwood Forest would not be green enough."

It would be early 2009 before filming finally got under way, by which time the movie was effectively *Robin Hood* in retitled name alone.

Echoing the 1976 Sean Connery movie, the action begins on the battle-field with King Richard in Normandy, at what would become the monarch's final battle, the siege of Chateau de Chaulus Chabral.

In Ridley Scott's version of the story, however, the army is still *on its way* to the Holy Land, an utterly mystifying chronological shift that effectively wipes the entire Third Crusade from history. And that is only one of the anachronisms and inaccuracies that rattle through the film.

Neither is our hero the man we expect him to be. No heroic lieutenant or chivalrous knight, Robin Longstride is just another archer in Richard's army, one who falls into the king's bad books following a gambling dispute with some of the other men. He and they are shackled, but the chaos that follows Richard's death allows them to escape, and prepare to return to England.

As they journey, Longstride and his companions fall in with a nobleman, Robert Loxley, as he, too, hurries home. Loxley bears dire news, however: the King of France, in league with a treacherous nobleman named Godfrey, is planning to invade England.

But Loxley is seriously injured, and fears (rightly, as it happens) that he will die before he is able to deliver the information. So he hands his sword to Longstride, asking the archer to deliver it to his, Loxley's, father, Sir Walter—who, in turn, asks Longstride not only to keep the news of his son's demise a secret, but also to take his place; to maintain the pretense that the heir is alive so that the lands might then pass to Loxley's daughter, Marian, upon the old man's death.

So far, so absurdly convoluted and, in storytelling terms, matters really don't improve after Longstride becomes Loxley. Too much plotting and too much talking make it far too easy for one's attention to wander—which is not a problem to which Robin's audiences are accustomed. Oscar Isaac's King John and Eileen Atkins's Queen Eleanor are both superlative in their roles, but they have far too little to do, while Crowe continues an especially unlikable hero, with Cate Blanchett a none-too-sympathetic Marian.

Furthermore, the notion that this entire affair, all two-and-a-half hours of it, should be considered a mere *prequel* to the familiar Robin Hood story is a conceit too far. Every retelling of the story offers its own interpretation of Hood's personality, but central to them all is an innate altruism. Not this time. Crowe's Robin is essentially little more than a thug, with another decidedly distracting accent.

It's not wholly disappointing. As always with a Ridley Scott movie, the sets and effects are, without exception, amazing, offering up as realistic (or, at least, what we might consider realistic) a depiction of medieval life and warfare as has ever been sccn on the big screen.

The opening siege, with its boiling oil and broiling corpses, battering rams and exploding portcullis, and even an unfortunate Frenchman taking an arrow in the eye (revenge for the death of King Harold at Hastings!), looks terrific; the costuming is solidly excellent, and the cast and extras hurl themselves into the action scenes with gusto.

Just another archer . . . only this one carries an axe.   *Photofest*

But one cannot help but feel the same way as Claude Rains did about the 1922 Douglas Fairbanks extravaganza, as he reflected upon "a light taste of the real Robin Hood story . . . dragged in as a tag at the end to justify the use of the name."

Or, as critic Roger Ebert asked, "Have we grown weary of the delightful aspects of the Robin Hood legend? Is witty dialogue no longer permitted? Are Robin and [Marian] no longer allowed to engage in a spirited flirtation? Must their relationship seem like high-level sexual negotiations? How many people need to be covered in boiling oil for Robin Hood's story to be told these days? How many parents will be misled by the film's PG-13 rating? Must children go directly from animated dragons to skewering and decapitation, with no interval of cheerful storytelling?"

The answer, hopefully, is no. Not yet. And not for a long time, either.

Robin Hood didn't do badly at the box office—it cost $200 million to make, but it is ranked second only to *Prince of Thieves* among Hollywood's most successful medieval movies of all time. (*Braveheart*, *Ever After*, and *Willow* complete the top five.)

But Ebert was not a voice in the wilderness. Other critics, too, were largely unimpressed, and those online sites that catalog audience appreciation tend not to praise *Robin Hood* too highly, either—in May 2016, the Rotten Tomatoes site gave it a meager 43 percent approval rating.

But Scott and Crowe both declared themselves amenable to a sequel, and Hollywood in general remains a happy hunting ground for writers with a little Robin in their quiver.

Hood is, after all, unquestionably an industry mainstay and, no less than James Bond, Tarzan, and Dracula, someone somewhere will always be plotting a new variant on his story—for better or worse.

Both Sony (*Hood*) and Disney (*Nottingham & Hood*) have both mooted fresh looks at the legend, and others are surely in a pipeline somewhere.

And if the big screen doesn't deliver, the small screen certainly will.

Robin in Your Living Room

From Lincoln Green to Richard Greene

Compared with the haste with which he bestrode the silver screen, it took Robin Hood some time to make his mark on television. A failed US TV pilot notwithstanding, it took until 1952 before English actor Patrick Troughton became the first actor to don the green for a small screen audience, and just one single six episode season would elapse before he removed it again.

Anyone who doubted Robin's ability to make his home in the living rooms of the western world was swiftly disavowed of such doubts, however. In 1955, *The Adventures of Robin Hood* flashed for the first time across the cathode tube, and it would continue to do so for the next four years. Decades of repeats testify to its ongoing popularity, multiple DVD releases ensure its ubiquity. It might not be the *best* Robin Hood series ever shot, but it is certainly the best known and the best loved, and it boasted the best theme music, too.

Robin Hood, Robin Hood, Riding Through the Glen

It's a curious creature, though. Made for British television, packed with British actors, *The Adventures of Robin Hood* was largely written by Americans. And not just any Americans, either. These were naughty Americans!

If any single event can be said to have shaped and molded the nature of American entertainment through the 1950s, it was Senator Joseph McCarthy's belief that Hollywood-and-beyond was a nest of Communist spies and sympathizers.

In many ways, it was the first of what we might call a modern media circus. We are all familiar with the way in which tabloid press and television will seize upon a controversial topic, and then elevate it to peaks of world-shattering importance; McCarthy's belief that great swaths of America were indulging in unAmerican activities was a lot like that.

The difference was that he was a senator, and he held sway. Soon, he had convened a senate committee to investigate his findings; and soon, Hollywood was reeling beneath his conclusions and accusations. Indeed, while the senator's own methods were swiftly dismissed as the witch-hunt that they unquestionably were, the fears that he stirred up continued to percolate.

In Hollywood, a blacklist of anyone suspected of having leftist leanings was rumored to remain in force long after the House Un-American Activities Committee concluded its hearings—as late as 1961, Rod Serling, the creator of *The Twilight Zone*, was recalling how he once asked to have two actors work for him and found out they were blacklisted:

> We submitted their names to the network *[which]* told us that these two actors were not hirable, and I found out later that one was a mistake in name, which happens all the time. In the other case it was a guy—you know—a little, two-bit walk-on that I wanted to use. I picked him because I liked his face, I didn't know what his politics were. And then all hell broke loose. The network knocked his name off the cast list. The agency said they didn't have a blacklist and yet these men remain un-hirable. So there must be somebody's list.

Serling was not alone in his frustration. Across television and the movies, once in-demand actors, writers, and crew members found work had mysteriously dried up for them as the suspicions leavened by McCarthy, and the fears that afflicted their employers, proved an insurmountable barrier to their continued careers.

They could never have expected Robin Hood to ride to their salvation. In 1954, American producer Hannah Weinstein approached the British impresario Lew Grade about a projected Robin Hood series. It would comprise thirty-six half-hour (including commercials) episodes, and Grade's ITC production would both finance the series and air it on Britain's soon-to-be-launched independent television network. Weinstein and the US distribution company Official Films Inc. would see to its American broadcast.

Grade agreed, and with Weinstein having already contracted the English actor Richard Greene, work began on gathering scripts—the majority of which Weinstein and script editor Howard Koch purposefully farmed out to writers whom they knew had been hard hit by the blacklist-that-wasn't-a-blacklist: Waldo Salt, Robert Lees, Ring Lardner Jr., Adrian Scott, and more (Koch himself was also on the list).

Each writer selected a pseudonym under which to work, to avoid the ruse being revealed by some eagle-eyed do-gooder; and each, it seemed, was given permission for their own political views and feelings to impact, in some way, upon their scripts.

Lardner later admitted the show offered him "plenty of opportunities to comment on issues and institutions in Eisenhower-era America," while the constant threat of betrayal under which the outlaws lived was, of course, a reflection of the lives that the blacklisted writers had themselves experienced. (For a fictionalized but throughly engrossing account of the subterfuge, see author Michael Eaton's HBO movie *Fellow Traveler*.)

Of course, much of this would have been lost on viewers, few of whom could ever have guessed the true identity of the writers; and even fewer of whom would have cared. *The Adventures of Robin Hood* was a children's show, written for and appealing to an audience that wanted nothing more from the program than twenty-plus minutes on the edge of their seats, thrilling and cheering as Robin and his Merry Men led the sheriff on another merry dance.

It succeeded, too. For four long seasons it ran, three of thirty-nine episodes apiece, one of twenty-six, for a total of 143 stories—all of which have survived to beguile modern audiences. And they are timeless.

No matter what hidden meanings and messages the modern sociologist might be able to read into the blacklisted writers' scripts, each story is exquisitely paced to extract the maximum drama, laughter and excitement from its running time; each one *feels* authentic, a genuine day-in-the-life of the Robin Hood with whom we are most familiar.

History is not rewritten (although it is ridden roughshod on occasion); heroes are left undented. Most of the familiar balladic tales are dramatized, great swaths of English history are revisited. Episodes concerned themselves with the laws of the land, as they stood at that time, and the politics, too. The Robin and sheriff whom we know from the fables are those that battle on the television screen, the men and Marian are true to tradition.

A more sophisticated modern audience might cringe at some of the more romantic moments—but so did the boys and girls who watched them at the time, shouting "soppy" at the screen and pulling disgusting faces whenever Robin and Marian allowed their feelings to show.

But that was part of the fun. *The Adventures of Robin Hood* was not merely a way to shut the kids up while Mom got on with making dinner. It was a way of dispatching the scamps to Sherwood for half an hour, knowing that they'd not get up to any mischief because Robin and Marian would look out for them.

It was after the show that you had to keep your eyes open, as entire neighborhoods disgorged their under-elevens, with staves and bows and swords and daggers, to play out the action they had just been sitting through.

Comics in the Hood

In his autobiography *Shell-Shocked*, singer Howard Kaylan of the sixties pop band The Turtles recalls how he and his brother would have Robin Hood fights in a neighboring hayloft; and toy stores of the day groaned beneath the merchandising—everything from Robin Hood jigsaws to Robin Hood shoes (with Richard Greene's face imprinted in the heel!), Robin Hood bubble gum cards and, inevitably, Robin Hood bow and arrow sets—the latter mercifully tipped with red rubber suckers, as opposed to the more lethal points that young imaginations might have preferred.

There were three movies created by combining and colorizing selected episodes (the series was, of course, shot in black and white); plus the Hammer Studio's *Sword of Sherwood Forest* which hit the cinema circuit soon after the series came to an end. (See chapter 21.)

There was even a flurry of comic books published, themselves echoing the wholesome values of the television series with remarkable fidelity.

They still read well today, too, and while none of them outlived the show that spawned them, nevertheless they augmented it with exquisite élan.

Sussex Publishing's *Robin Hood* sets the scene, a ruggedly handsome clean-shaven hero just like Richard Greene, and a series of adventures that might have been torn straight out of the pages of *TV Guide*, then *and* now.

"The Warrior Maid," for example, goes some way towards predicting Maid Marian's future (2006) escapades as the Nightwatchman, when a mysterious armored figure ambushes three of Robin's men, defeats them singlehandedly and mocks them mercilessly while it does so.

> So you're the merry men of Robin Hood, are you? Ha! I'm disappointed! I think little of your prowess as fighting men!
>
> In faith! If your leader be no better than you, I've come a long way in vain! On your feet! Take me to him! We'll see if Robin Hood can fight any better than his men!

Only when this mysterious assailant unmasks does anybody recognize her—Lady Edith Harwell, the Warrior Maid of Northumberland. "Some say she fights better than a man!" it is declared. And so she does.

Across pages bright with color, and festooned with advertisements for Charles Atlas bodies and five-dollar rocket ships ("the most sensational toy in America—over seven feet long"), Edith battles barbarians, punishes Picts, and even finds time to romance Robin.

Or so another of the merry men, her old friend Edwin of Warkworth, believes. How was he to know it was all a cunning plot to make him forget his crippling shyness and declare his love for the woman who adores him?

Four stories per issue, and a few pages of historical fact to lay down further background; *Robin Hood* was a riot of excitement, but it was not the only one on the magazine racks. From Charlton Comics, *Robin Hood and his Merry Men* followed suit with a bevy of short, three-or-four page adventures, more fascinating facts, and more gloriously purple prose.

Robin Hood—Classic Comic Appearances

1912 *Puck* (UK) (text serial)
1920 *The Rainbow* (UK) (text serial)
1922–1941 *Bubbles* (UK)
1923 *The Chick's Own* (UK)
1930 *Merry and Bright* (UK)
1931 *Sunbeam* (UK) (text serial)
1937 *Sparkler* (UK)
1941 *More Fun Comics* #73 (first appearance of Green Arrow) (National, US)
1941–1946 *Robin Hood and Company* (Canada)
1942 *Classic Comics* #1 (aka *Classics Illustrated* many reprints) (US)
1951 *Thriller* (UK)
1955 *Walt Disney's Robin Hood* (Dell, 1955)
1956 *The Brave and the Bold* vol. 1 #5–14 (National, US)
1956 *Young Heroes* #35–37 (American Comics Group, US)
1956–1958 *Robin Hood Tales* (DC, US)
1956–1958 *Robin Hood and his Merry Men* (Charlton, US)
1956–1960 *The Adventures of Robin Hood Annual* (six annual issues) (Adprint, UK)
1957 *Robin Hood and His Merry Men* (Quality/DC, US)
1957 *Robin Hood* (Sussex, US)
1957 *The Adventures of Robin Hood* (Sussex, US)
1957–1959 *Robin Hood Annual* (three annual issues) (Amalgamated Press, UK)
1958 *Robin Hood* (IW Publications, US)
1963 *Robin Hood* (Dell Comics) (US)

A selection of comics published during the rip-roaring run of the 1950s Richard Greene television series.

"You'll hang, Robin Hood, or I'm not the Sheriff of Nottingham."
"You'd better seek another office, then. I have no intention of hanging, today or any other day, Sheriff."

From Quality Comics, *Robin Hood Tales* ran for six issues beginning in February 1956, before being taken over by National/DC the following year (DC's own *The Brave and the Bold* carried a single Robin story through this same period; and, of course, the superhero The Green Arrow was unmistakably based on the hero).

Disney and Dell published further adventures. But the big daddy of them all was another Sussex publication, officially licensed from (and titled for) the television show, and delivered monthly, resplendent with a photo of its hero on the cover.

Into the Seventies, and Out of Them Again

The Adventures of Robin Hood was nearing the end of its televised lifespan when at least an element of the Robin story resurfaced in the 1958–1959 UK series *Ivanhoe*, starring a young Roger Moore as the titular Sir Wilfred of Ivanhoe.

However, it would be a decade before the outlaws returned to the small screen when, in 1968, Douglas Fairbanks Jr. finally got to walk in the partial footsteps of his father by appearing as the Sheriff of Nottingham in *The Legend of Robin Hood*, a ninety-minute musical produced by NBC.

All of which means the Richard Greene series was twenty years old before anything came along to truly dislodge it from the affections, as the BBC turned the cameras onto *The Legend of Robin Hood*.

This new retelling was conjured by Robert Banks Stewart, one of the mainstays of British television writing of the era—he was responsible, too, for two of the most popular *Doctor Who* stories ever aired, "Terror of the Zygons" and "The Seeds of Doom," as well as the creator of such beloved series as *Bergerac*, *Shoestring*, and *The Darling Buds of May*—the show that made a star of Catherine Zeta-Jones.

The Legend of Robin Hood was not Robert Banks Stewart's first dip into English mythology; in 1973, he was among the writers of *Arthur of the Britons*, a vivid recreation of the turmoil that wracked Britain in the centuries immediately following the Roman withdrawal in 410 AD.

Arthur is portrayed as a Celtic king, desperately trying to unite the disparate tribes against the invading Saxons. Now *The Legend of Robin Hood* allowed him to turn that around, with the victorious and now-settled Saxons involved in their own fight against continental invaders.

The Robin of this tale is the son and heir of the Earl of Huntingdon, left to be raised by a forester while his father is at war. As he comes of age, he is informed of his true identity, and journeys to London to meet with King Richard on the eve of the monarch's departure for the Holy Land.

But he also meets Marian, the daughter of a local Saxon nobleman, whose dream of securing peace between Saxons and Normans is predicated around the impending marriage of Marian to Guy of Gisborne, renowned as one of the most brutal and execution-happy men in the land.

Beautifully written and paced, the series is as much concerned with period politicking as it is with unabashed action, but—unlike other attempts to cram history onto adventure—it works, as much through Banks Smith's storytelling prowess as through a magnificent cast.

Diane Keen is never less than superlative as what one period observer described as "an implausibly lovely" Maid Marian; William Marlowe is a Gisborne whom one cannot help but love to hate; and there could be no better Prince John than David Dixon (a future Ford Prefect in the BBC's adaptation of *Hitch Hiker's Guide to the Galaxy*). Oozing over-privilege from every pouting pore, he makes it difficult to watch any other actor's portrayal of the character.

In fact the only weak link is Robin (Martin Potter), who is rarely more than adequate throughout; it is hard to shake the feeling that he leads his gang *not* because he's the right man for the job, but because they can't be bothered to argue with him, and will do what they want to regardless.

Nevertheless, even if you know the old stories, his failings do not lessen the shock of his death at the hands of Gisborne's prioress sister; while we are also witness to the demises of Will Scarlet, Friar Tuck, and Much—killings that have little to do with any version of the legend we had hitherto enjoyed, but which guaranteed *The Legend of Robin Hood* would have a powerful impact not only on those who watched it, but also upon those who strove to recreate it in later decades.

It was certainly a successful series; *Supersonic* magazine even persuaded a band called Arrows (best remembered for writing "I Love Rock and Roll" for Joan Jett) to don full Robin Hood garb for a photo spread in an upcoming issue. Admittedly, they didn't get any closer to Nottingham than the garden of a West London hotel but, according to the feature, they nevertheless "got their bows out . . . and went on the rampage."

Members of the Anglo-American pop group Arrows were persuaded to don the Lincoln green for this mid-1970s teen magazine photo spread.

The Hooded Man and Other Stories

Another comedic waltz through Sherwood entertained fans of made-for-TV movies in 1984, with George Segal taking the lead in *The Zany Adventures of Robin Hood*; Roddy McDowell playing Prince John; and Tom Baker a gloriously larger-than-life Guy of Gisborne—all of them hamming their hearts out as they struggle to raise (or not raise) the ransom being demanded for the captive King Richard.

And then came *Robin of Sherwood*.

It is impossible to overstate the impact of this series—or, at least, of its first two seasons. (The third, sadly, might have been just a little Robin too far).

No matter that, watching it today, one cannot help but remember that it *was* the 1980s, with half the cast's hairstyles auditioning for walk-on roles in *The Breakfast Club*; with Michael Praed (Robin)'s preening surely serving as his audition tape for his subsequent stint on *Dynasty*; and with Clannad's soundtrack effectively blueprinting everything that would become intensely annoying about so-called New Age music.

At the time, via weekly broadcasts through 1984–1985, *Robin of Sherwood* was perfect. More than that, it brought to the legend the aspects of pagan mystery and darkness for which it had cried out so long.

It is true that the Herne of *Robin of Sherwood* is little more than a gnarly old man with an old deer's head perched rather precariously on his own. Our first glimpse of him rising out of the mist, vivid light refracted in the swirling clouds, a silhouette surmounted by giant antlers, is the one that we remember—and the one that finally binds Robin Hood to a legacy founded firmly within his homeland's pagan past; to a landscape of ancient stones and burial mounds, lost beliefs and forgotten ceremonies, to the traditions of which the very first minstrels, singing their songs, would surely have been aware.

The American author Marion Zimmer Bradley had executed a similar reinterpretation of King Arthur just a year previous—1983's *Mists of Avalon* is often cited (at least by cynics) as one of the cornerstones of the modern pagan revival in both the UK and the US, a novel that depicted with breathless vivacity the turmoil that wracked the land as Christianity fought its final duel with the old gods and beliefs.

Carpenter illustrated the same conflict, but in his world, the old gods—maybe they didn't win. But they at least fought to an honorable draw, accepting that they might never stand center-stage again, but would forever be lurking in the shadows, there for whoever might need them.

Even this new Robin's name echoed mystery—Robin Hood no longer, he was now Robin *in the* Hood, a mysterious, cloaked and shrouded avenger who wreaked vengeful havoc on all who opposed him.

How could the remainder of the series even hope to compete?

Two seasons saw Praed fight as Robin; for the third, with the original Robin killed in battle, Herne the Hunter chose a successor, the renegade nobleman Robert of Huntingdon—now played by Jason Connery, the son of the 1976 movie's Sean.

It was a brave recasting and not, on its own terms, unsuccessful. But Praed's brooding Hood, so readily capable of swinging from fey to fierce, was a hard act to follow and the series ran to just one final season under Connery's blonde-maned management. A fourth season, however, was being considered, and creator Carpenter had already written one episode, "The Knights of the Apocalypse," before the series was canned. It was this lost epic that relaunched *Robin of Sherwood* in audio form in 2016.

The affection with which the show is remembered was not confined to its audience; more or less the full cast of the Connery era returned for the production, including the original cast, including Clive Mantle, Ray Winstone, Judi Trott, Nickolas Grace, Mark Ryan, Phil Rose, and Philip Jackson. Connery spoke for them all when he joyously proclaimed:

> My time in Sherwood was spent working with wonderful actors who became lifelong friends, and behind it all was Richard "Kip" Carpenter's brilliant writing, whose scripts we brought to life.

Another thrilling paperback adventure to tie in with the 1980s TV series.

After many false dawns, I can finally say that *Robin of Sherwood* is coming back. And so am I! The Hooded Man is ready to face the evil machinations of the Sheriff of Nottingham again, surrounded by my wonderful band of Merries, in a brand-new audio adventure written by Kip himself.

We may be a little older and wiser in real life but, on audio, we're forever young and golden-haired.

Richard Carpenter became the latest author to retell the legend, around the time of the *Robin of Sherwood* TV series.

The perceived poor judgment of that third season notwithstanding, the success of *Robin of Sherwood*, so quickly followed as it was by *Prince of Thieves*, precipitated a veritable deluge of fresh retellings.

Another comedy, in the form of *Maid Marian and Her Merry Men*, reduced "Robin of Kensington" to a mere buffoon, while elevating Marian to the role of leader; and a Japanese anime series, *Robin Hood no Daibōken*, transformed the familiar cast as children (albeit children with super powers).

There was the *Young Robin Hood*, an animated Canadian/American children's show, with Robin frequently aided by a local witch; and *The New Adventures of Robin Hood*, a French/American collaboration that adds a menagerie of mystic creatures to the outlaws' litany of foes.

Princess of Thieves was a TV movie with Kiera Knightley reprising the old role of Robin's heroic daughter; and *Back to Sherwood* saw Aimee Castle playing a modern-day descendent of the outlaw, flashing back in time with the help of a magic talisman . . .

It was time to find a new Robin. And a new way to tell the tale.

Back to Basics

The notion of recreating the legends of Robin Hood in something approaching a traditional manner seemed quaintly old-fashioned when it was first made public.

Created by Dominic Minghella and Foz Allan, and first mooted during the summer of 2005, the BBC's latest retelling of the tale was commissioned that fall, but few observers seemed overly excited at the prospect.

That same year had seen the network triumphantly relaunch the old *Doctor Who* series in twenty-first-century clothing, at the same time re-establishing early-evening Saturdays (at least in the UK) as the traditional slot for good-natured family entertainment. *Robin Hood* was purposefully designed to fill that niche.

As with the rebooted *Doctor Who*, casting was courageous. Jonas Armstrong would appear in the title role, a twenty-five-year-old Dubliner better-known for theatre work than television; as Marian, Lucy Griffiths—just nineteen at the time—was another comparative unknown; and Sam Troughton as Much was best known for his role as a demented priest in the supernatural drama *Hex*, and as the grandson of the first television Robin Hood, Patrick Troughton.

The "stars" of the show, then, were the bad guys—Richard Armitage, as Guy of Gisborne, had most recently starred in *North and South*; while Keith

Jonas Armstrong, as Robin, in 2006.   *Photofest*

Allen (the sheriff, Vaisey) had been working in stand-up comedy since the late seventies, and was a founding member of London's Comedy Store, the alternative comedy workshop that produced such television legends as *The Young Ones* and *the Comic Strip Presents . . .*

Since then, he had become a familiar funny face on British television (while also watching on as his daughter, Lily, carved herself a remarkably enjoyable pop career), but he does not play the sheriff strictly for laughs. He achieved them, though, painting the lawman as a vain, self-centered, and sarcastic blatteroon, shot through with a weighty dose of knowing camp. This is a sheriff, we quickly discover, who is as likely to be painting his nails as he signs a felon's death warrant, as he is to be wearing the robes of state.

His humor is cruel, his demands unreasonable, and his boredom thresh-old so low that even his loftiest and most crucial pronouncements are apt to fade off with a laconic "yadda yadda blah-de-blah." His victims know he's going to subject them to torture, so why bother wasting breath telling them?

Gisborne despises him, but goes along with Vaisey's every whim because his ambition and greed are (generally) greater than his conscience and even his common sense; and Robin seems simply to be amused by him, taunting him at every opportunity and taking so much delight in confounding the sheriff's latest scheme that the remainder of his career (the robbing, the giving, and the courting of Marian) feels almost secondary to his primary goal—to precipitate another of the sheriff's legendary tantrums.

The chemistry between the cast is electrifying; a fission that is evident not only in the traditionally tangled triangle of Robin, Gisborne, and Marian, but also the ties that bind the Merry Men themselves. To borrow a phrase from the Three Musketeers, they truly are "all for one and one for all."

The show takes few liberties with tradition. Much, Allen a Dale, Will Scarlet, and Little John are the heart and soul of the gang, to be joined late in season one by Djaq, a Saracen woman who masqueraded on the battlefield as a man; and in season three by Friar Tuck and a ferociously combative villager named Kate.

And so the first two, two-and-a-half, seasons play out more or less by the book, reprising the best of the old ballads and legends, but seeding other elements into the storyline.

Robin's personal origins certainly conform to what we would expect—a heroic knight returning to his home following the Crusades, to discover his lands have been expropriated by the sheriff and handed to Gisborne. He takes to the forest, gathers a gang, and continues to court his childhood sweetheart Marian, even as she is romanced by the black-hearted Sir Guy.

But slowly, other elements come to the fore—Marian's career as the Nightwatchman, caring for the poor long before Robin returned to Loxley; Gisborne's involvement in a plot to murder King Richard in the Holy Land (see chapter seven), and Robin's shocking discovery of that fact; a second attempt to kill the king, with Robin and his men following Gisborne back to the Holy Land for a climactic showdown. During which, shockingly, Marian is killed.

There is also room, during the third season, for Gisborne to be given a sister, Isabelle (played by the superlative Lara Pulver), who enjoys a brief fling with Robin before rising to the rank of sheriff herself, after Vaisey is apparently murdered by her brother. And suddenly intrigue is positively piling upon intrigue, as the writers raced to wrap up their story. Armstrong had annouced his intention to quit following the latest series, prompting the BBC to pull the plug on the entire series. There were a lot of loose ends to tie up.

Twisting one of *Robin of Sherwood*'s most remarkable twists, that Robin and Gisborne should discover themselves to be half brothers, we now learn that Gisborne's mother and Robin's father had an affair when the boys were younger, and that a son, Archer, was born from the union.

Cementing a most uneasy truce so that they might obey Robin's father's dying wish, the pair sets out to locate him, only for Archer to slip away from their care and join forces instead with his half sister, the now power-crazed sheriff Isabelle, in Nottingham Castle.

Robin and Gisborne combine forces to take back the castle in the name of King Richard, only to fall into a cunningly laid trap. But then Isabelle and Archer have a falling-out; he releases his half brothers and they resume their assault against Isabelle, only for a *third* army to appear, led by the not-as-dead-as-we-thought former sheriff Vaisey.

What follows is quite possibly the most apocalyptic conclusion to any telling of the legends of Robin Hood.

Allan a Dale is first to perish, cut down by a hail of arrows. Vaisey kills Gisborne; Isabelle runs Robin through with a poisoned sword; and then she and Vaisey perish when the castle's store of Byzantine Fire (gunpowder) is ignited by a flaming arrow.

Knowing his end is near, Robin escapes back to the forest with Archer and commands him to take over the leadership of the Merry Men. Then he drifts away to an afterlife where Marian already awaits him.

On paper, it all reads very pat. Spread across two consecutive Saturday nights, however, or viewed seamlessly on DVD, it's heart-pounding (not to mention, at the end, heart-breaking) stuff, and the show's audience loudly declaimed its anguish over the show's cancellation. But even without the BBC's decision, the experiences of *Robin of Sherwood*, replacing an accepted Robin with a new one, cast an impenetrable shadow over any thoughts of continuing.

No, *Robin Hood* ended as it ought to have, going out with the biggest bang Nottingham has ever seen or heard. And besides, it wasn't as if Robin was really dead.

How could he be?

Epilogue

mmortality, at least in terms of popular entertainment, is an awkward attribute to quantify.

Is James Bond immortal, simply because he is the figurehead of a commercial franchise that extends over more than a half century? Batman or Superman? *Star Trek* and Doctor Who?

The creativity that was poured into those characters' birth and development, after all, was long ago subsumed within the mechanics of profit; in terms of blockbuster movies and ever-more groaning bookshelves, all are just a few fallow years, and a major flop or two, away from being mothballed for a very long time.

Robin Hood is different; Robin Hood is all but unique. Only King Arthur can convincingly argue to having enjoyed as long (if not longer) a lifespan as Robin, and to have spent it in as many different media. Like Robin, the Arthurian legend devours ancient ballads, medieval plays, Renaissance fantasy, Victorian romanticism, modern merchandising, and dedicated scholarship; like Robin, his stories involve sacred quests and scheming monks, vicious foes, and unquenchable love, and hanging over all of them, one essential, unanswerable question.

Is any of it actually true?

Of course they are not alone in stepping out of the mists of some mysterious past to bask in the glow of mass popularity and awareness. But those other long-dead figures who have transcended their traditional place in the history books—Rob Roy and William Wallace, Spartacus and Henry VIII—they rise and fall according to the whims of authors and filmmakers, editors and audiences.

Robin (and Arthur) ride on regardless. He cares no more for public taste than he does for the Sheriff of Nottingham's dignity. If a new action hero proves a miserable flop, it is because the audience has tired of that particular hero. If a new Robin Hood should fail to take off, it's because there was something wrong with the story. Robin himself is bullet proof.

Perhaps that, after all the other theorizing is done, is the real reason Robin Hood is likely just as popular today, almost nine hundred years after his assumed birth, as he was at any other time in his history.

Novels, movies and television shows have replaced ballads and May games as the primary source for hearing old legends and conjuring new, but that is simply a shift in technology; the media might change, but the message remains identical.

In terms of entertainment, there is not the slightest difference between a group of medieval peasants gathered to listen to a troubadour performing his songs of Robin Hood, and a auditorium full of modern cinemagoers thrilling to the latest celluloid reinvention; and one could tie oneself into an impossible knot attempting to understand (let alone explain) how a story first told in the 1300s, as "A Lyttel Geste of Robyne Hood," should still be told, and loved, today.

People try, of course they do. Elsewhere in this book, you will read of the unquenchable values of humanity that Robin Hood represents; of the never-ending struggle for freedom and happiness; of his unwavering commitment to justice and equality. And these elements all play a part in the legend's survival.

The stark simplicity of his love for Marian; the absolute devotion and togetherness of his followers; the unparalleled excitement of his adventures. Courage and honesty, strength and heroism, every admirable quality that the human race can manifest is bound up in Robin Hood, and if his fight for freedom should oft-times butt heads with the demands and requirements of the state, then who is really at fault? Robin, for wanting the best for everyone? Or the state, for caring only about itself?

So he is invoked in times of war and rebellion, a beacon for us all; but he is no less present in times of peace, when lesser affairs concern us. He is a friend to the poor and the needy, but an ally, too, of those politicians and administrators who themselves recognize the plight of those less fortunate than themselves, and resolve to do something about it. And the fact that their opponents frequently outnumber them and certainly out-shout them is one that Robin himself would recognize from his own time. He did not give up the fight. Neither should we.

At the beginning of this book, discussing the manifold theories of who Robin Hood might really have been, "the question of Robin Hood's reality" was described as one "that this book will not be answering."

But, in many ways, it has done so anyway.

Robin Hood the person, if such a person ever lived, is less than dust today.

But Robin Hood the spirit is alive and well in everyone who wants to breathe it in. And that is why we love him still.

Robin Hood is within the mirror that man looks into every day, and when we see his reflection, we see ourselves.

Unless, of course, we see the Sheriff of Nottingham. Because he's in there, as well.

Appendix One
Robin in Song

Part One—The Child Ballads

The following offers a selection of available recordings of the ancient ballads, as collected by Francis James Child in *The English and Scottish Popular Ballads* (aka *The Child Ballads*). Child's original numbering, still recognized by artists and scholars alike, is included.

Child Ballad 117: A Lyttel Geste of Robyn Hode
Bob Frank: CD *A Little Gest of Robin Hood*—2001

Child Ballad 118: Robin Hood and Guy of Gisborne
Hester NicEilidh: CD *The Robin Hood Ballad Project*—2006

Child Ballad 119: Robin Hood and the Monk
Hester NicEilidh: CD *The Robin Hood Ballad Project*—2006

Child Ballad 120: Robin Hood's Death
Art Thieme: LP *Songs of the Heartland*—1980
Dan Keding: CD *MacPherson's Lament and Other Ballads*—1995
Ed McCurdy and Michael Kane: LP *The Legend of Robin Hood*—1973
Hermes Nye: LP *Ballads Reliques: Early English Ballads from the Percy and Child Collections*—1957
Regal Slip: CD *Bandstand*—1999
Roxanne and Dan Keding: LP *From Far and Near*—1980
Wallace House: LP *Robin Hood Ballads*—1953

Child Ballad 121: Robin Hood and the Potter
no recordings known

Child Ballad 122: Robin Hood and the Butcher
Ed McCurdy and Michael Kane: LP *The Legend of Robin Hood*—1973
Hester NicEilidh: CD *The Robin Hood Ballad Project*—2006

Child Ballad 123: Robin Hood and the Curtal Friar
Estampie: CD *Under the Greenwood Tree*—1997
Wallace House: LP *Robin Hood Ballads*—1953

Child Ballad 124: Jolly Pinder of Wakefield
Wallace House: LP *Robin Hood Ballads*—1953

Child Ballad 125: Robin Hood and Little John
Ed McCurdy and Michael Kane: LP *The Legend of Robin Hood*—1973
Edith Cummings Taylor: the Ben Gray Lumpkin Digital Folk Music
    Collection, University of Colorado, Boulder
Gilbert Flemming: the Helen Creighton Collection
John Strachan: LP *The Folk Songs of Britain, Vol 5: Child Ballads 2*—1961
Matt Schwarz: LP *The Lost Way*—2003
Roy Harris: LP *By Sandbank Fields*—1977
Wallace House: LP Robin Hood Ballads—1953

Child Ballad 126: Robin Hood and the Tanner:
L. Lloyd: LP *The English and Scottish Popular Ballads (The Child Ballads)
    Vol. 2*—1956
Broadside Electric: CD *Amplificata*—1997
Bob Lewis: CD *Old Songs & Bothy Ballads: There's Bound to Be a Row*—2010
English Heritage: CD *A Minstrel's Music*—1998
Estampie: CD *Under the Greenwood Tree*—1997
Martin Best: LP *William Shakespeare: Ages of Song*—1979
Michael Raven and Joan Mills: LP *The Dutch Connection*—1976
Richard Searles: CD *Scarborough Faire*—1997
Roy Harris: LP *The Bitter and the Sweet*—1972
Sherwood Rise: LP *From the Wood*—1981
St. George's Canzona: LP *A Tapestry of Music for Robin Hood and His
    King*—1976
Steve Jordan: CD *Folk Songs from Hampshire and Dorset*—2005
Wallace House: LP *Robin Hood Ballads*—1953

Child Ballad 127: Robin Hood and the Tinker
no recordings known

Child Ballad 128: Robin Hood Newly Revived
no recordings known

Child Ballad 129: Robin Hood and the Prince of Aragon

Ed McCurdy and Michael Kane: LP *The Legend of Robin Hood*—1973

Child Ballad 130: Robin Hood and the Scotchman

Hester NicEilidh: CD *The Robin Hood Ballad Project*—2006

Child Ballad 131: Robin Hood and the Ranger

Wallace House: LP *Robin Hood Ballads*—1953

Child Ballad 132: Bold Pedlar and Robin Hood (aka Gamble Gold and Robin Hood)

L. Lloyd: *The English and Scottish Popular Ballads (The Child Ballads)*—Vol. 4—1956

Barry Dransfield: LP *Barry Dransfield*—1972

Belle Luther Richards: The Helen Hartness Flanders Collection:

Ben Henneberry: The Helen Creighton Collection:

Benji Kirkpatrick: CD *Dance in the Shadow*—1998

Brass Farthing: CD *More Songs About Dogs and Beer*—2010

Carrie Grover: LP *Old Mother Hippletoe—Rural and Urban Children's Songs*—1978

Caswell Carnahan: LP *New Leaves on an Old Tree*—1981

Denny Smith: CD *Band of Gold*—2000

Ed McCurdy: LP *Bad Men and Heroes*—1955

Ed McCurdy and Michael Kane: LP *The Legend of Robin Hood*—1973

Emily and Hazel Askew: CD *Six By Two*—2005

Geordie Roberston: CD *Scottish Tradition 5: Muckle Sangs: Classic Scottish Ballads*—1992

Jon Pfaff: CD *It's Jon Goddammitt*—1998

June Tabor: LP *Folkweave 11*—1978

Margaret MacArthur: CD *Ballads Thrice Twisted*—1999

Oliver Bootle: CD *Oliver Bootle*—1997

Peter Shepheard: CD *Old Songs & Bothy Ballads: Nick-knack on the Waa*—2008

Shepheard, Spiers and Watson: CD *Over the High Hills*—2012

Stanley Robertson: CD *The College Boy*—2010

Steeleye Span: LP *All Around My Hat*—1975

Steve Chandler: CD *The Span of Time*—2005

The Owl Service: CD *Garland Sessions*—2012

Child Ballad 133: Robin Hood and the Beggar I

Child Ballad 134: Robin Hood and the Beggar II

Child Ballad 135: Robin Hood and the Shepherd
no recordings known

Child Ballad 136: Robin Hood's Delight
Hester NicEilidh: CD *The Robin Hood Ballad Project*—2006

Child Ballad 137: Robin Hood and the Pedlars
Hester NicEilidh: CD *The Robin Hood Ballad Project*—2006

Child Ballad 138: Robin Hood and Allen a Dale
Sherwood Rise: LP *From the Wood*—1981

Child Ballad 139: Robin Hood's Progress to Nottingham
Dave Goulder, Liz Dyer and The Broken Consort: LP *The Raven and the Crow*—1970
Ed McCurdy and Michael Kane: LP *The Legend of Robin Hood*—1973
John Goodluck: LP *The Suffolk Miracle*—1974

Child Ballad 140: Robin Hood Rescuing Three Squires
Charles Finnemore: LP *Burly Banks of Barbry O: Eight Traditional British-American Ballads*—1953
Dean Robinson: LP *Unto Brigg Fair: Joseph Taylor and Other Traditional Lincolnshire Singers*—(1972)
Jim and Lynette Eldon: CD *Jim & Lynette Eldon*—1997
John Kirkpatrick: CD *Ballads*—1997
Margaret MacArthur: CD *Ballads Thrice Twisted*—1999
The Songwainers: LP *The Songwainers*—1971
Wallace House: *Robin Hood Ballads*—1953*

Child Ballad 141: Robin Hood Rescuing Will Stutly
Ed McCurdy and Michael Kane: LP *The Legend of Robin Hood*—1973

Child Ballad 142: Little John a Begging

Child Ballad 143: Robin Hood and the Bishop
no recordings known

Child Ballad 144: Robin Hood and the Bishop of Hereford

A. L. Lloyd: LP *The English and Scottish Popular Ballads (The Child Ballads):Vol. 3*—1956

Heather Wood: CD *The English and Scottish Popular Ballads: The Digital Child Companion*—2003

John Roberts and Tony Barrand: CD *A Present from the Gentlemen: A Pandora's Box of English Folk Songs*—1992

Tim Laycock: CD *Fine Colours*—1999

Tony Rose: LP *Young Hunting*—1970

Child Ballad 145: Robin Hood and Queen Katherine

Child Ballad 146: Robin Hood's Chase

no recordings known

Child Ballad 147: Robin Hood's Golden Prize

Ed McCurdy and Michael Kane: LP *The Legend of Robin Hood*—1973

Hermes Nye: LP *Ballads Reliques: Early English Ballads from the Percy and Child Collections*—1957

Kathleen Danson Read: LP *Spoken Literature of Early English Ballads*—1956

Child Ballad 148: Noble Fisherman or Robin Hood's Preferment:

no recordings known

Child Ballad 149: Robin Hood's Birth, Breeding, Valor and Marriage (aka Robin Hood's Xmas at Gamwell Hall)

Ed McCurdy and Michael Kane: LP *The Legend of Robin Hood*—1973

Hester NicEilidh: CD *The Robin Hood Ballad Project*—2006

Child Ballad 150: Robin Hood and Maid Marian

Ed McCurdy and Michael Kane: LP *The Legend of Robin Hood*—1973

Estampie: CD *Under the Greenwood Tree*—1997

Wallace House: LP *Robin Hood Ballads*—1953

Child Ballad 151: King's Disguise, and Friendship with Robin Hood

no recordings known

Child Ballad 152: Robin Hood and the Golden Arrow

Ed McCurdy and Michael Kane: LP *The Legend of Robin Hood*—1973

Laura Berlage: CD *Legends of the Troubadours*—2006

Child Ballad 153: Robin Hood and the Valiant Knight
no recordings known

Child Ballad 154: A True Tale of Robin Hood
Wallace House: LP *Robin Hood Ballads*—1953

Part Two—Other Medieval and Traditional Ballads

With certain obvious exceptions, references to Robin within these are often vague and largely conjectural.

c1250—"A Lutel Soth Sermun" (author unknown)

c1260—"Dixieme Pastourelle" (attributed to Gilbert de Berneville)

c1283—"Le Jeu de Robin et de Marion" (by Adam de la Halle)

c1376—"Mirour de l'Omme" (by John Gower) late fourteenth century—"King Edward and the Shepherd" (author unknown)

c1520—"A Robyn" (by William Cornysh)

c1535—"A Robyn" (by Thomas Wyatt)

1608—"Since Robin Hood" (by Thomas Weelkes)

1609—"In Sherwood Lived Stout Robin Hood" from *A Musicall Dreame or Fourth Booke of Ayres* (by Robert Jones)

1632—"A True Tale of Robin Hood" (by Martin Parker—see also Child 154)

Part Three—Soundtracks, Stage, and Spoken Word

1784 *Robin Hood or Sherwood Forest* (stageshow)
(music by William Shield)

A version of "Her Hair is Like the Golden Clue, Drawn from Minerva's Loom" was recorded, in 1989, by Patricia Wright and John A. Gillaspie—CD *Jane Austen Songs* (Pearl SHECD 8613)

1891 *Robin Hood* (stageshow)
(music and lyrics by Harry B. Smith and Reginald De Koven)
"The Armorer's Song"
"Brown October Ale"
"The Country Dance"
"The Forest Song"
"In Greenwood Fair"
"Maid Marian's Song"
"Oh, Promise Me"
"The Tinker's Song"
"A Time Will Come"
"Though It Was Within This Hour We Met"
"A Troubadour Sang to His Love"
"When a Maiden Weds"
"The Hunting Song"
"The Legend of the Chimes"
Two 78s were later released comprising medleyed selections from this opera:

1912—Arthur Pryor's Band: *Robin Hood Favorites* (Victor 16919)

1915 Victor Light Opera Company – *Gems From Robin Hood* (Victor 35413)
"Hey Hey! For the Merry Greenwood"/"Brown October Ale"/"Come, Dream So Bright"/"Tinkers' Chorus"/"Oh, Promise Me"/"Come Away To The Woods"/ "Ho Ho Then For Jollity"/"Ye Birds In Azure Winging"/"Armorer's Song"/"A Hunting We'll Go"/"Ah! I Do Love You"/"Sweetheart, My Own Sweetheart"/"Love, Now We Never More Will Part"

1891 *Ivanhoe* (opera)
(music and lyrics by Sir Arthur Sullivan)
Act 1. Scene 1. Introduction
Act 1. Scene 1. "Each day this realm of England faints and fails . . ."
Act 1. Scene 1. "Good Thane, most noble Thane, I pray . . ."

Act 1. Scene 1. "Welcome, Sir Knights!"

Act 1. Scene 1. "Drink, drink ye all . . ."

Act 1. Scene 1. "The Palmer! The holy Palmer!"

Act 1. Scene 1. "Is she not fair? And she is rich withal . . ."

Act 1. Scene 2. "O moon, art thou clad in silver mail . . ."

Act 1. Scene 2. "Good Palmer, thou didst speak of one I know . . ."

Act 1. Scene 2. "Like mountain lark my spirit upward springs . . ."

Act 1. Scene 3. "Will there be no more fighting?"

Act 1. Scene 3. "Plantangenesta!"

Act 1. Scene 3. "Isaac, my Jew, my purse of Gold . . ."

Act 1. Scene 3. "'Tis from our Royal brother, Louis of France . . ."

Act 1. Scene 3. "What means his motto?"

Act 2. Scene 1. "Strange lodging this for England's King . . ."

Act 2. Scene 1. "There is a custom in the East . . ."

Act 2. Scene 1. "I ask nor wealth nor courtier's praise . . ."

Act 2. Scene 1. "Not bad, say I, nor badly sung!"

Act 2. Scene 1. "The wind blows cold across the moor . . ."

Act 2. Scene 1. "And now for combat! Where's this friend of mine?"

Act 2. Scene 2. "Will not our captor dare to show his face?"

Act 2. Scene 2. "Welcome, Sir Templar! But I may not stay . . ."

Act 2. Scene 2. "Her southern splendour, like the Syrian Moon . . ."

Act 2. Scene 3. "Whet the keen axes . . ."

Act 2. Scene 3. "O awful depth below the castle wall!"

Act 2. Scene 3. "Lord of our chosen race . . ."

Act 2. Scene 3. "Take thou these jewels; here is wealthenow . . ."

Act 2. Scene 3. "What sound is that?"

Act 3. Scene 1. "Happy with winged feet . . ."

Act 3. Scene 1. "Tend thou the Knight thou lovest . . ."

Act 3. Scene 1. "Ah, would that thou and I might lead our sheep . . ."

Act 3. Scene 1. "But hark! what sound is in mine ear?"

Act 3. Scene 1. "I see them now; the dark wood moves with bows . . ."

Act 3. Scene 1. "How canst thou know what pain it is to lie . . ."

Act 3. Scene 2. "Light foot upon the dancing green . . ."

Act 3. Scene 2. "Maurice de Bracy, faithless knight . . ."

Act 3. Scene 2. "Look, where thy moody father walks apart . . ."

Act 3. Scene 2. "Knight, Knight of Ivanhoe, I come for thee!"

Act 3. Scene 3. "Fremuere principes . . ."

Act 3. Scene 3. "Thou Jewish girl, who art condemned to die . . ."

Act 3. Scene 3. "It shall not be . . ."

Act 3. Scene 3. "A champion! A champion! A champion!"

Act 3. Scene 3. "A judgment! A judgment!"

Act 3. Scene 3. "See where the banner of England floats afar . . ."

This entire score was recreated/recorded in 2010 by David Lloyd Jones and the BBC National Orchestra of Wales (Chandos 10578)

1892 *The Foresters*

(music by Arthur Sullivan; lyrics by Alfred, Lord Tennyson)

"The Warrior Earl Of Allendale"

"Love Flew in at the Window"

"Long Live Richard!"

"To Sleep! To Sleep!"

"There Is No Land Like England"

"Evil Fairy! Do You Hear?"

"By All the Deer That Spring"

"The Bee Buzz'd Up in the Heat"

"Now the King Is Home Again"

This entire score was recreated/recorded in 2004 by the New London Orchestra, the London Chorus and soloists conducted by Ronald Corp (Hyperion CDA 67486)

1902—*Maid Marian* (stageshow)

(music and lyrics by Harry B. Smith and Reginald De Koven)

"Annabel Was Fairest"

"The Cobbler and the Flies"

"Never in the Wide, Wide World"

"The Cellarer's Toast"

"Can I Forget?"

"The Dew Is on the Heather"

"The Forester's Song"

"The Monk and the Magpie"

"Song of the Falcon"

"The Sheriff's Song"

"Serenade"

"Song of the Outlaw"

"Song of the Crusader"

"Tell Me Again, Sweetheart"

"True Love Is Not for a Day"

"Under the Mistletoe Bough"

No recordings known

1921 Robin Hood (light opera)

music and lyrics by Bernard and Norman Page
No recordings known

1926 *Bad Habits of 1926* (Broadway)

The Student Robin Hood Of Pilsen (music by Randall Thompson; lyrics by Perry Ivins)

1937—And On We Go (Broadway)

Includes the original version of "The Night Is Young and You're So Beautiful" (music by Dana Suesse; lyrics by Irving Kahal; Billy Rose)—see *Robin Hood: Men In Tights*

1938—*The Adventures of Robin Hood*

Main Title
"New Taxes / The Poaching Miller"
"Nottingham Castle"
"The Confrontation / Fight and Chase"
"Little John and Robin Hood"
"The Pledge"
"Friar Tuck and Robin Hood"
"Capturing Sir Guy"
"Romantic Theme / Love Theme"
"Lady Marian / Love Theme"
"The Tournament"
"The Capture / Robin Hood in Chains"
"The Escape"
"Robin Hood Visits Marian"
"Marian Caught / King Richard and Robin Hood"
"The Procession"
"The Fight"
"Victory / The End"
King Richard's Theme
Available recordings of this soundtrack include BMG RCA Victor 60863-2-RG, 1972 and BMG RCA Victor 0912-2-RG, 1975 (both conducted by Charles Gerhardt and performed by the National Philharmonic Orchestra); DCC Compact Classics GZS-1094 (originally recorded in 1961, conducted by Lionel Newman and Kurt Graunke, and performed by an uncredited Munich orchestra); and Marcoi Polo

8.225268 (recorded in 2003 by William T. Stromberg and the Moscow Symphony Orchestra)

1950s—Basil Rathbone—*Robin Hood/Treasure Island* (spoken word)

Robin Hood
Treasure Island
Released on LP as Columbia CL 673

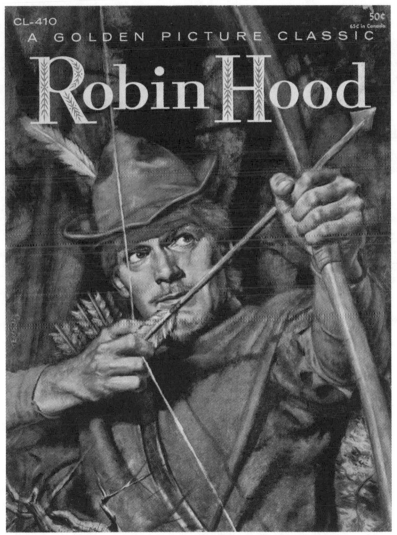

First published in 1883, Howard Pyle's *The Merry Adventures of* Robin Hood *of Great Renown in Nottinghamshire* ranks among the most beloved Robin books.

1952—*Walt Disney Presents the Story of Robin Hood* (movie soundtrack)
"Riddle De Diddle De Day"
"Come Sing Low, Come Sing High"
"Ballad of Robin Hood"
"Riddle De Diddle De Day"
Released on 7-inch extended play (EP) as Disneyland LLP 342

1952—Children's Record Guild/Ray Abrashkin and Herbert Haufrecht – *Robin Hood* (spoken word)
Robin Hood (four parts)
Released on two 10-inch EPs as CRG 1010/11

1959—*Clown Jewels* (stageshow)
Robin Hood (music and lyrics by Carl Sigman)
No recording known

1960s—*Tale Spinners for Children: Robin Hood*
Performed by Robert Hardy and the Famous Theatre Company with the
     Hollywood Studio Orchestra
Robin Hood (two parts—spoken word)
Released on LP as United Artists UAC 11001

1962—Full Cast And Orchestra – *Robin Hood / Young Folks Favourites*
Robin Hood
Three other songs
Released on 10-inch EP as Cricket C28

1963—Anthony Quayle: The Ballad of Robin Hood
Parts one and two
Released on LP as Caedmon TC 1177

1964—General Electric Show 'n' Tell Picturesound Program: Robin Hood
"Robin Hood"
"When Johnny Comes Marching Home"
Released on 7-inch single as General Electric Show 'n' Tell NST 114

1964—Bret Morrison and Leroy Holmes and His Orchestra—*Tom and Jerry Meet Robin Hood*

Tom and Jerry Meet Robin Hood
Tom and Jerry Find Aladdin's Lamp
Released on 7-inch single as MGM EPO 7509

1964—*Robin And The 7 Hoods* (Original Score From The Motion Picture Musical Comedy)

Robin And The 7 Hoods—Overture (Nelson Riddle Orchestra)
"My Kind Of Town (Chicago Is)" (Frank Sinatra)
"All For One and One For All" (Peter Falk)
"Don't Be A Do-Badder" (Bing Crosby)
"Any Man Who Loves His Mother" (Dean Martin)
"Style" (Sinatra/Crosby/Martin)
"Mister Booze" (chorus)
"I Like to Lead When I Dance" (Sinatra)
"Bang Bang" (Sammy Davis Jr.)
"Charlotte Couldn't Charleston!" (chorus)
"Give Praise!!" (chorus)
"Don't Be A Do-Badder" (Finale)
Released on LP as Reprise FS 2021

1968—The Legend Of Robin Hood (US TV movie)

(music and lyrics by James Van Heusen and Sammy Cahn)
"Out in the Open Air"
"Prithee Please"
"A Happy Happenstance"
"Ever So Softly"
"Nottingham Fair"
"The Star Beyond the Star"
No recording known

1970s—London Theatre Company—Robin Hood (spoken word)

Adventures of the Outlaw of Sherwood Forest (two parts)
Released on LP as Beano BE12 012

1973—*Stories and Songs from Robin Hood* (movie soundtrack)

"Whistle Stop" (by Roger Miller)
"Oo-De-Lally" (by Roger Miller)

"Love"
"The Phony King of England" (by Phil Harris)
"Not in Nottingham" (by Roger Miller)
Reprise: "Whistle Stop" (by Roger Miller)
Finale: "Oo-De-Lanny"
Released on LP as Disneyland 3810

1973—Ed McCurdy and Michael Kane—*The Legend of Robin Hood* collection of Child Ballads

"Robin Hood's Birth"
"Robin Hood and the Fifteen Foresters"
"Robin Hood and Little John"
"Robin Hood Rescues Will Stuttley"
"Robin Hood and Maid Marion"
"Robin Hood and The Butcher"
"Robin Hood's Golden Prize"
"Robin Hood and the Prince Of Aragon"
"Robin Hood and the Pedlar"
"Robin Hood and the Golden Arrow"
"Robin Hood's Death"
Released on LP as Wonderland RLP 1458

1977—*Robin Hood in Story and Song with Top Cat*

Song: "Top Cat"
Story: Robin Hood (Pt. 1)
Song: "M-O-N-E-Y"
Story: Robin Hood (Pt. 2)
Song: "Robin Hood"
Song: "Dibble"
Story: Robin Hood (Pt. 3)
Story: Robin Hood (Pt. 4)
Song: "Buddies"
Released on LP as Columbia Special Projects P13864

1979—*Never Mind the Bullocks* (stageshow)

The Ballad of Robin Hood (music and lyrics by CP Lee)
No recording known

1979—St. George's Canzona—*Musica Para Robin Hood Y Su Rey*
Spanish act performing on medieval instruments
"La Estampida Inglesa—Robin Y Marian"
"Fanfarria"
"Ja Nuns Nos Pris—Lamento De Tristan"
"Estampida A Dos Voces: A La Fontenella"
"Quan Je Plus—Redit Aetas Aurea"
"The Maid in the Moon"
"Robin Hood and the Tanner"
Released on LP as Enigma S90-105

1981—*Robin Hood* (stageshow)
(music and lyrics by Dave Arthur; Toni Arthur; David Wood)
No recording known

1984—*Legend* (*Music from the TV series Robin of Sherwood*)
(music and lyrics by Clannad)
"Robin (The Hooded Man)"
"Now Is Here"
"Herne"
"Together We"
"Darkmere"
"Strange Land"
"Scarlet Inside"
"Lady Marian"
"Battles"
"Ancient Forest"
Released on CD as RCA 07863

1991—*Robin Hood: Prince of Thieves* (*Original Motion Picture Soundtrack*)
Overture and "A Prisoner of the Crusades" (From Chains to Freedom)
"Sir Guy of Gisborne and the Escape to Sherwood"
"Little John and the Band in the Forest"
"The Sheriff and His Witch"
"Maid Marian"
"Training—Robin Hood, Prince of Thieves"
"Marian at the Waterfall"
"The Abduction and the Final Battle at the Gallows"

"(Everything I Do) I Do It For You"
"Wild Times"
Released on CD as Morgan Creek 2959-20004-2

1993—Robin Hood: Men In Tights (Music from the Original Motion Picture Soundtrack)

"Marian" (Duet Version – Cathy Dennis, Lance Ellington)
Main Title
"Sherwood Forest Rap #1" (Kevin Dorsey, The Merry Men Singers)
"Escape from Kahlil Prison"
"Robin's Pledge / The Great Voyage"
"Stick Fight with Little John"
"Prince John's Party / Robin's Entrance"
"The Great Hall Fight"
"Men in Tights" (The Merry Men Singers)
"The Witch in the Tower"
"Villagers' Training Sequence"
"The Night Is Young" (Arthur Rubin, The Merry Men Singers)
"Romantic Marian"
"Royal Country Fayre / The Abbot's March"
"Villagers To The Rescue"
"The Wedding"
"Marian" (Solo Version—Debbie James)
"Sherwood Forest Rap #2" (Kevin Dorsey, The Merry Men Singers)
Released on CD as Milan 74321-17639-2

2001—Paul O'Dette—Robin Hood: Elizabethan Ballad Settings

"I Cannot keepe my wyfe at howme"
"Up tails all"
"The Spanish Pavane"
"Robin Hoode"
"John come Kisse me now"
"Chromatica Pavana"
"Galliard"
"Sueit smyling Katie loves me" (Scottish)
"Put on your sark on Monenday"
"Buckinghames branle"
"The Laydie Louthians lilte"
"La Volta"

"Wolsey's Wilde"
"Pavana Bray" set by Fr. Cutting
"Galiarda"
"Will yow walke the woods soe wylde"
"My Lord willoughbies welcome home"
"Pavin"
"Galliard"
"Lusty Gallant"
[A Ground]
"Home again, market is done"
"Trenchmore"
"Mall Symes"
Released on CD as Harmonia Mundi HM 90

2006—Robin Hood (Music from the BBC TV Series)

"Robin Hood Theme"
"Journey Home"
"Run Master Run"
"Locksley"
"Marian's Theme"
"Your Eyes"
"Rescue"
"The Sheriff Gets His Man"
"Scaling the Walls"
"Outlaws"
"From the Rich to the Poor"
"Chasing the Nightwatchman"
"Flush Him Out"
"Proving His Innocence"
"A Noble Deed"
"Gisborne's Trap"
"Shooting Pies"
"Robin and Marian"
"Marian's Punishment"
"Two Mothers"
"Where Is She?"
"Him I Liked"
"Different Directions"
"Silver Arrow"

"Gisborne Woos Marian"
"The Sheriff's Plan"
"A Love That Cannot Be"
"Lucky George"
"He's My Brother"
"The Nightwatchman"
"The Hanging"
"No Way Out"
"I Never Told Her I Loved Her"
Robin Hood End Credits
Released on CD as EMI 381 0292

2010—Hood the Musical (stageshow)
(music and lyrics by Andy Brown and Steve Williamson)
No recording known

2010—Robin Hood (Original Motion Picture Soundtrack)
"Destiny"
"Creatures"
"Fate Has Smiled Upon Us"
"Godfrey"
"Ambush"
"Pact Sworn in Blood"
"Returning the Crown"
"Planting the Fields"
"Sherwood Forest"
"John Is King"
"Robin Speaks"
"Killing Walter"
"Nottingham Burns"
"Siege"
"Landing of the French"
"Walter's Burial"
"Preparing for Battle"
"Charge"
"Clash"
"The Final Arrow"
"The Legend Begins"
"Merry Men"
Released on CD as Varèse Sarabande 302 067 020 2

2013—*Robin des Bois: Le Spectacle Musical—Ne renoncez jamais* (stageshow)

(music and lyrics by Patrice Guirao and Lionel Florence)

"Le jour qui se rêve"
"Devenir quelqu'un"
"Tes blessures"
"À nous"
"J'ai dit oui"
"Un monde à changer"
"Si l'amour existe"
"La flèche ou la cible"
"Quinze ans à peine"
"Lui sait qui je suis"
"Laissez-nous vivre"
"Notting Hill Nottingham"
"Terre"
Released on CD as Parlophone 5053105983124

Part Four—A Selection of Other Songs about Robin Hood

All released as 7 inch 45s. (Titles in *italics* are not Robin Hood related).

1945—Charles Norman Orkester: "Robin Hood"/"*Sentimental Journey*" (Columbia DS 1570)

1955—Nelson Riddle and His Orchestra: "*Lisbon, Antigua*"/"Robin Hood" (Capitol F3287)

1955—Gary Miller: "Robin Hood"/"*The Ballad of Davy Crockett*" (Pye Nixa N 15020)

1956—Dick James: "*The Ballad of Davy Crockett*"/"Robin Hood" (Parlophone R4117)

1963—Louis Prima with Gia Maione and Sam Butera and the Witnesses: "*Angelina*"/"Robin Hood" (Funckler PR 42.755)

1963—Baba Brooks: "Robin Hood"/"*I Shall Wear a Crown*" (Dutchess no cat #)

1964—Inga Cabor: "Robin Hood"/"*Dolce Vivere*" (Polydor NH 52337)

1967—Los Pekenikes: "Robin Hood"/"*Felices '20*" (Hispavox H 164)

1973—The Pastors: "Robin Hood" (mono/stereo) (Alithia AR 6058)

1979—Fox and Promes: "Robin Hood"/"*Mr Reggae Man*" (CBS 7955)

1979—The Charlie Parkas: "The Ballad of Robin Hood"/"*Space Invaders*" (Paranoid Plastics PPS 001)

1979—Loredana Bertè: "Robin Hood" + other artist (CGD YD 554)

1980—Barrington Levy: "Robin Hood"/"Rob In Dub" + *2* (Jah Guidance JG 014)

1983—The Chaps: "The Legend of Robin Hood"/"*Jock the Rapper*" (Dakota DAK 16)

1983—Bogart: "Robin Hood"/"*Telefonkoks*" (Artic 6.19012)

1983—Sina: "Robin Hood"/"*Daddy's Dattelmonopol*"(Jupiter Records 6.13783)

1985—Lamu: "Robin Hood"/"*Mancher Mann*" (CBS CBSA 6311)

1986—William King: "Robin Hood" (vocal)/(instrumental) (Modern Music MDN 1002)

1988—La Voz De Los Señores—"Robin Hood"/"*Obsesion*" (Dame Dame DD 005)

1991—Fish and Roses: *Fish & Roses' Friar Tuck Record*—"Monks Hate You"/"Robin Hood 4" (Ajax Records AJAX 012)

1992—FYAH: "*Rock Don't Fall*"/"Robin Hood" (Ruption Records SSM 223)

1996—General Degree: "Robin Hood"/instrumental (VP Records VPRD 5985)

2001—Jenny Rom: "Robin Robin Hood" (extended version + mixes) (Interdance DAN 19022)

2006—Jamie Taylor: "Robin Hood"/"*Sycophant*" (Cluster Records 81)

2007—DJ Brasco: "*Go Hard*"/"Robin Hood" (Greenstone GS 0004)

2011—Edguy: "Robin Hood" (album version)/(single version) (Nuclear Blast NB 2777)

Appendix Two
Robin on Screen

1908: *Robin Hood and His Merry Men* (UK)

1908: *Robin Hood* (US)

1912: *Robin Hood—Outlawed*
   Cast:
   A. Brian Plant—Robin Hood
   Ivy Martinek—Maid Marian
   George Foley—Friar Tuck
   Edouard Durant—Will Scarlet (as Edwin Durant)
   Jack Houghton—Sir Hubert de Boissy
   J. Leonard—Abbot of Ramsey
   Harry Lorraine—Little John

1912: *Robin Hood* (US)
   Cast:
   Robert Frazer—Robin Hood
   Barbara Tennant—Maid Marian
   Alec B. Francis—Sheriff of Nottingham
   Julia Stuart—Sheriff's Housekeeper
   Mathilde Baring—Maid at Merwyn's
   Isabel Lamon—Fennel
   Muriel Ostriche—Christabel
   M. E. Hannefy—Friar Tuck
   Guy Oliver—Guy Oliver
   George Larkin—Allen a Dale
   Charles Hundt—Will Scarlet
   John Troyano—Much
   Arthur Hollingsworth—Richard the Lion-Hearted
   Lamar Johnstone—Guy of Gisborne
   John G. Adolfi—Thomas Merwin

1913: *Ivanhoe* (US)
Cast:

King Baggot—Wilfred of Ivanhoe
Leah Baird—Rebecca of York
Herbert Brenon—Isaac of York
Evelyn Hope—Lady Rowena
Walter Craven—Richard, the Lion-Hearted
Wallace Widdicombe—Sir Brian de Bois—Guilbert
Walter Thomas—Robin Hood
Wallace Bosco—Sir Cedric, Ivanhoe's Father
Helen Downing—Elgitha
Jack Bates—Reginald Front-de Boeuf
R. Hollies—Friar Tuck
George Courtenay—Prince John
William Calvert—Gurth
A. J. Charlwood—Athelstane
Maurice Norman—Wamba, the Jester

1913: *Robin Hood and Maid Marian*
Cast:

William Russell—Robin Hood
Gerda Holmes—Maid Marian
Harry Benham—Allen a Dale
John Dillon—Sheriff of Nottingham
Ernest Redding—Friar Tuck
Mignon Anderson—Ellen
David Thompson—Hardfast
Sidney Bracy—The Baron
Walter Gibbs— King Richard

1922: *Douglas Fairbanks in Robin Hood*
Cast:

Douglas Fairbanks—Earl of Huntingdon/Robin Hood (It was
    Fairbanks's custom to place his name last.)
Wallace Beery—King Richard the Lion-Hearted
Sam De Grasse—Prince John
Enid Bennett—Lady Marian Fitzwalter
Paul Dickey—Sir Guy of Gisborne
William Lowery—The High Sheriff of Nottingham
Willard Louis—Friar Tuck

The book version of the 1922 movie.

Alan Hale—The Squire/Little John
Bud Geary—Will Scarlet
Lloyd Talman—Allen a Dale
Billie Bennett—Servant to Lady Marian

1923: *Robin Hood Jr*

Cast:
Frankie Lee—The Boy, later Robin Hood
Peggy Cartwright—The Girl, later Maid Marian
S. J. Bingham—The Father, later King Richard (as Stanley Bingham)
Edward Cooper—The Doctor, later Prince John
Harry Lamont—Sir Guy of Gisborne

Phillip Dunham—High Sheriff of Nottingham

1925: *Lady Robin Hood* (aka *Amazon of the Hills*)
Cast:
Evelyn Brent—Señorita Catalina / La Ortiga
Robert Ellis—Hugh Winthrop
Boris Karloff—Cabraza
William Humphrey—Governor
D'Arcy Corrigan—Padre
Robert Cauterio—Raimundo

1932: *The Merry Men of Sherwood*
Cast:
John J. Thompson—Robin Hood
Aileen Marson—Maid Marian
Eric Adeney—Sheriff of Nottingham
Patrick Barr—Torturer

1938: *The Adventures of Robin Hood*
Cast:
Errol Flynn—Sir Robin of Locksley
Olivia de Havilland—Lady Marian Fitzwalter
Basil Rathbone—Sir Guy of Gisborne
Claude Rains—Prince John
Patric Knowles—Will à Gamwell
Eugene Pallette—Friar Tuck
Alan Hale—John Little
Herbert Mundin—Much, the Miller's Son
Melville Cooper—the High Sheriff of Nottingham
Una O'Connor—Bess
Ian Hunter—King Richard
Montagu Love—the Bishop of the Black Canons
Harry Cording—Dickon Malbete
Ivan F. Simpson—the proprietor of the Kent Road Tavern
Leonard Willey—Sir Essex
Robert Noble—Sir Ralf
Kenneth Hunter—Sir Mortimer
Robert Warwick—Sir Geoffrey
Colin Kenny—Sir Baldwin

Lester Matthews—Sir Ivor
Lionel Belmore—Humility Prin
Frank Hagney—a man-at-arms
Holmes Herbert—the archery referee at the tournament
Howard Hill—Elwen the Welshman
Crauford Kent—Sir Norbett
Carole Landis—a guest at the banquet
Leonard Mudie—the town crier
Reginald Sheffield—the herald at tournament
Trigger—Lady Marian's horse

1946: *The Bandit of Sherwood Forest*
Cast:
Anita Louise—Lady Catherine Maitland
Jill Esmond—The Queen Mother
Edgar Buchanan—Friar Tuck
Cornel Wilde—Robert of Nottingham
Henry Daniell—The Regent. William of Pembroke
George Macready—Fitz-Herbert
Russell Hicks—Robin Hood, Earl of Huntington
John Abbott—Will Scarlet
Lloyd Corrigan—Sheriff of Nottingham
Eva Moore—Mother Meg
Ray Teal—Little John
Leslie Denison—Allen a Dale
Ian Wolfe—Lord Mortimer
Maurice Tauzin—The King
Miles Mander—Lord Warrick
Mark Roberts—Robin Hood's Man

1948: *The Prince of Thieves*
Cast:
Jon Hall—Robin Hood
Patricia Morison—Lady Marian Claire
Adele Jergens—Lady Christabel
Alan Mowbray—The Friar
Michael Duane—Sir Allan Claire
H. B. Warner—Gilbert Head
Robin Raymond—Maude

Lowell Gilmore—Sir Phillip
Belle Mitchell—Margaret Head
Gavin Muir—Baron Tristram
Walter Sande—Little John
Syd Saylor—Will Scarlet
Lewis Russell—Sir Fitz-Alwin

1950: *Rogues of Sherwood Forest*

Cast:

John Derek—Robin Hood
Diana Lynn—Lady Marianne de Beaudray
George Macready—King John
Alan Hale—Little John
Paul Cavanagh—Sir Giles
Lowell Gilmore—Count of Flanders
Billy House—Friar Tuck
Lester Matthews—Allen a Dale
Billy Bevan—Will Scarlet (as William Bevan)
Wilton Graff—Baron Fitzwalter
Donald Randolph—Archbishop Stephen Langton
Matthew Boulton—Abbot

1951: *Tales of Robin Hood* (TV pilot)

Cast:

Robert Clarke—Robin Hood
Mary Hatcher—Maid Marian
Paul Cavanagh—Sir Gui de Clairmont
Wade Crosby—Little John
Whit Bissell—Will Stutely
Ben Welden—Friar Tuck
Robert Bice—Will Scarlet
Keith Richards—Sir Alan
Bruce Lester—Allen a Dale
Tiny Stowe—Sheriff of Nottingham
Lester Matthews—Sir Hugh Fitzwalter
John Vosper—Earl of Chester
Norman Bishop—Mitch
Margia Dean—Betty
Lorin Raker—Landlord

1952: *The Story of Robin Hood and His Merrie Men*

Cast:

Richard Todd—Robin Hood

Joan Rice—Maid Marian

Peter Finch—the Sheriff of Nottingham

James Hayter—Friar Tuck. (Hayter would later reprise his role in the 1967 Hammer film *A Challenge for Robin Hood*.)

James Robertson Justice—Little John

Martita Hunt—Queen Eleanor of Aquitaine

Hubert Gregg—Prince John

Elton Hayes—Allen a Dale

Anthony Eustrel—the Archbishop of Canterbury

Patrick Barr—King Richard I

Anthony Forwood—Will Scarlet

Bill Owen—Will Stutely

Louise Hampton—Tyb, aged nurse of Maid Marian

Richard Graydon—Merrie Man

1952: *Ivanhoe*

Cast:

Robert Taylor—Sir Wilfred of Ivanhoe

Elizabeth Taylor—Rebecca

Joan Fontaine—Rowena

George Sanders—Sir Brian De Bois-Guilbert

Emlyn Williams—Wamba

Robert Douglas—Sir Hugh De Bracy

Finlay Currie—Cedric

Felix Aylmer—Isaac

Francis de Wolff—Front De Boeuf (also Francis DeWolff)

Norman Wooland—King Richard

Basil Sydney—Waldemar Fitzurse

Harold Warrender—Locksley—Robin Hood

Patrick Holt—Philip DeMalvoisin

Roderick Lovell—Ralph DeVipont

Sebastian Cabot—Clerk of Copmanhurst (Little John)

John Ruddock—Hundebert

Michael Brennan—Baldwin

Megs Jenkins—Servant to Isaac

Valentine Dyall—Norman Guard

Lionel Harris—Roger of Bermondsley
Carl Jaffe—Austrian Monk
Guy Rolfe—Prince John
Jack Churchill—Archer on the Walls of Warwick Castle

1952: *Miss Robin Hood*
Cast:
Margaret Rutherford—Miss Honey
Richard Hearne—Henry Wrigley
Edward Lexy—Wilson
Frances Rowe—Marion
Michael Medwin—Ernest
Eunice Gayson—Pam
Sidney James—Sidney
Dora Bryan—Pearl
Eric Berry—Lord Otterbourne
Peter Jones—Lidstone
James Robertson Justice—Macalister

1953: *Robin Hood* (UK TV)
Cast:
Patrick Troughton—Robin Hood
Wensley Pithey—Friar Tuck
Kenneth Mackintosh—Little John
Dudley Jones—Much
John Breslin—Allen a Dale
David Kossoff—Sheriff of Nottingham
Philip Guard—Will Scarlet
David Markham—King Edward I

1954: *The Men of Sherwood Forest* (UK)
Cast:
Don Taylor—Robin Hood
Reginald Beckwith—Friar Tuck
Eileen Moore—Lady Alys
David King-Wood—Sir Guy Belton
Douglas Wilmer—Sir Nigel Saltire
Harold Lang—Hubert
Ballard Berkeley—Walter

Patrick Holt—King Richard
Wensley Pithey—Hugo
Leslie Linder—Little John
John Van Eyssen—Will Scarlet

1955–1959: *The Adventures of Robin Hood* (UK TV)

Cast:

Richard Greene—Robin Hood
Alan Wheatley—Sheriff of Nottingham
Archie Duncan—Little John
Bernadette O'Farrell—Maid Marian (seasons one/two)
Patricia Driscoll—Maid Marian (seasons three/four)
Alexander Gauge—Friar Tuck
Ronald Howard—Will Scarlet (season one)
Paul Eddington—Will Scarlet (season four)
Victor Woolf—Derwent
Simone Lovell—Joan
Ian Hunter—Sir Richard of the Lea
Patricia Burke—Lady Leona
John Arnatt—Deputy Sheriff
John Schlesinger—Allan a Dale
Donald Pleasance—Prince John
Patrick Barr—King Richard
Jill Esmond—Queen Eleanor
Zena Walker—Isabella of Angouleme

1955: *Robin Hood, the Movie* (UK movie compiled from *The Adventures of Robin Hood*)

1956: *Robin Hood's Greatest Adventures* (UK movie compiled from *The Adventures of Robin Hood*).

1958: *Robin Hood: The Quest for the Crown* (UK movie compiled from *The Adventures of Robin Hood*)

1958–1959: *Ivanhoe* (UK TV series)

Cast:

Roger Moore—Sir Wilfred of Ivanhoe
Robert Brown—Gurth (Ivanhoe's armorer)

Peter Gilmore—Waldo Ivanhoe
Andrew Keir—Prince John
John Pike—Bart
Bruce Seton—King Richard
Anthony Dawson—Sir Maurice
Norah Gorsen—Lady Rowena
Henry Vidon—Sir Cedric

1958: *The Son of Robin Hood*
Cast:
David Hedison—Jamie (as Al Hedison)
June Laverick—Deering Hood
David Farrar—Duke Simon Des Roches
Marius Goring—Earl of Chester
Philip Friend—Baron Charles Dorchester
Delphi Lawrence—Lady Sylvia
George Coulouris—Alan A. Dale
George Woodbridge—Little John
Humphrey Lestocq—Blunt
Noel Hood—Prioress
Shelagh Fraser—Constance
Jack Lambert—Will Scarlet
Oliver Johnston—Apothecary
Russell Napier—Squire Miles
Alastair Hunter—1st Woodsman

1960: *Sword of Sherwood Forest* (UK movie)
Cast:
Richard Greene—Robin Hood
Sarah Branch—Maid Marian
Peter Cushing—the Sheriff of Nottingham
Richard Pasco—Edward, Earl of Newark
Nigel Green—Little John
Niall MacGinnis—Friar Tuck
Jack Gwillim—Archbishop Hubert Walter
Edwin Richfield—The Sheriff's Lieutenant
Oliver Reed—the Lord Melton
Patrick Crean—Lord Ollerton
Vanda Godsell—The Prioress

Dennis Lotis—Allen a Dale
Derren Nesbitt—Martin of Eastwood

1964: *Robin and the 7 Hoods*

Cast:
Frank Sinatra—Robbo
Dean Martin—Little John
Sammy Davis Jr.—Will
Bing Crosby—Alan A. Dale
Peter Falk—Guy Gisborne
Barbara Rush—Marian Stevens
Victor Buono—Deputy Sheriff Alvin Potts
Robert Foulk—Sheriff Octavius Glick
Edward G. Robinson—Big Jim (uncredited)
Chet Allen—one of the Hoods
Hank Henry—one of the Hoods, "Six Seconds"
Phil Crosby—Hood
Allen Jenkins—"Vermin"
Jack La Rue—"Tomatoes"
Phil Arnold—"Hatrack"
Bernard Fein—"Bananas"
Richard Simmons—Prosecutor
Joseph Ruskin—"Twitch"
Maurice Manson—Dignitary
Barry Kelley—Police Chief
Harry Wilson—Hood
Richard Bakalyan—Hood
Hans Conried—Mr. Ricks
Sig Ruman—Hammacher
Bill Zuckert—Prosecutor

1967: *A Challenge for Robin Hood* (UK movie)

Cast:
Barrie Ingham—Robin de Courtenay
Peter Blythe—Sir Roger de Courtenay
John Arnatt—the Sheriff of Nottingham
Gay Hamilton—Lady Marian Fitzwarren
John Gugolka—Stephen Fitzwarren
James Hayter—Friar Tuck

Eric Flynn—Allen a Dale
Reg Lye—Much
Leon Greene—Little John
Douglas Mitchell—Will Scarlet
Eric Woofe—Henry de Courtenay
John Harvey—Wallace, Sir Roger's chief henchman
Arthur Hewlett—Edwin, the castle steward
John Graham—Justin, a loyal guard
Jenny Till—The Imposter Lady Marian
William Squire—Sir John de Courtenay
Norman Mitchell—Dray Driver
Alfie Bass—The Pie Seller
Donald Pickering—Sir Jamyl de Penitone

1968: *The Legend of Robin Hood* (US TV movie)

Cast:
David Watson—Robin Hood
Leigh Beery—Maid Marian
Victor Buono—Sir Guy
Douglas Fairbanks Jr.—King Richard
Steve Forrest—Sheriff of Nottingham
Noel Harrison—Allen a Dale
Harvey Jason—Will Scarlet
Arte Johnson—Much
Roddy McDowall ... Prince John
Walter Slezak—Friar Tuck
Bruce Yarnell—Little John

1969: *Wolfshead: The Legend of Robin Hood* (UK TV pilot, 1973 movie)

Cast:
David Warbeck—Robert of Locksley
Kathleen Byron—Katherine of Locksley
Dan Meaden—John Little of Cumberland
Ciaran Madden—Lady Marian Fitzwalter
Kenneth Gilbert—Friar Tuck
Joe Cook—Much
Derrick Gilbert—Wat

David Butler—Will Stukely
Patrick O'Dwyer—Tom
Peter Stephens—Abbot of St. Mary's
Christopher Robbie—Roger of Doncaster
Roy Boyd—Geoffrey of Doncaster
Pamela Roland—Adele
Inigo Jackson—Legros
Will Knightley—Abbot's Secretary

1969: *The Ribald Tales of Robin Hood* (aka *The Erotic Adventures of Robin Hood*)

Cast:
Ralph Jenkins—Robin Hood
Dee Lockwood—Maid Marian
Lawrence Adams—Prince John (as Lawrence Adams)
Danielle Carver—Lady Sallyforth
Scott Sizemore—Young Robin
C. S. Poole—The Sheriff
Frank Nathan—Little John
James Brand—Sir Guy
Eddie Nova—Friar Tuck
Ray Renard—Robin's father
Barbara Sanders—Robin's Mother
Bambi Allen—Polly
L Cranston—Allen a Dale (as L. Cranston)
Paul Smith—Will Scarlet
Terry Sands—Tina
Ingrid Young—Robin's sister

1971: *Up The Chastity Belt* (UK movie)

Cast:
Frankie Howerd—Lurkalot / Richard the Lionheart
Graham Crowden—Sir Coward de Custard
Bill Fraser—Sir Braggart de Bombast
Hugh Paddick—Robin Hood
Anna Quayle—Lady Ashfodel
Eartha Kitt—Scheherazade
Roy Hudd—Nick the Pick
Godfrey Winn—Archbishop of all England

Anne Aston—Lobelia
Lance Percival—Reporter
Royce Mills—Knotweed
Fred Emney—Mortimer
Dave King—Landlord of the Blue Boar
David Prowse—Sir Grumbel de Grunt
Nora Swinburne—Lady in Waiting
Judy Huxtable—Gretel
Lally Bowers—The Voice (voice)
Derek Griffiths—Saladin
Iain Cuthbertson—Teutonic Knight
Fred Griffiths—Father
Billy Walker—Chopper
Rita Webb—Maid Marian
Long John Baldry— Little John
David Kernan—Troubador
Frank Thornton—Master of Ceremonies
David Battley—Yokel
Chris Sandford—Mutch
Norman Beaton—Blacksmith
Sam Kydd—Locksmith
Aubrey Woods—Vegetable Stall Owner
Christopher Timothy—Vendor

1973: *Walt Disney's Robin Hood*

Cast (voices only):
Brian Bedford—Robin Hood
Monica Evans—Maid Marian
Phil Harris— Little John
Roger Miller—Allen a Dale
Andy Devine—Friar Tuck
Peter Ustinov—Prince John and King Richard
Terry-Thomas—Sir Hiss
Carole Shelley—Lady Kluck
Pat Buttram—The Sheriff of Nottingham
George Lindsey—Trigger
Ken Curtis—Nutsy
John Fiedler—Friar Tuck's Sexton
Barbara Luddy—Sexton's Wife

Billy Whitaker—Skippy
Dana Laurita—Sis
Dori Whitaker—Tagalong
Richie Sanders—Toby
Barbara Luddy—Mother Rabbit
Candy Candido—Captain of the Guard
J. Pat O'Malley—Otto

1975: *The Legend of Robin Hood* (UK TV)
Cast:
Martin Potter—Robin Hood
Diane Keen—Lady Marion
John Abineri—Sir Kenneth Neston
William Marlowe—Sir Guy of Gisborne
Paul Darrow—Sheriff of Nottingham
Michael-John Jackson—Richard I
David Dixon—Prince John

1975: *When Things Were Rotten* (US TV)
Cast:
Dick Gautier—Robin Hood
Misty Rowe—Maid Marian
Henry Polic II—Sheriff of Nottingham
Bernie Koppell—Allen a Dale
Dick Van Patten—Friar Tuck
David Sabin—Little John

1976: *Robin and Marian*
Cast:
Sean Connery— Robin Hood
Audrey Hepburn—Lady Marian
Robert Shaw—the Sheriff of Nottingham
Nicol Williamson—Little John
Richard Harris—Richard the Lionheart
Denholm Elliott—Will Scarlet
Ronnie Barker—Friar Tuck
Kenneth Haigh—Sir Ranulf
Ian Holm—King John
Bill Maynard—Mercadier

Esmond Knight—Old Defender
Veronica Quilligan—Sister Mary
Peter Butterworth—Surgeon
John Barrett—Jack
Kenneth Cranham—Jack's Apprentice
Victoria Abril—Queen Isabella

1982: *Ivanhoe* (UK TV)
Cast:
Anthony Andrews—Wilfred of Ivanhoe
James Mason—Isaac of York
Sam Neill—Brian de Bois-Guilbert
Michael Hordern—Cedric the Saxon
Olivia Hussey—Rebecca
Lysette Anthony—Lady Rowena
Julian Glover—King Richard
Michael Gothard—Athelstane
Tony Haygarth—Friar Tuck
George Innes—Wamba
Philip Locke—Grand Master
Ronald Pickup—Prince John
John Rhys-Davies—Front de Bœuf
David Robb—Robin of Locksley
Stuart Wilson—Maurice de Bracy

1984: *The Zany Adventures of Robin Hood* (US TV)
Cast:
George Segal—Robin Hood
Morgan Fairchild—Lady Marian
Roddy McDowall—Prince John
Janet Suzman—Eleanor of Aquitaine
Tom Baker—Sir Guy of Gisborne
Neil Hallett—the Sheriff of Nottingham
Robert Hardy—King Richard
Roy Kinnear—Friar Tuck
Robin Nedwell—Will Scarlet
Michelle Newell—Rebecca
Pat Roach—Little John
Kenneth Griffith—Isaac of York

Melvyn Hayes—Father Luther
Michael Hordern—Rupert
Aubrey Morris—Archbishop
Bruce Purchase—Moishe
Roger Ashton-Griffiths—1st Coachman
Paul Brooks—2nd Coachman
Angus Lennie—Scott Kelly
Tony Steedman—Bank President
Fenella Fielding—Molly
John Louis Mansi—Reuben
Kelly Summers—Miss Jones
Melanie Hughes—Miss Sanders
Colin Higgins—Irving
Peter Brayham—Yehoudi
Marc Boyle—Bernie
Andrew Lodge—Lord Exeter
Angela Grant—Lady Exeter
Su Elliot—Alice
Chris Webb—1st Merryman
Del Baker—2nd Merryman
Terence Plummer—3rd Merryman
Steve Dent—4th Merryman
Peter Brace—Captain of Guards
Fred Haggerty—1st Guard
Fred Powell—2nd Guard
Dinny Powell—3rd Guard
George Lane Cooper—4th Guard
Derek Lyons—5th Guard
William Morgan Sheppard—Saxon thief

1984–1986: *Robin of Sherwood* (UK TV)

Partial cast:
Michael Praed—Robin of Loxley
Peter Llewellyn Williams—Much
Ray Winstone—Will Scarlet
Clive Mantle—Little John
Judi Trott—Lady Marion
Phil Rose—Friar Tuck
Mark Ryan—Nasir

Jason Connery—Robert of Huntingdon
John Abineri—Herne the Hunter
Nickolas Grace—Robert de Rainault, Sheriff of Nottingham
Philip Jackson—Hugo de Rainault, Abbot of St. Mary's
Robert Addie—Sir Guy of Gisburne
Anthony Valentine—Baron Simon de Belleme
Phil Davis—Prince John
Richard O'Brien—Gulnar
John Rhys-Davies—King Richard

1989–1994: *Maid Marian and Her Merry Men* (UK TV)
Cast:
Kate Lonergan—Maid Marian
Wayne Morris—Robin of Kensington
Danny John-Jules—Barrington
Mike Edmonds—Little Ron
Howard Lew Lewis—Rabies
Forbes Collins—Prince John, King Richard, Queen Eleanor
Tony Robinson—Sheriff of Nottingham
Mark Billingham—Gary
David Lloyd—Graeme
Ramsay Gilderdale—Guy of Gisborne
Siobhan Fogarty—"Rotten" Rose Scargill

1991: *Robin Hood: Prince of Thieves*
Cast:
Kevin Costner—Robin Hood (Robin of Locksley)
Morgan Freeman—Azeem
Christian Slater—Will Scarlet
Alan Rickman—George, Sheriff of Nottingham
Mary Elizabeth Mastrantonio—Marian Dubois
Geraldine McEwan—Mortianna
Mike McShane—Friar Tuck
Brian Blessed—Lord Locksley
Michael Wincott—Guy of Gisborne
Nick Brimble—Little John
Harold Innocent—the Bishop of Hereford
Walter Sparrow—Duncan
Daniel Newman—Wulf

Sean Connery—King Richard
Jack Wild—Much the miller's son
Daniel Peacock—Bull

1991: *Robin Hood*

Cast:

Patrick Bergin—Sir Robert Hode / Robin Hood
Uma Thurman—Maid Marian
Jürgen Prochnow—Sir Miles Folcanet
Edward Fox—Prince John
Jeroen Krabbé—Baron Roger Daguerre
Owen Teale—Will Scarlet
David Morrissey—Little John
Jeff Nuttall—Friar Tuck
Danny Webb—Much the Miller
Carolyn Backhouse—Nicole, Roger's Mistress
Barry Stanton—Miter
Conrad Asquith—Lodwick
Phelim McDermott—Jester
Caspar De La Mare—Sam Timmons the Carpenter
Cecily Hobbs—Mabel
Gabrielle Reidy—Lily
Stephen Pallister—Jack Runnel

1993: *Robin Hood: Men in Tights*

Cast:

Cary Elwes—Robin Hood
Richard Lewis—Prince John
Roger Rees—Sheriff of Rottingham
Amy Yasbeck—Maid Marian
Dave Chappelle—Ahchoo
Mark Blankfield—Blinkin
Eric Allan Kramer—Little John
Matthew Porretta—Will Scarlet O'Hara
Isaac Hayes—Asneeze
Tracey Ullman—Latrine
Patrick Stewart—King Richard
Dom DeLuise—Don Giovanni
Steve Tancora—Filthy Luca

Joe Dimmick—Dirty Ezio
Dick Van Patten—The Abbot
Mel Brooks—Rabbi Tuckman
Megan Cavanagh—Broomhilde
Brian George— Dungeon Maitre d'
Robert Ridgely— Boris, the hangman
David DeLuise— a Villager
Avery Schreiber— Tax assessor
Chuck McCann—Villager
Marc Ian Sklar—Merry man
Tim Storms—Merry man

1994: *Robin Hood: Prince of Sherwood*
Cast:
Jason Braly—Robin Hood
Steve Barker—Sheriff of Nottingham
Caroline Duncan—Maid Marian
John Neely—Friar Tuck
Mark S. Faulkner—Guy of Gisborne
Brad Letson—Will Scarlet
Scott Knoblach—Little John
Mary Dobbs—Witch of Prophecy
Ronnie Prince—Wulf
Mike Pollick—King Richard
Rick Wright—Baron of Doncaster
James W. Hunter Jr.—Knight
Dick Tait—Priest

1996: *Robin of Locksley* (US TV movie)
Cast:
Devon Sawa—Robin McAllister
Sarah Chalke—Marion Fitzwater
Billy O'Sullivan—Will Scarlet
Tyler Labine—Little John
Colin Cunningham—Walter Nottingham
Josh Jackson— John Prince Jr.
Chad Todhunter—Warner Jr.
Kevin Hansen—Gibson Jr.
Tom Butler—John Prince Sr.

Annie Charles—Rosie
Michael St. John Smith—Agent Seals
James Bell—Father Tuck
Julie Bond—Sister Angelina
Robert Thurston—Dean Harvey
Sean Milliken—Mr. Anderson
Alfred E Humphreys—Grant McAllister)
Elizabeth Carol Savenkoff—Janet McAllister
Fred Henderson—Sullivan Warner Sr.
L. Harvey Gold—Lyle Gibson Sr.
Robert Fox—Tommy Tarla
Donald Morin—Mark Tarla
Donald Gordon—Doctor
Sheri-D Wilson—Lucille Pettigrew
Tom Anderson—Fifth Grader
Jared Van Snellenberg—Jimmy Brandenberg
Dan Muldoon—Allan Fitzwater
Kelsa Kinsly—Reporter
Heather Hanson—Secretary
Diana Stevan—Bank Manager
Chris Eastman—FBI Agent

1997–1998: *The New Adventures of Robin Hood* (US TV)
Cast:
Matthew Poretta—Robin Hood (seasons one/two)
John Bradley—Robin Hood (seasons three/four)
Anna Galvin—Lady Marion Fitzwalter (season one)
Barbara Griffin—Lady Marion Fitzwalter (seasons two-four)
Richard Ashton—Little John
Martyn Ellis—Friar Tuck
Christopher Lee—Olwyn
Hakim Alston—Kemal
Andrew Bicknell—Prince John
Christie Lee Woods—Rowena

1997: *Ivanhoe* (US TV mini-series)
Cast:
Steven Waddington—Ivanhoe
Ciaran Madden—Urfried

Ciarán Hinds—Bois Guilbert
Susan Lynch—Rebecca
Jimmy Chisholm—Wamba
Nick Brimble—Front de boeuf
Valentine Pelka—Maurice de Bracy
David Nicholls—Little John
James Cosmo—Cedric
Chris Walker—Athelstane
Simon Donald—Louis Winklebrand
Roger Ashton Griffiths—Prior Aymer
Dermot Keaney—Brother Ambrose
Trevor Cooper—Gurth
Ron Donachie—Friar Tuck
Aden Gillett—Robin of Locksley
David Horovitch—Issac
Rory Edwards—King Richard
Victoria Smurfit—Rowena
Peter Guinness—Montfitchet
Christopher Lee—Beaumanoir
Jack Klaff—Malvoisin
Peter Needham—Abbot
David Barrass—Hubert
Renny Krupinski—Bardon
Ralph Brown—Prince John
Ronald Pickup—Fitzurse
Siân Phillips—Eleanor of Aquitaine

1999: *Back to Sherwood* (US TV)
Cast:
Alexa Dubreuil—Joan Little
Aimée Castle—Robyn Hood
Larry Day—Guy of Gisborne
Angela Galuppo—Tanya
Carl Alacchi—Shardwell
Eugene Brotto—Tavern Peasant
Dawn Ford—Peasant
Adam Frost—Phil Scarlet
Ruby Ann King—Alana Dale
Anik Matern—Brenan
Swede Swensson—Peasant

Andrew W. Walker—William de Gisborne
Gillian Ferrabee—Mrs. Hood
Christopher B. MacCabe—Robin Hood
Dennis St. John—The Abbot

2001: *Princess of Thieves* (US TV movie)
Cast:
Keira Knightley—Gwyn
Stephen Moyer—Prince Philip
Stuart Wilson—Robin Hood
Del Synnott—Froderick
Malcolm McDowell—Sheriff of Nottingham
Jonathan Hyde—Prince John
Crispin Letts—Will Scarlet

2006–2009: *Robin Hood*
Partial cast:
Jonas Armstrong—Robin Hood
Gordon Kennedy—Little John
Sam Troughton—Much
Joe Armstrong—Allan a Dale
Richard Armitage—Guy of Gisborne
Keith Allen—Sheriff of Nottingham
Lucy Griffiths—Marian
Harry Lloyd—Will Scarlet
Anjali Jay—Djaq
Michael Elwyn—Edward
David Harewood—Tuck
Joanne Froggatt—Kate
Mike Kelly—Sheriff's Man
Mark Rhino Smith—Karim
Lara Pulver—Isabella
Matt Devere—Elite Guard
Ben O'Brien—Castle Guard
William Beck—Roy
Teresa Banham—Rebecca
Péter Geltz—Jailer
Clive Standen—Archer
Toby Stephens—Prince John

John Carlisle—Thornton
Alexis Latham—Abel
Mark Phoenix—Jailer
Lee Ross—Sir Jasper
Mark Bagnall—Forrest
Fraser James—Blamire
Juliet Seal—Alice Little

2010: *Robin Hood*

Cast:
Russell Crowe—Robin Longstride
Cate Blanchett—Marion Loxley
Mark Strong—Sir Godfrey
Velibor Topic—Belvedere
Oscar Isaac—Prince John
William Hurt—William Marshal
Max von Sydow—Sir Walter Loxley
Danny Huston—King Richard the Lionheart
Mark Lewis Jones—Thomas Longstride
Mark Addy—Friar Tuck
Eileen Atkins—Eleanor of Aquitaine
Jonathan Zaccaï—King Philip of France
Matthew Macfadyen—the Sheriff of Nottingham
Kevin Durand—Little John
Léa Seydoux—Isabella of Angoulême
Scott Grimes—Will Scarlet.
Alan Doyle— Allan A'Dayle
Douglas Hodge—Sir Robert Loxley
Denis Menochet—Adhemar
Jessica Raine—Isabel of Gloucester

2012: *Robin Hood: Ghosts of Sherwood 3D*

Cast:
Martin Thon—Robin Hood
Ramona Kuen—Maid Marian
Kane Hodder—Little John
Kai Borchardt—Friar Tuck
Dennis Zachmann—Will Scarlet

Tom Savini—Sheriff of Nottingham
Claude-Oliver Rudolph—Guy of Gisborne
Anika Neubauer—The Witch
Andrea Glowig—The Young Witch
Martin Hentschel . . .Transformed Will Scarlet
Carolina Grigorov—Transformed Maid Marian
Thorsten Paladin Bareck—Transformed Robin Hood

2014: *Doctor Who—Robot of Sherwood* (UK TV)
Cast:
Peter Capaldi—the Doctor
Jenna Coleman—Clara Oswald
Tom Riley—Robin Hood
Roger Ashton-Griffiths—Quayle
Sabrina Bartlett—Quayle's Ward (Marian)
Ben Miller—Sheriff of Nottingham
Ian Hallard—Allen a Dale
Trevor Cooper—Friar Tuck
Rusty Goffe—Little John
Joseph Kennedy—Will Scarlet
Adam Jones—Walter
David Benson—Herald
David Langham—Guard
Tim Baggaley—Knight
Richard Elfyn —Voice of the Knights

Index

Adventures of Robin Hood, The (comic book), 132

Adventures of Robin Hood, The (US 1938), xii, 26, 107, 230-34, 263-66

Adventures of Robin Hood, The, (1955– 1959 TV series), 166, 182, 244

Adventures of Robin Hood, Earl of Huntingdon, and his Mate Little John, The, 199

Ainsworth, William Harrison, 79, 139, 141–47, 162, 204–5

Allen, Keith, 98, 103, 105, 276–79

Andrew of Wyntoun, 2–3

Armitage, Richard, 105, 276–77

Armstrong, Jonas, 4–5, 14, 58, 135, 276–78

Back to Sherwood (US TV), 276–77

Bandit of Sherwood Forest, The, 90, 235

Bell, Adam, 12–13, 202–3

Blanchett, Cate, 97, 260

"Bold Pedlar and Robin Hood," 287

Brooks, Mel, xvi, 88, 219, 258

Carpenter, Richard, 87, 149–50, 248, 255, 273–75

Challenge for Robin Hood, A, (UK movie), 48, 66, 165, 246–47

Child Ballads, the. See Child, Francis James

Child, Francis James, 84, 93, 104, 166–70, 173–78, 181, 183–84, 187, 189, 191, 204, 212–14, 257

Connery, Jason, 273–74

Connery, Sean, 7, 253, 260, 273

Costner, Kevin, 9, 58, 219, 256–58

Crowe, Russell, 33, 259–60, 262

de Havilland, Olivia, 97, 107, 219, 231

Douglas Fairbanks in Robin Hood (US 1922), 223–32, 234, 239, 262

Egan, Pierce, 74–75, 205, 207, 221

English and Scottish Ballads. The. See Child, Francis James

English and Scottish Popular Ballads. See Child, Francis James

Erotic Adventures of Robin Hood, The. See Ribald Tales of Robin Hood, The

Fairbanks, Douglas, 34, 58, 99, 109, 188, 210, 219, 223–32, 234, 239, 262

Fairbanks Jr, Douglas, 231, 270

Flynn, Errol, vii, 26, 59, 107, 172, 219, 223, 230–33, 235, 238–39, 256, 258

Foresters, The (Tennyson), 214–18

"Gamble Gold and Robin Hood," 72

Gay, John, 142, 199–200

Gordon, Adam, 5, 6, 41

Greene, Richard, viii–ix, xiv–xv, 58, 86, 244, 247, 263–64, 266, 268–70

Griffiths, Lucy, 89, 97, 276

Hale Sr, Alan, 232, 237

Hepburn, Audrey, 7, 219, 253

Hereward the Wake, xvi, 39–46, 89, 113, 121, 147, 232

Hereward the Wake: Last of the English, 45

Herne the Hunter, 139–50, 153, 273

In the Days of Robin Hood, 221

Ivanhoe (1913), 220

Ivanhoe (1952), 238

Ivanhoe (1958–1959) 270

Ivanhoe (opera), 218

Ivanhoe, A Romance, 19, 76, 81, 192–95, 199, 209, 211, 225, 232

"Jolly Pinder of Wakefield, The," 84–86
Jonson, Ben, 135–36, 138, 202

Keats, John, xi, 195
Keen, Diane, 96–97, 271
"King's Disguise, and Friendship with Robin Hood, The," 112, 183
Kingsley, Charles, 39–46, 163

Lady Robin Hood (aka *Amazon of the Hills*) (US 1925), 229
Legend of Robin Hood, The, (UK TV series 1975), 69, 109, 126, 129, 227, 270–71
Little John and Will Scarlet; or, The Outlaws of Sherwood Forest, 201
"Lyttel Geste of Robyn Hode, A," 6, 32, 112, 128, 169, 247

Maid Marian (1822), 195–99
Maid Marian (1891), 203
Maid Marian (1901), 203
Maid Marian and her Merry Men, 88, 95, 122, 276–77
Maid Marian, or The Huntress of Arlingford, 199
Maid Marian, the Forest Queen, 207
Men of Sherwood Forest, The, 243
Merry Adventures of Robin Hood of Great Renown in Nottinghamshire, The, 192, 209
Merry Men of Sherwood, The, 207, 229
Miss Robin Hood (US 1948), 236–37
Munday, Anthony, 18–20, 22, 24, 33, 70, 84, 91, 171

New Adventures of Robin Hood, The, 88, 276–77
"Noble Fisherman, or Robin Hood's Preferment, The," 47–49
Noyes, Alfred, 131, 133, 219

Praed, Michael, 272–73
"Prince Edward and Adam Gordon," 4–5

Prince of Thieves, The (1948), 236–37
Princess of Thieves (US TV movie 2001), 276–77
Pulver, Lara, 278
Pyle, Howard, 13, 70, 73, 192, 209–11, 214, 221

Rains, Claude, 57, 107, 232, 234, 262
Rathbone, Basil, 107, 231, 235
Ribald Tales of Robin Hood, The (aka *The Erotic Adventures of Robin Hood*) (US 1969), 250
Rickman, Alan, 257
Ritson, Joseph, 93, 110, 161–62, 176, 183, 195, 207
Robin and Marian (US 1976), 253, 254, 256
Robin and the 7 Hoods (US, 1964), 250
Robin Hood (1860), 203
Robin Hood (1908), 219
Robin Hood (1912), 221
Robin Hood (1953), 243
Robin Hood (1991), 257–58
Robin Hood (2006), 75, 88–89, 95, 98, 104–5, 109, 112–13, 126, 135, 189, 209, 266, 276–79
Robin Hood (2010), 259–62
Robin Hood: A Comic Opera (1891) 203
Robin Hood (comic), 266
"Robin Hood and Allen a Dale," 84
"Robin Hood and Guy of Gisborne," 106, 209
Robin Hood and His Merry Men (1908), 219
"Robin Hood and Little John," 199
"Robin Hood and Maid Marian" (1913), 222
"Robin Hood and Maid Marian" (ballad), 93, 170
"Robin Hood and Queen Katherine," 170, 187
"Robin Hood and the Beggar," 189
"Robin Hood and the Bishop of Hereford," 113, 170
"Robin Hood and the Bishop," 189
"Robin Hood and the Butcher,"189
"Robin Hood and the Curtal Friar," 80–82, 201

"Robin Hood and the Golden Arrow,"
    180–82
"Robin Hood and the Monk," 74–75,
    123, 172–73, 177
"Robin Hood and the Potter," 44, 189
"Robin Hood and the Prince of
    Aragon," 73, 87, 183
"Robin Hood and the Ranger," 86
"Robin Hood and the Scotchman," 86
"Robin Hood and the Shepherd," 189
"Robin Hood and the Tanner," 69,
    170, 213
"Robin Hood and the Tinker," 185
"Robin Hood and the Valiant Knight,"
    30
Robin Hood Jr., 229
"Robin Hood Newly Revived," 70
Robin Hood or Sherwood Forest (stage-
    show), 201
"Robin Hood Rescuing Three
    Squires," 86–97
"Robin Hood Rescuing Will Stutly," 73
Robin Hood, Prince des Voleurs, 201
Robin Hood—Outlawed (US 1912), 221
Robin Hood: Ghosts of Sherwood 3D, 132
Robin Hood: Men In Tights (US 1993),
    xvi, 88, 258
Robin Hood: Prince of Thieves, 166, 194,
    256–58, 262, 276
Robin Hood's Barn, 126
Robin Hood's Bay, 126
"Robin Hood's Birth, Breeding, Valor
    and Marriage," 12–13, 72, 91,
    201
Robin Hood's Butts (Herefordshire),
    124
Robin Hood's Butts (Somerset), 124
Robin Hood's Cave, 125
Robin Hood's Chair, 125
"Robin Hood's Chase," 170
Robin Hood's Cross, 125
"Robin Hood's Death," 32, 177
"Robin Hood's Delight," 190
Robin Hood's Fountain, 128
"Robin Hood's Golden Prize," 190, 213
Robin Hood's Hills, 126
Robin Hood's Leap, 126
Robin Hood Meadow, 126
Robin Hood's Penny Stone, 128

Robin Hood's Picking Rods, 125
Robin Hood Pit, 126
"Robin Hood's Progress to
    Nottingham,"16
Robin Hood's Steed, 124
Robin Hood's Stride, 125
Robin Hood's Tor, 124
Robin Hood's Well (Lancs), 125
Robin Hood's Well (Notts), 126,
Robin of Sherwood, 69, 87, 102, 139–40,
    149–50, 182, 248, 255, 272–76
"Robot of Sherwood," (*Doctor Who*),
    126–27, 182
Rogues of Sherwood Forest, 236
Rutherford, Margaret, 237

*Sad Shepherd: or, A Tale of Robin-Hood,
    The*, 135–39
Scott, Sir Walter. See *Ivanhoe*
Sinatra, Frank, 219, 249–52
*Story of Robin Hood and His Merrie Men,
    The*, 92, 176, 239
Sullivan, Sir Arthur, 215, 217–18
Sword of Sherwood Forest, The, 266

Tales of Robin Hood (TV pilot), 236, 238
Taylor, Elizabeth, 238
Taylor, Robert, 238
Tennyson, Alfred, Lord, 214 18
Todd, Richard, 239
    Troughton, Patrick, 243, 263,
    276
Troughton, Sam, 75, 276
    "True Tale of Robin Hood, A"
    (1632) 186–87

Up The Chastity Belt (UK 1971), 251

Walt Disney's Robin Hood (US 1973),
    239–41
When Things Were Rotten (US TV series
    1975), 258
*Whole Life, and Merry Exploits of Bold
    Robin Hood, Earl of Huntington
    (etc., etc.), The*, 195
Wolfshead: The Legend of Robin Hood, 316

Zany Adventures of Robin Hood, The (US
    TV movie) 272

Johnny Cash FAQ
by C. Eric Banister
Backbeat Books
9781480385405 .... $24.99

KISS FAQ
by Dale Sherman
Backbeat Books
9781617130915 .... $24.99

Led Zeppelin FAQ
by George Case
Backbeat Books
9781617130250 .... $22.99

Lucille Ball FAQ
*by James Sheridan
and Barry Monush*
Applause Books
9781617740824 .... $19.99

M.A.S.H. FAQ
by Dale Sherman
Applause Books
9781480355897 .... $19.99

Michael Jackson FAQ
by Kit O'Toole
Backbeat Books
9781480371064 .... $19.99

Modern Sci-Fi Films FAQ
by Tom DeMichael
Applause Books
9781480350618 .... $24.99

Monty Python FAQ
*by Chris Barsanti, Brian Cogan,
and Jeff Massey*
Applause Books
9781495049439 .... $19.99

Morrissey FAQ
by D. McKinney
Backbeat Books
9781480394483 .... $24.99

Neil Young FAQ
by Glen Boyd
Backbeat Books
9781617130373 .... $19.99

Nirvana FAQ
by John D. Luerssen
Backbeat Books
9781617134500 .... $24.99

Pearl Jam FAQ
*by Bernard M. Corbett and
Thomas Edward Harkins*
Backbeat Books
9781617136122 .... $19.99

Pink Floyd FAQ
by Stuart Shea
Backbeat Books
9780879309503 .... $19.99

Pro Wrestling FAQ
by Brian Solomon
Backbeat Books
9781617135996 .... $29.99

Prog Rock FAQ
by Will Romano
Backbeat Books
9781617135873 .... $24.99

Quentin Tarantino FAQ
by Dale Sherman
Applause Books
9781480355880 .... $24.99

Robin Hood FAQ
by Dave Thompson
Applause Books
9781495048227 .... $19.99

**The Rocky Horror
Picture Show FAQ**
by Dave Thompson
Applause Books
9781495007477 .... $19.99

Rush FAQ
by Max Mobley
Backbeat Books
9781617134517 .... $19.99

Saturday Night Live FAQ
by Stephen Tropiano
Applause Books
9781557839510 .... $24.99

Seinfeld FAQ
by Nicholas Nigro
Applause Books
9781557838575 .... $24.99

Sherlock Holmes FAQ
by Dave Thompson
Applause Books
9781480331495 .... $24.99

The Smiths FAQ
by John D. Luerssen
Backbeat Books
9781480394490 .... $24.99

Soccer FAQ
by Dave Thompson
Backbeat Books
9781617135989 .... $24.99

The Sound of Music FAQ
by Barry Monush
Applause Books
9781480360433 .... $27.99

South Park FAQ
by Dave Thompson
Applause Books
9781480350649 .... $24.99

Star Trek FAQ
(Unofficial and Unauthorized)
by Mark Clark
Applause Books
9781557837929 .... $19.99

Star Trek FAQ 2.0
(Unofficial and Unauthorized)
by Mark Clark
Applause Books
9781557837936 .... $22.99

Star Wars FAQ
by Mark Clark
Applause Books
9781480360181 .... $24.99

Steely Dan FAQ
by Anthony Robustelli
Backbeat Books
9781495025129 .... $19.99

Stephen King Films FAQ
by Scott Von Doviak
Applause Books
9781480355514 .... $24.99

Three Stooges FAQ
by David J. Hogan
Applause Books
9781557837882 .... $22.99

TV Finales FAQ
*by Stephen Tropiano and
Holly Van Buren*
Applause Books
9781480391444 .... $19.99

The Twilight Zone FAQ
by Dave Thompson
Applause Books
9781480396180 .... $19.99

Twin Peaks FAQ
*by David Bushman and
Arthur Smith*
Applause Books
9781495015861 .... $19.99

UFO FAQ
by David J. Hogan
Backbeat Books
9781480393851 .... $19.00

Video Games FAQ
by Mark J.P. Wolf
Backbeat Books
9781617136306 .... $19.99

The Who FAQ
by Mike Segretto
Backbeat Books
9781480361034 .... $24.99

The Wizard of Oz FAQ
by David J. Hogan
Applause Books
9781480350625 .... $24.99

The X-Files FAQ
by John Kenneth Muir
Applause Books
9781480369740 .... $24.99

HAL•LEONARD®
PERFORMING ARTS
PUBLISHING GROUP

FAQ.halleonardbooks.com

0117

Prices, contents, and availability subject to change without notice.